The C͟ ͟ ͟ial o͟ ͟ Television ͟nd Radi͟

The Classic Serial on Television and Radio

Robert Giddings

and

Keith Selby

First published 2001 by
PALGRAVE
Houndmills, Basingstoke, Hampshire RG21 6XS and
175 Fifth Avenue, New York, N. Y. 10010
Companies and representatives throughout the world

PALGRAVE is the new global academic imprint of
St. Martin's Press LLC Scholarly and Reference Division and
Palgrave Publishers Ltd (formerly Macmillan Press Ltd).

Outside North America
ISBN 0–333–71387–7 hardback
ISBN 0–333–71388–5 paperback

In North America
ISBN 0–312–23598–4 hardback

This book is printed on paper suitable for recycling and made from fully managed and sustained forest sources.

A catalogue record for this book is available from the British Library.

Library of Congress Cataloging-in-Publication Data
Giddings, Robert.
    The classic serial on television and radio / Robert Giddings and Keith Selby.
        p. cm.
    Includes bibliographical references and index.
    ISBN 0–312–23598–4 (cloth)
        1. Television serials—Great Britain—History and criticism. 2. Radio serials—Great Britain—History and criticism. 3. Television adaptations. 4. Radio adaptations. 5. English fiction—Film and video adaptations. I. Selby, Keith. II. Title.

    PN1992.3.G7 G44 2000
    791.45'6—dc21
                                                                    00–030893

10   9   8   7   6   5   4   3   2   1
10   09 08 07 06 05 04 03 02 01

Printed in Great Britain by Antony Rowe Ltd, Chippenham, Wiltshire

Contents

Acknowledgements

This book could not have been written without the help of the library staff of the following institutions: Bournemouth University, the London Library, Poole Public Reference Library and Southampton City Library. We are particularly grateful to Anne Salenieks of Parkstone Library, Poole, for her help in tracing a number of video recordings. We are indebted to Janice Cake, for secretarial support, who transcribed many hours of recorded interviews. For additional help with recordings, our thanks are due to the staff of Media Services, Bournemouth University. Particular thanks are due to Tim Preece and Catherine Wearing for their help in arranging interviews with many media professionals, and to Charmian Hearne for her encouragement and endurance. We acknowledge the great help we had from the BBC Written Archives Centre, Caversham Park, Reading, BBC Sound Archives at Broadcasting House, and the BBC Reference Library Service. Parts of this book first appeared in *The Dickensian* and appear by kind permission of the Editor.

List of Plates

Introduction

> Unceasingly contemplate the generation of all things through
> change, and accustom thyself to the thought that the Nature
> of the Universe delights above all in changing the things that
> exist and making new ones of the same pattern. For every-
> thing that exists is the seed of that which shall come out of it.
>
> Marcus Aurelius [1]

This book evolved naturally as a result of teaching English, media and communication, and researching and writing *Screening the Novel*. We found that little work had actually been done on the ways in which the broadcast classic serial as a genre had been initiated, pioneered and developed to become an accepted broadcasting genre. We found that it had developed not only as the creation of early radio drama producers, but had partly evolved as the result of the expressed wishes of the BBC radio audiences before the Second World War. As a result, the BBC declared its intention in *Radio Times* to broadcast faithful serial dramatisations of classic novels, adhering to the original as much as possible. Radio audiences enjoyed dramatisations of novels, and particularly relished the opportunities radio offered in bringing classic novels alive on the airwaves. Serialised classic novels were consumed as special treats associated with weekends and high holidays. Friday evening was at first scheduled for their transmission but this was soon transferred to Sunday evenings which became firmly established as their slot. With the advent of television early Sunday evening was taken over as appropriate scheduling for those serials suitable for family viewing and the more adult novel dramatisations were scheduled in the late evening slot on Saturday or sometimes on a weekday evening.

When television took on the classic serial the genre had been well established by the BBC. By classic novel was usually meant a British novel of the Victorian or Edwardian period, with occasional forays into Jane Austen or occasionally into the eighteenth century. The intention was to serialise this fiction but to treat it with respect in an attempt to do justice to the original work. This is an important point. These were not adaptations. They were dramatisations. As far as possible these versions stuck to character, plot and dialogue as closely as broadcasting allowed, and they were essentially translations from the printed page into broadcast drama.

There are several ways in which a media genre may be regarded. It can be evaluated aesthetically. An attempt may be made to define the genre in terms of a system of conventions that permit artistic expression. We would need to establish what constitutes a classic serial, as broadcast drama. What qualities does it have, which might differentiate it from other costume dramas or adaptations of novels? We would need to establish what constitutes the conventions which governed the manner in which novels were dramatised and scheduled for broadcasting.

When we look at the origins of the genre, it is clear that in the main it was nineteenth- or early twentieth-century British novels which tended to be selected, although there were occasional American, French or Russian classics. These were serialised in several episodes and treated with respect. An effort was made to preserve as much of the original dialogue as possible. Productions gave great care to good diction and historical accuracy. Much of the attention which the BBC had always given to historical feature programmes was transferred to classic serial production – sound effects, music and general production values – in a genuine attempt to recreate a convincing sense of the past. This sometimes erred towards the precious, for example, a peculiarly crisp and careful elocution-teacher style of pronunciation became the done thing in Jane Austen.

Additionally, classic serials may also be seen as examples of broadcasting ritual, which involves an examination of the genre as a means by which a culture speaks to itself, and incorporates an evaluation of shared beliefs and values as transmitted by the form. Two aspects of classic serial form in particular need pondering: the 'classic serial' prototype, and the type of narrative prose fiction selected for the 'classic serial' treatment. The form itself, the drama serial in episodes of equal length broadcast in weekly instalments, was created to establish audience loyalty. It provided good wholesome family listening, particularly for autumn weekends, and fitted comfortably into the construction of the Reithian Sunday. This considerably affected the choice of material, which has to be seen as worthy and morally wholesome, even uplifting. The form has been a staple of British broadcasting for decades and continues to thrive, though its history has not been entirely free of ups and downs. Ritual theory though suggests how genre connects with the evolving social order. The broadcast classic serial becomes a means by which past literature is identified as being worthy of classical status and this contributes to the construction and maintenance of the literary canon. This may work imperceptibly. For example, Charles Dickens, Charlotte Brontë, Henry James and George Eliot have assumed the status of classical authors. Not an eyebrow would be raised at the announcement that one of their novels had been currently dramatised as a classic serial. But being broadcast as a classic serial in itself becomes an accolade which dubs a work as a classic. Adapting a novelist's work for broadcasting as a classic serial was accepted as an important stage towards literary canonisation. Thus, if it is given out that Evelyn Waugh's *A Handful of Dust* or John Le Carré's *The Spy Who came in From the Cold* is to be 'the new classic serial on Radio Four' then those authors and those works have taken significant steps towards achieving classical status. Being processed by this genre is one of the stages by means of which novels become classic novels, and may continue and by due process join the literary canon, become part of the valued cultural heritage and inherited by subsequent generations.

Finally the classic serial may be examined ideologically. Here the genre might be seen sociologically as an instrument of control on several levels.[2] At the industrial level, particularly on commercial television in the UK and USA, the genre might assure advertisers of an audience for their messages. The need to guarantee the delivery of particular audiences with disposable income would influence the choice of particular novels for the treatment. It is important to consider these significant changes in production policy now consequent upon these market imperatives. Up until a few years ago the tendency was to market ready-made English programmes to the United States – this was the case with *Henry VIII and his Six Wives*, *Upstairs Downstairs*, *The Duchess of Duke Street*, *Henry VII*, *Elizabeth R*, *The Pallisers*, *The Forsyte Saga* and many more. The American television market was offered a choice and it took what it wanted. These were emphatically English programmes, and would be transmitted on Public Service Broadcasting with acknowledged sponsorship from such giants as Exxon, Rank Xerox, Mobil, Monsanto Chemicals or General Motors, who are happy to acquire quality by association with what are perceived as high-culture products. The link between the commercial complex and the media was proclaimed by Time-Life's marketing information: 'We would like to tell you about the benefits of underwriting quality programming... and how an exclusive association with one of our new productions can be of significant value to your company....'[3] The tendency now is for works to be selected for dramatisation or adaptation because they might well appeal to the US, in the hope of attracting a co-production deal which would underwrite production costs.

At the time of writing it continues to be the BBC and the major commercial television companies who make classic serials – the only discernible infiltration seems to have been in satellite broadcasting, where the Disney Channel, curiously enough reviving the classic novel serial as an item in junior programming reminiscent of much earlier BBC traditions, has transmitted wholesome family Disney versions of *Oliver Twist* (with Richard Dreyfuss as Fagin), *The Old Curiosity Shop* (with Peter Ustinov as Grandfather Trent) and *Great Expectations* (with Anthony Hopkins as Magwitch). But it is important to remember that these productions are usually made by a British television company in a co-production deal with the Disney Corporation. As far as the major players are concerned, these circumstances have worked together in creating a set of conditions highly suitable for the successful production of a particular style of classic novel adaptation by the major television companies. This has ensured the healthy survival of the classic serial well into the age of satellite television, cable, deregulation and digital broadcasting.

1
Definitions, Early History: the Classic Drama Serial

The broadcast classic serial, the serialised adaptation of a 'classical' literary text, does not exist as an immutable, unchanging, permanent media form. The form has changed over the years as broadcasting technology has changed, as economic and commercial imperatives have developed and as taste and style have altered.

Origins

The prototype of the BBC classic serial, upon which all subsequent classic serial adaptations and dramatisations have been to a greater or lesser extent based, was put together in the early days of radio drama between the wars. The genre emerged in the context of the BBC monopoly which enabled John Reith to initiate public service broadcasting – the Reithian trinity of Information, Education and Entertainment. The classic serial as we know it today is part of that Reithian legacy, of that extraordinary endeavour to use radio broadcasting not only for our amusement but also for our betterment. Reith is on record as wanting to use the wireless to 'part the clouds of ignorance'. From some perspectives it might have seemed slightly silly. This Auntie BBC tendency was well captured in 1940 by E.M. Forster, who wrote in *Does Culture Matter?*

> Today, people are coming to the top who are, in some ways, more clear-sighted and honest than the ruling classes of the past, and they refuse to pay for what they don't want; judging by the noises through the floor, our neighbour in the flat above doesn't want books, pictures, tunes, runes, anyhow doesn't want the sorts which we recommend. Ought we to bother him? When he is hurrying to

1

lead his own life, ought we to get in his way like a maiden-aunt, our arms, as it were, full of parcels, and say to him 'I was given these specially to hand on to you... Sophocles, Valesquez, Henry James... I'm afraid they're a little heavy, but you'll get to love them in time, and if you don't take them off my hands I don't know who will... please ... please... they're really important, they're culture'. His reply is unlikely to be favourable, but, snubbing or no snubbing, what ought we to do? That's our problem...[1]

John Reith wanted the BBC to act in the role of a good parent to the nation, to bring us up to be good citizens. Part of this good citizenship was to be a sound knowledge of our culture, both past and present. Consequently, the creative and performing arts always played an important part in BBC schedules. Drama, it was early believed, was particularly well suited to radio broadcasting.

British radio drama was created and pioneered by the BBC. There was only one broadcasting service, the BBC, and the BBC broadcast on only one station. Reith proclaimed in 1928: 'Broadcasting in this country is a striking example of the advantages which are gained through being able to be definite – it may appear even arbitrary – in the pursuit and execution of a line of policy capably but deliberately chosen.'[2]

The BBC's income from the licence fee – guaranteed as long as people bought and used wireless sets – freed the Corporation from the need either to pay out dividends to shareholders obtained from profits or from the need to satisfy audiences in order to gain advertising revenue. The BBC could employ professional programme makers, who in effect were able to work without dependence on either state, patron or box office, on the task of inventing radio drama. But this monopoly position nevertheless required some diplomacy in practice. In effect, the BBC had a captive audience, who had little by way of choice – the BBC or nothing. This captive audience was considerable – out of a population of 46 000 000 by 1930 there were 3 092 000 wireless licences in the United Kingdom (compared to 1 996 000 telephone subscribers). The Corporation had no need to fear financial loss which might result from dishing up unpopular plays on the airwaves. But, on the other hand, it was a monopoly which relied on artists to supply the goods, and artists are sustained by applause. As Reith's Head of Drama, Val Gielgud put it:

You could maintain that the listener should be consistently given what he ought to like, but it was difficult to suggest with confidence that he should consistently be given what he actively disliked, and impossible to deny that a public service had to supply accepted popular standards of entertainment.[3]

The result was an interesting and influential compromise. Scheduling and programming had been built into the British experience from the very earliest days – the result of the need to create, build and to maintain audiences. The art of British broadcasting as conceived by John Reith was to please audiences but at the same time lead them a bit further than they themselves might have originally wished to go. This can clearly be seen in action in the early history of BBC radio drama.

Radio drama, and in the larger sense, broadcast drama, is certainly to be ranked among the great pioneering achievements of the BBC. Fortuitously the BBC went right to the centre of the matter when in February 1923 they decided that excerpts from plays by Shakespeare were to be among the first drama broadcast on the wireless in Britain. Cathleen Nesbitt adapted several major scenes from the plays and these were directed by C.A. Lewis – the quarrel scene from *Julius Caesar*, the trial from *The Merchant of Venice*, the Hubert and Arthur scene from *King John*, as well as excerpts from *Romeo and Juliet* and *Henry VIII*. On 28 May 1923 *Twelfth Night* was broadcast more or less complete starring Nigel Playfair, Cathleen Nesbitt and Gerald Lawrence.[4] Significantly, a production of this play starring Alec McCowen, Dilys Laye and Andrew Sachs was broadcast by Radio Four to mark the BBC's Diamond Jubilee in 1982. An important step was taken as early as 1924 when a separate department was established for producing plays, managed by R.E. Jeffrey.

It would not seem to stress the argument too far to say that Shakespeare seems to be at the heart of British radio drama. Shakespeare, the world's greatest dramatist, relied on the power of words. Radio drama offered audiences a theatrical experience which they could hear but not see. In radio broadcasting the entire dramatic import would have to be delivered in words and sounds. Radio drama pointed the way to an entirely new kind of drama. There was no point taking a well-made West End success and hoping somehow to transform it into radio drama. This was, of course, briefly attempted – in much the same way as the early film-makers initially attempted cinematigraphically to replicate stage drama until pioneers such as Griffith and Eisenstein realised that film was an entirely new language with its own grammar, vocabulary and syntax.

It is usually claimed that Richard Hughes's *Danger* (January 1924) was the first play actually written for the wireless, but another claimant might be a play written for children by Phyllis Twigg, *The Truth About Father Christmas*. Hughes's play was, in fact, a very interesting experimental work which seems to grasp the secret of radio's effectiveness. It begins with the line: 'The lights have gone out.' The writer hoped that listeners would sit in the dark and share the experience of the characters in the play, and identify with their situation. The BBC broadcast a new stereo production of this play, again to mark the Diamond Jubilee.

John Reith was highly critical of the attempts of radio drama productions to duplicate 'theatrical' effects in wireless terms. Within two years he had recorded the comment: 'It seems to me that in many of our productions there is too much striving for theatre effect and too little attempt at actually discovering the actual radio effect when the play is received in distant homes.'[5] There was originally an attempt to leech off traditional literature. *Westward Ho!* (1924) was the first classical novel to be adapted for radio, followed the next year by Conrad's *Lord Jim*. This is more interesting than it seems. Conrad's novels seem 'classic' to us, but in the 1920s they would be regarded as modern. The BBC early established almost a proprietary right over the adaptation, production and broadcasting of the British literary classics[6] and it is frequently asserted by media pundits that most British citizens owe their initial awareness of the masterpieces of their own language to versions of them broadcast by the BBC.[7]

Gradually the BBC evolved the language and technique of drama in terms of sound. This was not stage drama relayed to the listening audience by means of the wireless: it was a new kind of drama altogether. Radio drama, as a new kind of radio, was conceived and brought into being as the BBC settled down after the early years of struggling simply to fill their schedules. As social historians of radio have commented, this was at a propitious moment:

> ... by the late twenties the BBC's system of distribution and the content of its programme service had begun to settle. Attention was now turned towards a more defined social purpose and towards more considered forms of expression. Radio began to be talked of not only as a new form of communication, but also as a potential art-form. It was linked in discussion with film, especially the pioneering work of contemporary Russian film-makers ...[8]

Cecil A. Lewis, one of the pioneer writers of dramas for the BBC, wrote as early as 1929 that the task of the wireless playwriter differs from that of the writer for the stage because:

... although in broadcasting limitations of inaudible 'stage business' are very narrow, the limitations of actions and *mis en scene* are bounded only by the imagination of the listener himself. The stage author deals in scenes and situations which can be presented to the eye. The wireless author may make use of practically any scene or situation which can be conceived by human thought and imagination.[9]

The ability of radio so easily to cut from one scene to another with an almost Shakespearean immediacy was attractive to these early pioneers. Howard Rose, one of Gielgud's earliest colleagues, had experience of acting in broadcast Shakespeare. The analogy with Shakespeare went further – the concentration of dialogue and quick-fire effects proved very tempting and initially led to some ineffective gimmickry. The amount of material by Shakespeare broadcast in these early days is impressive evidence of the case. Gradually, radio drama writers and producers perceived that the concentration entirely on sound was to open up new territory to be explored. Technical mastery of the control of sound enabled the producers and directors of radio drama to create in radio terms something closely equivalent to Eisenstein's achievement of montage, with fades and cross-fades giving similar technical effects as that in the editing of film. And writers were certainly willing to experiment with this new medium. Among the earliest were several of quite outstanding ability – Richard Hughes, Lance Sieveking, Tyrone Guthrie and L. Du Garde Peach.

Sieveking, who joined the BBC in 1924 after serving as a flyer in the First World War, was assistant to the Director of Education, and had a very deep and involved fascination with the possibilities of radio as a mass medium. He became the BBC's first head of outside broadcasts, which was to give him invaluable experience in creating and transmitting convincing audio constructions of dramatic events. He made the opening announcement at the England versus Wales rugby international in January 1927 at Twickenham, the first sporting occasion covered by the BBC. His technique was impressive. He hired a blind rugby fan from St Dunstan's to sit with the commentator, H.B.T. Wakelam, who then explained the game as it unfolded, thus providing a vivid and parallel account for listeners at home – 'And back to square one.'[10] Sieveking was keenly aware, as were many of the early BBC personnel, of what could be distinctively achieved by radio, and he carried these interests with him when he was moved to radio drama at a formative stage in its development. He began to make an early impression with such productions as *Kaleidoscope I*, which he described as a rhythm 'representing the Life of Man From the Cradle to the Grave' broadcast in 1929 – 'a play too purely radio to be printed for reading' which was greeted by reviewers as real wireless drama at last.[11] His output was prolific: he was to have over ninety works to his credit, among them some of the earliest adaptations especially written for radio, including work by Somerset Maugham, Evelyn Waugh and H.G. Wells's *War of the Worlds*.[12]

Tyrone Guthrie, a cousin of Tyrone Power, brought considerable stage experience to radio production, and was fascinated by the possibilities of presenting drama in terms of sound and words. His *Squirrel's Cage* (1929) represents the dilemma of modern industrial/commercial man trapped in his world of unremittingly repeated routines. This nightmare modern world was brilliantly created in radio terms, and the production was hailed as a major contribution to real 'radio' drama. Tyrone Guthrie seized on the opportunities for surrealism, interior monologue, stream of consciousness and a whole battery of non-realistic dramatic effects to present visions of life almost expressionistically.

The extraordinary work of Lawrence Du Garde Peach developed radio drama in equally important directions, which had a significant influence on the style and content of radio drama. Peach initially worked on short plays and ballad operas, which used narrative.[13] *Up the River* was a kind of historical scrap book devoted to the life and work of Shakespeare. *London's a-Calling*, *The True History of Henry VIII* and *A Pageant of the Tower* moved even further in the direction of using radio drama as a pageant of popular historical mythology, and foreshadowed the colourful work of such writers as Charles Chiltern. This obviously took on and developed in radio the then contemporary fashion for civic and theatrical historical pageants, founded by Napoleon Parker.[14] Another aspect of this unusual writer's work is found in his hard-hitting social-problem radio dramas *Bread* and *Three Soldiers*. The former was a family chronicle which concerned characters who leave England in the 1840s during the agricultural depression and become farmers in the New World. The latter dealt with the then contemporary issue of men who served their country only to be thrown on the dole. Peach's work made two considerable contributions to the development of radio drama. One was the use of a variety of sound effects to reconstruct the past using all the resources of radio features and documentaries, where the aim was to give documentary the feel of actuality in terms of sound.[15] This is significant: radio drama grew up at the same time as radio documentary, and both learned from each other. Peach's other contribution was the realisation of a convincingly natural everyday speech for characters from the past which replaced the conventional stage 'Tushery' of Wardour Street English – 'Pray tell me madam, how came you by this intelligence' and 'wither away so fast', and so on. It is interesting that Val Gielgud resisted attempts by BBC regions to produce plays for radio, and strived to centralise BBC drama production in London.[16]

Val Gielgud recorded the fact that he always felt he had a free hand in the way he developed radio drama.[17] But he was aware, at least as early as 1931, that just as radio drama was a new art which was still, in a sense, in the process of being invented, radio listeners would have patiently to learn the art of listening. The BBC seemed to be advancing at a faster rate than the taste of their audience. A newspaper poll revealed that radio drama was the least popular programme: Gielgud accepted that the audience for radio plays would continue to be modest until listeners learned the required concentration:

... Radio drama, by its demand upon the listener's imagination, implies a concentrated degree of listening which is as yet confined to an enthusiastic minority. As soon as the wireless play is generally regarded not as a substitute for the stage or a screen play, but as a distinct form of art demanding a distinct form of approach on the part of the listener, the audience for drama will be as large as it is now faithful and enthusiastic. [18]

Radio drama continued to exploit fully the resources. *The Flowers Are Not For You To Pick* (1930) was based on the idea of one's life flashing before one's eyes at the moment of drowning. A young clergyman, *en route* for China, falls overboard and as he drowns rehearses his entire life in his mind, each episode separated by the lapping of the waves. The same year the BBC broadcast a much acclaimed adaptation of Karael Capek's *R.U.R.* This bizarre and frightening glimpse into a future of the triumph of mechanistic capitalism was well suited to radio. Words and sounds alone possibly painted a more terrifying reality than could be realised on stage. Productions of this kind foreshadow that semi-dream type of radio drama which was to culminate in such masterpieces as Louis MacNeice's *The Dark Tower* and Dylan Thomas's *Under Milk Wood*.

This first decade of radio drama produced impressive results. BBC scheduling was flexible, and did not restrict productions to a particular time or duration. Unlike, say, a commercial radio broadcasting system with the need to deliver a regular audience to sponsors or advertisers, BBC planners had considerable autonomy. At this stage no one particular night or time was put aside for any particular type of programme – say, variety, or talks or drama. The search was on for attentive rather than for lazy listeners. Consumers were expected to make deliberate choices from the published details in *Radio Times*.[19] Within twenty years BBC radio had produced works by authors which must now be ranked among the classics of radio broadcasting, Dorothy L. Sayers, Louis MacNeice.[20] In 1939 J.B. Priestley was the first author to be commissioned by the BBC to write a play for radio. His *Let the People Sing* was the astounding result.

It was during these early stages of the development of radio drama that the fist evidence of the prototypical classic novel serialisation begins to emerge. We can see that radio drama and costume drama developed in an interesting and significant context – feature programmes and plays were actually connected in production style, although strictly speaking the work of separate production departments. Features frequently presented historical documentaries, great moments in history, biographies of the great, celebrated trials and so on – the *Loss of the Birkenhead*, the *Tryall of Charles I*, the *Battle of Waterloo* – which attempted to recreate the past in sound (*son sans lumiere?*). This is very clear in such a landmark radio documentary production as D.G. Bridson's radio evocation of the Jacobite Rising and the catastrophe at Colludon Moor in *The March of the '45* broadcast in February 1936.[21] Historical, 'classical' or costume dramas and novel adaptations were part of the same production style and procedure.

As a medium, radio always had its own unique sense of the immediate. A newspaper gives you a written account by a reporter printed on the page. We perceive film and television as carefully reproduced moving pictures of events. But with radio, we are there as it happens. To this day, radio dines out on its triumph in reporting the Crystal Palace fire and the R101 disaster. But not only does radio have the geographical ubiquity of Prospero's Ariel, radio – from its earliest days – also undertook to transport us back across past years. The traditional BBC radio Christmas is interesting evidence in this respect, in which peoples from all over the world were united and the far-flung Empire brought together as we looked back at events of the past year in preparation for the Royal Christmas broadcast in which the heritage of the past was brought together to ponder in the light of the present. The BBC Scrapbook programmes, which began in 1933 with *Scrapbook for 1913*, were a characteristic and enduring example of these days of radio production. These popular programmes remained a feature of the schedules for the next forty years.

An end to experiment: beginnings of the classic serial

By the mid 1930s, it was clear that the BBC's unchallenged monopoly had allowed, certainly as far as radio drama was concerned, a lengthy period of experiment and development in which much about the nature and the possibilities and limitations of radio drama had been learned. As Val Gielgud himself commented:

> Plays were written – and produced on the air – less for their merits in terms of drama than because they offered opportunities for the simultaneous use of more and more studios, more and more ingenious electrical devices.... The radio play had so far always been among 'minority' programme items. At this particular stage it tended to grow progressively and self-consciously minority.[22]

From the very earliest days, long before the emergence of anything resembling the classic serial, the BBC had experimented with narrative prose fiction as the raw material for broadcasting. Dramatic readings were pioneered in the early 1920s. *Barkis is Willin'*, adapted from *David Copperfield*, was broadcast in July 1924.[23] In August the following year a radio anthology feature by R.E. Jeffrey, *Pages from Dickens*, was broadcast from London. *A Christmas Carol* was broadcast on 23 December 1925. This work featured in Christmas broadcasting again in 1928, 1929, 1933, 1934 and 1935. It has since become a firm and traditional Christmas holiday favourite. The link between stage performance and radio broadcasting is demonstrated by the fact that several of these early Dickens programmes were studio performances of Bransby Williams's celebrated stage shows. Early Dickens appeared to be favoured above the later more satirical and gloomy melodramatic novels – *Pickwick Papers* and *The Old Curiosity Shop* were radio favourites in early BBC schedules. Scenes from Jane Austen, Charles Kingsley, Walter Scott, Trollope and other respected novelists were broadcast from the very early days.[24] A serial reading of Trollope's *Barchester Towers* was broadcast on the London regional programme in the summer of 1938.

It was from this spirit of experiment that the enduring genre of the broadcast classic serial was to emerge. In 1937 Gielgud introduced *Experimental Hour*, which was it seems based on the Columbia

Broadcasting System of America's programme, *Workshop*. It was foreseen that these BBC productions might well not appeal to a large audience, so they were scheduled late at night They were experimental drama productions and early samples included a verse play by the American Archibald MacLeish, *Fall of the City*, W.B. Yeats's *Words Upon the Window Pane* and two versions of *Twelfth Night*, one in modern English and another in what was claimed to be Elizabethan pronunciation. Audiences were appreciative and, what was more interesting, proved to be in large numbers. *Experimental Hour* failed, not for lack of support, but from the lack of a good supply of suitable material. Nevertheless, Asa Briggs has convincingly distilled the main theoretical questions with which radio drama producers were at this stage apparently particularly concerned.[25]

One format of radio drama that struck a chord with consumers at the close of the decade was the serial, in which the story unfolded in a series of episodes. It aimed at the middle ground. Unlike American soap operas, it took itself seriously, but had few aspirations towards the intellectual or highbrow end of the market and we may in consequence date the beginning of the classic novel adaptation, as an ongoing feature of broadcast drama, from March 1939. The popularity of serial drama had clearly proved itself in *Send for Paul Temple* and a twelve part serial adaptation of *The Three Musketeers* in 1938. There were fundamental developments in thinking about programme schedules as a result of a listeners' questionnaire which asked about preferences for serial formats in drama, entertainment and talks. This was the beginning of the magazine format and serial drama. In *Radio Times* 31 March 1939 Val Gielgud's plans for radio drama and features were announced, in an article called 'Plays and Features: There Are Many Treats in Store for the Lovers of Radio Drama', readers learned:

> Extensive new plans covering the future output of the Features and Drama Department have been made by Val Gielgud and his staff of writers and producers. Hitherto plays and features have been planned in the short term policy, at the most three months ahead. Now the situation has been reviewed, and planning for the whole year ahead is to be put in hand.
>
> An essential part of this new plan is the giving of regular and fixed time to plays and features. Beginning in April, Friday night will become the big night of the week for drama and features. At least one important show will be broadcast each Friday.

Serial plays, which have been so popular a feature in broadcasting within the last two years, are to continue unabated. Starting this week is *The Prisoner of Zenda*. It will be followed by one that is likely to attract an entirely new public to this form of broadcast entertainment – T.H. White's *The Sword in the Stone*, which Walt Disney has bought with a view to making it his second full length feature film, the successor to *Snow White and the Seven Dwarfs*.[26]

The article goes on to announce radio productions of plays taken from the previous twenty years of the London theatre – Noel Coward, Priestley, Gordon Daviot, Edgar Wallace – plays from the USA and from the Continent. So radio drama emerged in an interesting celebratory context. The classic serial was born at a propitious moment. A full page feature with photographs of the stars in their roles announced *The Prisoner of Zenda* with a flourish: '*The Prisoner of Zenda* will be broadcast as a serial play, starting on Sunday. The explanatory article is by Jack Inglis, who has adapted the great romantic novel for radio.'[27] And it is very interesting to note that the adapter, Inglis, lays out what have become the golden rules of classic serial adaptation ever since:

> The story is simple, with clear cut characters, falls easily into nine episodes, and therefore seems ideally suited to radio serial form.... It always seems to me that it is the first duty of an adapter to reproduce in another medium the original flavour and atmosphere of the book. And so I have chosen the method which is nearest to the novel. Rudolph Rassendyll tells the story himself, introducing each episode. Once this is done, each instalment is complete in itself, and there is no 'narration' to break the interest.... I have stuck to the dialogue and, what is more important, I have stuck to the story....[28]

The only bits he altered, to make the story clearer on radio, were in rendering the two castles into one, to make the geography more immediately understandable to the listener. He had thought of having a plan of the castles printed in *Radio Times* so that listeners could follow the action as it unfolded, but this proved far too complicated. This epoch-making serial was transmitted on Sundays at 5.20 p.m. Sunday teatime was eventually to become the traditional time for the BBC classic serial and the tradition survived into the age of television drama sixty years later. This serial was the prototype.

Dickens made his appearance in classic serial form in 1939, but, as we have seen, had been identified as ideal material for public service broadcasting from the very earliest crystal set receiving Savoy Hill 2LO days of the BBC. Bransby Williams, who had toured the music halls with his impersonation of Dickens's characters since the end of the last century, broadcast several of his character monologues, and performed *Scrooge* with a small supporting company. In January 1930 the first serial reading of any Dickens novel on radio was transmitted, when *Great Expectations* was read as a solo turn by V.C. Clinton Baddeley in 16 instalments between January and April. These broadcasts proved very popular, and he followed them with serial readings of *Dombey and Son, David Copperfield, Nicholas Nickleby, Pickwick Papers, Martin Chuzzlewit* and *A Tale of Two Cities*. The significance of Dickens in our national culture and as suitable material for radio broadcasting was again demonstrated in 1936 when the BBC transmitted *Mr Pickwick's 100 Years Old*, scripted by V.C. Clinton Baddeley (also broadcast in Sweden and the USA). A similar celebration of the centenary of *Nicholas Nickleby* was broadcast in 1938, which contained dramatised scenes of the trial of William Shaw, the original Yorkshire school-master on whom the dreadful Wackford Squeers was based.

As the BBC began to establish the classic radio serial, *Pickwick Papers* was serialised in October 1939, adapted in twelve episodes by Philip Wade, with Bryan Powley as Pickwick. Philip Wade was Sam Weller and Geoffrey Wincott Tony Weller. The BBC radio classic serial seems to have got itself well-bedded down during the war.[29] In November 1940 *David Copperfield* was serialised in twelve episodes in a dramatisation by Audrey Lucas, who followed this with two serialisations in 1941 – *Oliver Twist* and *Edwin Drood*, both produced by Moray McLaren. The narrative problems in these adaptations were resolved by retaining the authorial voice of Charles Dickens, which was supplied by Ronald Simpson. A landmark production of *David Copperfield* on radio in 1943 featured Ralph Richardson as Micawber, a role he was memorably to reprise in the 1970 film.[30] Anthony Trollope's novels were to become a stable of the broadcast classic serial, and made their impact in the early days of the tradition. *Barchester Towers*, adapted by H. Oldfield Box, was broadcast in ten parts in 1943. Dickens's *A Christmas Carol*, which was also to take its part in the traditional schedules, was broadcast at Christmas 1944. The trial scene from *Pickwick Papers*, another stalwart, was broadcast on BBC radio in the adaptation by V.C. Clinton-Baddeley in 1945. In the same year Trollope's *Doctor Thorne* was serialised in thirteen episodes. Both *David Copperfield* and *Dombey and Son* were serialised in 1946.

Looking at the details of these early classic serial productions in *Radio Times* we can clearly see that the British classic serial tradition was based on certain assumptions. In the main the novels selected are in the nineteenth-century mainstream; although Jane Austen is a regular choice from the very earliest days, and there is an occasional Walter Scott, the novelists most favoured are Dickens, Thackeray, Hardy, Trollope, Collins, Mrs Gaskell, George Eliot, and the Brontës. John Galsworthy and Arnold Bennett were favoured from a slightly later period. Dickens was a very firm favourite. Several of the more adventurous nineteenth-century novels, such as *The Count of Monte Cristo, Les Miserables, Anna Karenina, Barlasch of the Guard, The Three Musketeers, Swiss Family Robinson*, were also serialised. Trollope continued to find an honourable place in the classic serial tradition with *The Warden, Phineas Finn, Orley Farm, The Small House at Allington, Barchester Towers* and *The Eustace Diamonds* all in the schedules between 1946 and 1953.

It is interesting to note that during this formative stage of the genre, these adaptations were not always whole, complete and entire, but were occasionally open ended. The version of *The Mystery of Edwin Drood*, broadcast in 1941 was in three parts, and came to an end at the point where Dickens's death interrupted the novel's composition. There was then a discussion between the Narrator ('Dickens') and the characters as to the likely solution to the mystery. It seems that Jasper had attempted to strangle his nephew with the black necktie (as shown in Luke Fildes's illustration to the published serial edition) but had only rendered him unconscious. Edwin was thus able to escape with his life from the quicklime into which he had been thrown. When *Edwin Drood* was again broadcast in December 1951, in an adaptation by Mollie Greenhalgh, a conclusion was provided to the story. Jasper is lured to the Sapsea tomb and hounded to confess, Edwin appears as white as a ghost, as he has escaped from the quicklime, and there is ambiguity as to whether Jasper hallucinates, whether Edwin is a real ghost, or whether he just seems like an apparition – an ambiguity to which radio is well suited as a medium.[31]

If the war had not intervened, the carry over from radio to television broadcasting of classic novels might well have been much smoother and much earlier. As early as July 1938 Dickens's fiction was broadcast on television. Stephen Harrison adapted the trial scene from *Pickwick Papers – Bardel Against Pickwick*. This adaptation was revived when television transmission resumed after the war and it was broadcast again in September 1946. Radio broadcasting was the great technical gift to humanity by means of which humanity would be not only entertained, but informed and educated also. Here, in radio drama, was the opportunity to give the British public *en masse* what they had so long been denied through illiteracy, poor education and the need to leave school early and seek gainful employment – the joy, solace and inspiration to be had from the classics of their own literature. Why stop at English literature? World literature could be rendered an open book.

These were the ideals which powered BBC radio's pioneering efforts in adapting classic novels to audio drama. The scheduling adopted by BBC programme planners was interesting and seems to have established principles which survived well into the era of television. Sunday was seen as the major day for such serious, meaty, weighty, well-established classic literature. It seems to epitomise the very spirit of public service broadcasting. There was a regular slot between 8.30 and 9.00p.m. for the adult classic novel. Here, come rain or shine every Sunday throughout the year, the BBC broadcast an endless run of classic novel serials. And at teatime, the time during weekdays devoted to *Children's Hour*, younger listeners had plays, stories adapted from the bible and occasionally classic novels considered suitable for them – *Treasure Island, Oliver Twist, Little Women, Tom Sawyer, The Secret Garden, Alice in Wonderland*.

The beginnings of BBC television drama

Television drama had very slow beginnings in Britain. The new medium was not seen in its early days as a suitable vehicle for drama. Performances were perforce live, in the days long before recording was possible. As the initial fashion was for excerpts from current West End productions, actors could not be in two places – studio and stage – at the same time. It was to be some time before television as an entity in itself became established. Gerald Cock, Director of Television, wrote in the *Radio Times* on 23 October 1936 that he did not believe there was much of a future for television drama as the public were 'already sated with entertainment'. He did not envisage television as a medium for entertainment, but that its future lay in the transmission of information: '...in my view, television is from its very nature, more suitable for the dissemination of all kinds of information than for entertainment as such, since it can scarcely be expected to compete successfully with films in that respect.'

Gradually, he was proved wrong. The first play televised by the BBC was Luigi Pirandello's *The Man With a Flower in His Mouth*, transmitted from the Long Acre Studio on 14 July 1930. When a regular television service began in 1936 drama featured strongly in the programming. The problems faced in television production of drama in the early days were considerable. Cameras were heavy and movement was difficult. The definition was such that picture quality was poor. Live production led to serious continuity problems. Initially the BBC took stage drama and simply transferred it to the domestic screen. Nevertheless there were some courageous experiments in these pioneering days.

In July 1938 the BBC broadcast scenes from Edgar Wallace's stage hit, *On the Spot*, and by using cameras at the limits of their cables, managed to incorporate exterior scenes played on the terrace at Alexandra Palace. On 12 November the same year the BBC broadcast *The White Chateau* and used military sound effects – rifle and artillery fire provided by the 7th Middlesex Regiment and the Royal Artillery. This did not work out quite as intended, perhaps: windows in houses adjacent to the studios at Alexandra Palace were shattered and the BBC received serious complaints. West End theatre productions were also featured on BBC television – *Little Ladyship*, with Lillie Palmer and Cecil Parker was broadcast from the Strand Theatre by the BBC on 5 March 1939, and *Rope* was broadcast in a studio production from Alexander Palace on 8 March 1939. The BBC ran a weekly series, *Theatre Parade*, which presented studio produced excerpts of West End plays then running.

On 16 November 1938 the BBC broadcast J.B. Priestley's *When We Are Married*, as an outside broadcast from St Martin's Theatre. Further loyalty to serious drama was demonstrated by the BBC's broadcasting of James Elroy Flecker's *Hassan*, Capek's *The Insect Play* and T.S. Eliot's *Murder in the Cathedral*. It is interesting to note that when *Journey's End* was broadcast, film sequences of the exterior battlefield were used between the various studio location sequences in the dug-out. Other interesting evidence of the BBC's willingness to experiment lies in the fact that as early as 1938 they used two studios to broadcast a production of Kaufman and Hart's *Once in a Lifetime*. This Christmas production had five sets, and the cast had to move from one set to another in the studios as fast as they could. This was the BBC's first ninety minute drama production.

Television also became recognized as a medium for drama in its own right. Initially, as with radio, the tendency had been for producers to avail themselves of material already written for the stage. But the first drama written for BBC television was J. Bissell Thomas's *The Underground Murder Mystery*, set in the Underground station at Tottenham Court Road. This thirty-minute play was broadcast on 19 January 1937. The following year the BBC broadcast their first full length West End play – *Magyar Melody* (with Binnie Hale) – from His Majesty's Theatre. Before the service closed at the beginning of the war in 1939 the BBC had broadcast a total of 326 dramas.

Postwar BBC television drama

The emphasis on works taken from the stage was initially continued in postwar television. The first drama televised after the war was Shaw's *Dark Lady of the Sonnets* on 7 June 1946. Other notable early television productions included Eugene O'Neill's *Anna Cristie*, Shakespeare's *Macbeth* (with Stephen Murray), Wilde's *Lady Windermere's Fan*, Shaw's *St Joan*, Patrick Hamilton's *The Duke in Darkness* and *Rope*. J.B. Priestley wrote a play especially for BBC television, *The Rose and the Crown*, and a courageous television adaptation of the celebrated French Resistance novel by 'Vercors' (Jean Bruller) *The Silence of the Sea* (*La Silence de la Mer*) was broadcast on 11 June 1946.

Robert MacDermot, Head of Drama in 1948, did not think it would be possible or desirable to concentrate exclusively on new work. Television audiences, in his opinion, would always require a consistent diet of dramas which had previously been tried and proved successful on stage. Nevertheless, he went so far as to hope that in time some 50 per cent of television drama output might be scripted as original for television.[32] This certainly seemed to be the case in the immediate postwar era. In April 1954 the BBC launched into drama series production with *The Grove Family*, the nation's earliest television soap opera, devised by John Pertwee.[33] *Dixon of Dock Green* began in 1955 and ran for over twenty years. As far as serious drama was concerned, direct continuity between the acknowledged pioneering success of BBC radio drama under Val Gielgud might have been carried over into BBC television drama, as Gielgud was, for a time, in charge of television drama. But he declined the opportunity to initiate production with the medium. He did not have a high opinion of television as a vehicle for drama, as his comment illustrates:

> I fail to see any sign of the establishment of theory as to television, its object and method. As far as I can judge, the camera is still supreme over the microphone, and the television producer tends to photograph a stage play rather than to illustrate a broadcast.[34]

Michael Barry became Head of Drama at the BBC in 1952. His policy was to move away from simply recycling West End stage successes in television terms, toward the creation of television drama as a free-standing art form. Barry expended his entire budget during his first year on one new work. The result was the celebrated series, *The Quatermass Experiment* by Nigel Kneale. The six-part work was produced by Rudolph Cartier, who is on record as saying he thought the viewers wanted something more than Dickens. The success of Kneale's first shocker was repeated in two more six-part series, *Quatermass II* in 1955 and *Quatermass and the Pit* in 1958. The undoubted success of Quartermass encouraged Cartier to seek further futuristic fantasy drama subjects and this led to the notorious BBC production of George Orwell's *1984*. This was studio bound and transmitted live but nevertheless was a landmark in television drama. The budget for the day was considered huge (£3000) and significantly enough this included original music, especially composed for this production by John Hodgkis. It was broadcast on 12 December 1954. In other respects this production was a landmark, with Cartier using filmed sequences between sections of live drama to create narrative continuity.

Nevertheless, the Reithian ideology of public service broadcasting was still extremely strong. As well as encouraging British contemporary writing, BBC television found time and money from its earliest postwar days to broadcast fine classical and foreign drama – there were outstanding productions of *The Man Who Came to Dinner*, *Rosmersholm*, Eugene O'Neil's *Mourning Becomes Electra* and *Strange Interludes*, Shakespeare's *The Merchant of Venice*, the medieval morality, *Everyman*, Congreve's *Love for Love*, Ibsen's *Peer Gynt* (with Peter Ustinov and Greig's music) and the French North African dramatist, Emannuel Robles' brutal drama of Simon Bolivar's revolt against the Spanish, *Monserrat* (with Stephen Murray). The BBC did not immediately transfer the genre of the classic serial from radio to television, but they certainly demonstrated their intentions towards adapting classic novels to screen very early in the postwar period. During the Christmas holiday in December 1946 the BBC televised *Alice*, a forty minute drama, based on scenes from Lewis Carroll's fantasy. It starred Vivian Pickles as Alice, but also featured the young Miriam Karlin.[35]

The state of television technology considerably influenced the actual quality of the broadcast product. Television broadcasting was monochrome. Location filming was very expensive, and therefore its use was extremely limited. Further, blending the low-definition image of the 405-line standard of broadcast television quality with the very different definition of film was a serious handicap. Due to the high cost of film stock, productions were therefore almost entirely broadcast live. This meant that none of the post-production editing and polishing we now take for granted was possible. Productions tended to be static, locked into one location at a time, and this implied considerable restrictions for practitioners:

> Limitation of space is paramount. Even in the larger studios where one really big set can be built, one gains little, for you cannot pack it all on the screen at once. The further back you take your camera, the less detail becomes recognisable. In the same way there should not be too many characters on the screen at once. Scenes between twos and threes are what television wants: quiet, intimate stuff which the camera can get right into. Five people on the set for any length of time is a producer's headache, meaning constant regrouping and cutting from shot to shot in order to show the viewers what the characters look like in close-up.[36]

The result was the establishing of a characteristic style of television drama. Its necessity to concentrate on interior work, the quality of its definition which made close-up a frequent resort, has meant that television drama accommodated close-up emotional cut and thrust as an essential part of its vocabulary. The very fact that it could not move easily has added considerably to its characteristic vocabulary. Often the most striking and successful moments in television drama are intimate, close-up dialogue between characters; great effect can be achieved by focusing attention on the reactions of one character, as another speaks. These effects are particularly useful in television drama and very hard to realise in stage drama. As so often, limitations often prove to be immense advantages.

Television adaptations had to accommodate the complex logistical problems of actors' mobility and moving the action from location to location. Performers obviously could not be in two places at once, nor could they move rapidly and with plausible continuity from one location to another, nor from one situation to another. It was not an easy life for actors. Stephen Murray here compares performing in television drama with that of radio in the early days:

> Compared with the unimaginable nightmare of the television studio – the lights, three or four times brighter and hotter than any one encounters in a film studio; the creeping, peering cameras, with their incredibly efficient, silent, headphoned crews, winding and

cranking and tracking in and out at the orders of the unseen, unheard producer; the wild rushes down the corridor from one studio to another, while dressers tear clothes off one's back and throw fresh ones on, and make-up girls mop one's streaming face – compared with this the peace and tranquillity of the broadcasting studio is like a rest-cure.[37]

These limitations were demonstrably clear in one of the earliest of the BBC television drama's postwar reaffirmations of loyalty to the classic novel – *Bardell versus Pickwick*, Stephen Harrison's adaptation of the trial scene from *Pickwick Papers*, transmitted in 1946. It was in three studio scenes – Mr Pickwick's sitting room, the Angel Inn and finally in the court. It was during these early days of BBC television drama that the first classic novel series were to emerge. Dashing about in time and place was out of the question. The result was that somehow or other texts were chosen or were treated so as mainly to be enacted by a limited cast and with dramatic action mostly set between just a few characters, in interior locations and in a limited number of places. Consequently, early postwar television drama tended to present drama as a 'special event'. The BBC was transmitting such quality drama regularly by the mid 1950s, including television productions of a number of plays originally written for the theatre but staged in studio conditions, as well as plays written exclusively for television production.

Dickens had made a triumphant return to BBC television when the veteran Bransby Williams starred in *A Christmas Carol* on Christmas Day 1946. Two years later Freeman Wills and Canon Langbridge's version of *A Tale of Two Cities*, *The Only Way*, was broadcast on BBC television, starring Marion Harvey. In 1950 Bransby Williams again appeared as Scrooge. The BBC broadcast versions of *Rebecca*, *Wuthering Heights* and other established novels, but these could not be categorised as classic serials. The classic serial tradition was initiated on BBC television in 1951 with Trollope's *The Warden* in six episodes. *Pride and Prejudice* was serialised in 1952 produced by Campbell Logan, with Peter Cushing as D'Arcy and Daphne Slater as Elizabeth Bennet. *Jane Eyre* (1955) was followed in the next few years by *Villette*, *Nicholas Nickleby*, *The Small House at Allington*, *Pride and Prejudice* again in 1958 (produced by Barbara Burnham, with Alan Badel and Jane Downs), *The Last Chronicle of Barset*, *The Railway Children*, *Blackarrow*, *The Three Hostages*, *David Copperfield*, *The Eustace Diamonds*, *Bleak House*, *The Children of the New Forest*, *Vanity Fair*, and *Kenilworth*. One of the best early BBC television Dickens serials was P.D. Cummins's version of

Great Expectations in 1959. Highly aware of the constraints of television production, Cummins sounds defensive of the potential limitations of his dramatisation: 'Alterations were necessary in order to make the story clear, but all concerned in the serial have done everything possible to keep it faithful to the spirit of Dickens, so we do most sincerely hope it will live up to your expectations.'[38] It starred Michael Gwynn as Joe Gargery and Colin Spaull as young Pip, and Dinsdale Landen as the mature Pip with Helen Lindsay as Estella. Jane Austen's *Emma* was serialised by Vincent Tilsley in February 1960, followed by Rex Tucker's adaptation of Stevenson's *St Ives* and C.E. Webber's *Tom Sawyer* in the summer of the same year.

The days of live drama on television, and all it had involved, were brought to an end by videotape recording. In 1956 the Ampex Corporation of Redwood City, California, demonstrated their videotape recording system at the convention of the National Association of Broadcasters held in Chicago. The first transmission by Ampex videotape, interestingly enough, was the three minute trailer on BBC Television for *A Tale of Two Cities* on 1 October 1958. In November 1960 the BBC televised a thirteen episode serialisation of Dickens's sprawling historical saga *Barnaby Rudge* by Michael Voysey. The foundations of the classic serial tradition on BBC television were certainly laid this year, which ended in the December 1960 four-episode dramatisation of Jane Austen's *Persuasion* by Michael Voysey and Barbara Burnham. Interest in Jane Austen was immediately renewed in January 1961 when the Corporation transmitted Theo Home's serialisation of *Mansfield Park*. The Home Service continued the tradition on radio with Sunday evening broadcasts of *Sense and Sensibility*, *The Trumpet Major*, *Return of the Native*, *The Woman in White*, *Great Expectations* and *Pendennis*. The use of Ampex videotape recording was having a marked impact on the production of television programmes, and obviously its effect on drama was considerable – especially noticeable in terms of continuity. Peter Vaughan, who has enjoyed an acting career in theatre, film, radio and television for nearly forty years, and starred in some of the earliest classic serials which used Ampex tape-recording, commented:

The basic difference is between film and Ampex taping. The Ampex taping is done after you have rehearsed, rather in the way you rehearse in the theatre. You would rehearse all your positions, moves etc. for a week or two. Or, in the case of a weekly show, material for that week, and you would then come into the studio. Here you would have the technicians for the first time, and maybe five or six cameras there on the studio floor. And there are Ampex tape cameras that move around, as opposed to film cameras which – unless they're on track – are static. So the whole process means that you can work in that way. You can do much longer sequences normally. So that in those days, what you did, was you worked on Ampex tape in that way. You would just have the odd film insert – you might go out and shoot a horse and carriage arriving – you know, one day's work. The rest of it would all be done on these sets inside in the television studios, so that the whole process of working was entirely different to filming. The main problem was that you couldn't get your lighting as clear cut and as accurate and it was sometimes quite difficult to organise the cameras in such a way that you could get the close-ups you wanted, so that the whole rhythm of shooting was entirely different. It was much like it might been in the theatre.[39]

Improvements in production technology were certainly a spur to the achievement of a more convincing realism in television drama. The signs were early on quite noticeable and were, for the most part, positive. But in some cases, there was a price to be paid. While BBC TV continued its good works in the now well-established Sunday teatime slot with *Rob Roy* and *Vice Versa*, it hit troubled waters with Constance Cox's serialisation of *Oliver Twist* which began in January 1962. This production of a popular classic was beautifully cast, with Max Adrian as Fagin and Peter Vaughan as Bill Sikes. It was the murder of Nancy which made this production controversial. Peter Vaughan noted: 'These classical roles are very rich to play. They're rich, and therefore you know you have something really to latch on to. The trick with them is to make them real, because I think they can be over drawn.'[40] But the endeavour to achieve realism did not please all viewers. There was a storm of protest, with letters in the national press, which mostly showed concern at so much violence being shown in a production watched by so many younger viewers. This production actually sparked off a row in the House of Commons, in which the Postmaster General described the murder scene as 'brutal and quite inexcusable'. The BBC wilted under pressure and cut the final scene, which showed the shadow of Sikes's body swinging from a rope. This raises questions which are ever present in adapting the classics for broadcasting. Bearing in mind the oft-proclaimed aim of being faithful to the integrity of the original text, to what extent should they be modernised and even censored in consideration of their potential audience's particular chronocentric prejudices? What may have been the world view of the nineteenth century may well not find favour with today's audience.

The Corporation's transmission of *The Old Curiosity Shop* in 1962, with a 15-year-old Michele Dotrice as Little Nell, Oliver Johnston as Grandfather Trent, Patrick Troughton as Quilp and Anton Rogers as Dick Swiveller, was much more happily received. In 1964 Constance Cox dramatised *Martin Chuzzlewit*, interestingly adding an opening sequence to explain the origins of the division between the Chuzzlewit brothers. This production starred a memorable Pecksniff – Richard Pearson, who made a splendid feature of his unctuously reiterated 'Mercy, my dear' – Gary Raymond as young Martin, Ilona Rodgers as Mary Graham and Barry Jones as old Martin. *A Tale of Two Cities* (starring Patrick Troughton as Dr Manette, Kika Markham as Lucie, Nicholas Pennell as Darnay, Rosalie Crutchley as Madame Defarge and John Wood as Carton) tiredly followed in 1965 – with a modest bunch of extras running round and round in the studio trying to look like a revolutionary mob storming the Bastille. The effect was not impressive.

Rivalry with ITV

In 1955 BBC television lost its monopoly when commercial television began. The assault on the BBC's monopoly began when, in 1946, the British Institute of Practitioners in Advertising lobbied for television advertising. In that same year the postwar Labour government had extended the BBC Charter only for a further five years, rather than the ten years that had been widely expected, and in 1949 a Government Commission, chaired by Lord Beveridge, met to discuss both the future of radio and television broadcasting in the United Kingdom and, more specifically, the question of the BBC's monopoly. In its written submission to the committee the BBC argued that the introduction of other programme services would inevitably result in the lowering of the broadcasting service as a whole because broadcasters would be forced to abandon their cultural goals in order to win larger audiences. The Beveridge Committee's findings echoed these sentiments: 'because competition in broadcasting must, in the long run, descend to a fight for the greatest number of listeners, it would be the lower forms of mass appetite which would more and more be catered for in programmes'. However, the Report also included substantial evidence pointing towards a future media environment in which the BBC would not have the sole monopoly. There was powerful interest shown by both the large advertising agencies – who foresaw that they would immediately find new outlets for their wares – and the electronics industry, who anticipated a boom in the sales of television sets. This was, in fact, borne out: despite the high price of television sets at this time, sales jumped from one million television sets in 1951 to over five million sets sold in 1955.

A minority report submitted by the Conservative MP Selwyn Lloyd proposed that although the BBC should continue to control radio, television should be financed by sponsored advertising under the control of the British Television Corporation. With an election in the air, the struggling Labour administration gave Ernest Bevin the job of preparing a new Charter for the BBC which would have enshrined in law the strength of its monopoly position for another ten years. This was a task he was never to complete. Bevin died suddenly, and before anything could be done, the election was over and the Conservatives were returned in 1951. The days of the BBC monopoly were numbered, and the critics now had the power and the will to attack both Beveridge and the BBC. The next real challenge to the BBC's monopoly came with the formation of the Conservative broadcasting study group in 1951 and soon the rights and wrongs of the monopoly were being discussed by the Church and the teaching profession. The extra-parliamentary commercial television lobby was channelled through the Popular Television Association, which was supported by a number of prominent business leaders (including Sir Robert Renwick, who quite co-incidentally, perhaps, held 14 directorships in the electricity supply and electronics industries), and by C.O. Stanley (chairman and managing director of the electronics company, Pye). Conservative backbench opinion was articulated by John Profumo MP, who argued that the press had supported the BBC because it feared a loss of advertising revenue, while the Labour Party had supported it because it was against competition.

Initially, it had not seemed that the debate about commercial broadcasting would be split wholly along party political lines: supporters of commercial television were to be found on both sides of the House. But when the opposition Labour Party stated that it would, if returned to power, dismantle any television station run solely for 'private profit', the issue quickly resolved itself into a party political one, thereby – given the Conservative's comfortable parliamentary majority – assuring the Bill's success. Mark Chapman Walker, head of research at the Conservative central office, suggested an innovative alternative to American-style programme sponsorship: a state authority would control independent commercial stations who would be responsible for producing their own programmes and recoup the production cost by selling advertising time during commercial breaks. The political and commercial pressures for the formation of commercial television proved overwhelming and, on 4 March 1954, the Bill to create the Independent Television Corporation was introduced. This involved a large grant being paid to the body to administer the new system. However, such government control outraged a number of Conservatives and during the committee stage of the Bill 206 amendments were tabled. In spite of this difficult beginning, the Bill became law on 30 July 1954, passing its second reading by the fairly narrow margin of 296 to 269 votes.

Although the advocates of commercial television argued that this was a service the public required, the public opinion polls conducted in the years leading up to the 1954 Act revealed that public opinion on whether the BBC's monopoly should be ended had remained fairly evenly split. The arrival of commercial television was, therefore, in fact determined by the lobbying of industrial and advertising groups who had recognized that television provided a central plank in developing the postwar consumer boom. And it very quickly appeared that this potential audience would soon be realised in fact: in September 1955 the ITV audience numbered 180 000; by 1956 that had risen to one-and-a-half million and had reached over four million the following year. The television audience ratings in the same year showed a similar movement towards TV: there were only three BBC programmes listed in the top ten programmes for each week that year against 536 ITV programmes.

When the ITC was established in 1954 the intention was to conduct a comprehensive review of British broadcasting a decade later. This review was undertaken by the Pilkington Committee on Broadcasting in 1960. Its findings were an attack on much that the commercial stations had done and its recommendations included a proposal to disenfranchise the contracting ITV companies, a proposal which the Conservative government chose to ignore. Much of the reaction against the ITV companies was a reaction against the rapid growth in television advertising, and it was felt by many that this commercialism extended to the mindless materialism of much of the ITV output. When the Pilkington Report on the future of radio and television broadcasting was published on 27 June 1962, its conclusions were that the BBC was successfully realizing the purposes of broadcasting as defined under its Charter, but that commercial television did not successfully achieve the purposes of television broadcasting as defined in the Television Act. The BBC's proposals for a second channel and to start a colour transmission were accepted in the government white paper of 4 July 1962.[41]

During the consideration of the evidence presented to the Pilkington Committee, television drama was discussed at some length, and space was timetabled for the discussion of drama (on 9 November 1960). There was concern that the BBC might have lowered its standards in the face of competition from the commercial channel, but it was, on the other hand, argued that changes in society had brought forth changes in playwriting – in the theatre, as well as for production on television.[42] The changes referred to may be discerned in the BBC's fine record in commissioning and producing new television dramas with this social awareness, in a rather more adult approach in bringing the classics to the small screen and in the commercial television's good record in new drama, pioneered especially in ABC's (later Thames Television's) *Armchair Theatre*. Under the guidance of Canadian Sydney Newman these Sunday night transmissions had concentrated on contemporary plays by contemporary writers. The model, while originally American and Canadian, *Armchair Theatre* soon acquired a stable of British writers, producers and directors. Dramatists included Alan Owen, Ray Rigby, Robert Muller. The concern for committed, socially relevant drama earned the nickname 'armpit theatre' but its influence was undeniable.

Sydney Newman was appointed to head BBC Television Drama in 1963 and thus began what many still regard as the beginning of the Golden Age of BBC Television drama. Newman was responsible at this time for fostering quality productions both in terms of single plays and drama series/serials. *The Wednesday Play* slot, (later called *Play for Today*) which attracted socially committed and often provoking material, had regular audiences of between ten and 12 million.[43] Some idea of the range and quality of the output during the 1960s may be gleaned from brief details of BBC television drama transmissions in just one year, 1965: new drama included Simon Raven's *Mr Jocelyn, the Minister*, David Mercer's *And Did Those Feet*, John Hopkins's *Horror of Darkness*, Neil Dunn's *Up the Junction* and four plays by Dennis Potter (including two of the Nigel Barton plays).[44] Serials included *For Whom the Bell Tolls* and series included *The Wednesday Thriller*, *Mogul*, *Sherlock Holmes* and *The World of Wooster*. Classical drama was well served with the television version of the Royal Shakespeare Company's *Wars of the Roses*. Peter Watkins's *The War Game* was produced but not transmitted.

With its fairly comfortable and growing audience figures, commercial television at first made little attempt directly to compete with BBC endeavours as far as televising the classics was concerned. The first noticeable shift in style or taste was that the BBC began to treat their classic novels in a more adult fashion. *Great Expectations* was adapted, courageously using Dickens's original unsentimental (and unhappy) ending. This production starred John Tate as Magwitch, Peter Vaughan as Jaggers, Francesca Annis as Estella and Gary Bond as Pip. *Pride and Prejudice* was serialised on BBC-1 in 1967, produced by Campbell Logan, starring Lewis Fiander and Celia Bannerman. A sound and convincing *Nicholas Nickleby*, dramatised by Hugh Leonard and starring Martin Jarvis followed in 1968, chiefly remembered for Jarvis's charming head of naturally curly hair and the splendidly eccentric Gordon Gostolow as Newman Noggs. The BBC, one might say, now grown up, cast around for classic literary texts which dealt seriously with socio-political issues. With serial versions of Zola's *Germinal* and *Nana* and Flaubert's *Sentimental Education* it was as if we had left the innocent world of *David Copperfield* and *Treasure Island* for good.

BBC-2 was launched in April 1964 and a new slot was allocated for classic serial adaptations (of a more adult kind) on Saturday evenings. This allowed for a more sophisticated and sometimes daring choice of novel, and a more adult treatment in longer episodes. The classic serial took a considerable step forward and the year 1967 was to prove a turning point in television drama history. *The Forsyte Saga* was screened, a massive undertaking and the last classic serial made in monochrome. *Vanity Fair*, made in ostentatious colour to launch BBC colour television on 2 December 1967, was the first classic novel serialised in colour.

A sign of things to come was the lavish BBC production of *The Forsyste Saga*, shown in 26 50-minute episodes in 1967. Dramatised by Lennox Philips (and others) it was directed by James Cellan Jones. Among its lavish cast were Eric Porter, Nyree Dawn Porter, Kenneth More, Susan Hampshire, John Welsh, Joseph O'Connor, Fay Compton, Margaret Tyzack, Lana Morris. The series was well planned; each episode was more or less free-standing and independent, but connected up with the general outline of the unfolding dramatic series as a whole. It proved a much honoured series – BAFTA Awards for Best Drama Series, Eric Porter, Nyre Dawn Porter as Best Actor and Actress, and Julia Trevlyan Oman for Best Design. This classic serial was also a landmark in the change-over from live drama transmission to monochrome videorecording. The series gathered an audience of over 18 million viewers per episode, (which would offer very considerable competition to Granada's *Coronation Street* today) and was hugely successful in the USA where it was shown on National Educational Television in 1979 – the first major breakthrough in selling BBC series to America. It was bought and shown all over the world, including the USSR and all told, world viewing figures are reckoned to have totalled 160 million.[45]

The Forsyte Saga seemed to have struck a particular chord with British viewers, reaching the same parts of the national psyche as those soon to be tickled by Granada's drama series created by John Hawksworth *Upstairs Downstairs* between 1970 and 1975 in 75 50-minute episodes. Fascination with the same period was demonstrated in Yorkshire Television's drama series *Tom Grattan's War* which ran from 1968 to 1970 and told the story of a young boy who was sent to work on a farm in Yorkshire when his father served in the Great War and his mother worked in munitions.[46] It should additionally be noted that BBC-2 had much success with their eight-part drama-biographies *The Edwardians* (1972) which featured notable Edwardian figures Conan Doyle, Lloyd George, (a fine starring, and stirring, performance by Anthony Hopkins as the Welsh Wizard), Horatio Bottomley, E. Nesbit, Rolls and Royce. In 1974 BBC ran *The Fall of Eagles*, a 13-part drama series about the Hapsburg dynasty covering the period from the mid-nineteenth century to the 1914–18 war which again appealed to the long sunset of the Old World.[47] Thames Television transmitted *Jennie, Lady Randolph Churchill*, a seven episode drama series biography of Jenny Jerome, Winston Churchill's mother. The series portrayed the period of Randolph's career and its tragic conclusion, the Boer War, and her various love affairs. It was shamelessly drenched in romantic nostalgia for an age of elegance long since lost.[48] ATV capitalised on this Edwardian craze with *Edward the Seventh* (13 50-minute episodes in 1975), their splendid complete life of Edward VII, written by various television dramatists, based on Philip Magnus's biography. Edward was notably played by Timothy West, with Annette Crosbie as Queen Victoria and Robert Hardy as Prince Albert. The BBC bought John Hawksworth's team of Edwardian re-enactment experts for their 1976–77 series *The Duchess of Duke Street*, with Gemma Jones the plucky working-class cook who makes a glorious go at running a fashionable London establishment, based on the true life story of the remarkable Rosa Lewis and the Cavendish Hotel, cheerfully recycling the same Edwardian period nostalgia. Another series which contributed to this 1970s pocket of Edwardianism[49] was Ken Taylor's 1974 drama series *Shoulder to Shoulder* (six 50-minute episodes) which devoted an episode apiece to the six leading Suffragettes.

Nostalgia for the glorious lingering sunset of Edwardianism was very strong at this time when both Labour and Conservative parties seemed to have lost the political will to cope with problems of the present day, and the West lacked the leadership it might otherwise have had from across the Atlantic while the USA was locked in the Indo-China debacle and the Watergate crisis. A particularly ideological version of the immediate pre-1914 war Edwardian period seemed a great comfort – its flavour founded in the indulgent sorrow of the Georgian poets, the meandering pastoralism of Vaughan Williams, Frederick Delius and their imitators, and that Elgarian melancholy which suggests that amid the glory is the passing of an age. Such feelings are powerfully present in the slow movements of the two great symphonies, with Jacqueline du Pre at this stage in her career immortalising her moving, nostalgic rendition of the great Elgar cello concerto. In 1973 Lord David Cecil looked back to the death of his grandfather, Lord Salisbury, in 1903:

My grandfather died that evening, as the sun was setting. This sunset, as subsequently historians have not failed to point out, was symbolic; and not just of my grandfather's death. To the contemporary observer his career had remained to its close a success story. He died still a revered national figure, with his party in power and his policies apparently successful: he had been Prime Minister of England at the Diamond Jubilee of 1897, which celebrated the highest point of dominion and glory ever attained by the English. In fact Fate, in a spirit of irony which my grandfather would have appreciated, if grimly, had designed these triumphs as though to provide a contrasting prelude to a period of spectacular catastrophe, which entailed, incidentally, the decline of most of what my grandfather had stood for: British greatness, aristocratic government, individual liberty and international peace. Within fifty years of his death, British greatness had dwindled, aristocratic government had disappeared, individual liberty had lost its prestige and England had been involved in the two greatest wars in the history of mankind.[50]

Peace, harmony, tranquillity, stability seem to have existed before the cataclysm of 1914. After it comes all that is 'modern'. As Samuel Hynes argues, we continue to live with the consequences of the First World War in a comprehensive way:

> The sense of a gap in history that the war engendered became a commonplace in imaginative literature.... Poets and novelists rendered it in images of radical emptiness – as a chasm, or an abyss, or an edge – or in images of fragmentation and ruin, all expressing a fracture in time and space that separated the present from the past.... The gap in history had entered post-war consciousness as a truth about the modern world.[51]

These ideological themes are very strong in Joseph Losey's 1970 film version of L.P. Hartley's *The Go Between*. It is to that seemingly enduring stability, that break in the heartbeat of time which is implied in that picture of Edwardianism we carry in our minds to which these series – *The Forsyte Saga, Upstairs, Downstairs, The Duchess of Duke Street* – appeal. As Philip Purser commented:

> For the British audience a hidden significance (of *The Forsyte Saga*) was its function as a kind of communal family history, replete with lots of births, deaths and juicy scandals but also a nostalgia for what were imagined to be better days.[52]

And the series was given a very elaborate and indeed adult treatment. This was not the last of the big-time classic serials to be made in monochrome, but it definitely pointed to new developments in the style and tone of television classic serials which were to be taken up after the advent of colour television. At the time, these new signs were easy to overlook. Viewed in retrospect, the elaboration, attention to detail, bravura acting and a general serious, adult tone are easy to detect. The impact of the series was immense. Viewing figures grew and grew; publicans and vicars bemoaned their diminishing custom. A clear landmark in the classic serial tradition had been reached, and passed.

The advent of colour television

The first classic novel to be dramatised and transmitted in colour was Rex Tucker's version of Thackeray's masterpiece, *Vanity Fair*, broadcast on BBC-2 in six episodes beginning on Saturday 2 December 1967. It was directed by David Giles, who also directed *The Forsyte Saga*. *Vanity Fair* was an elaborate undertaking, with 60 speaking parts, lavish costumes and conscientiously historical design by Spencer Chapman, conceived and developed to show off the new channel and the wonders and charms of colour television. One big set-piece, the Duchess of Richmond's famous pre-Waterloo ball, was based on the 'actual' building in Brussels where the event would 'actually' have taken place – as it were. This was no mean achievement. Historical source books differ in interesting detail. One assures posterity that the dance was held in a converted coach house, another says the ball was situated in the largest room in the house. So the designers compromised – they combined the two. Susan Hampshire was Becky, and already famous for her role as Fleur in *The Forsyte Saga*. Some indication of the splash the series was hoped to make may be judged from the fact that Miss Hampshire had 30 costume changes, culminating in her appearance at the ball. Marilyn Taylerson was Amelia, Dyson Lovell was Rawdon Crawley, Bryan Marshall Captain Dobbin and Roy Marsden George Osborne. It was rapturously received by reviewers. Maurice Wiggin in the *Times* spoke for many when he said: 'Yet how enchanting it all is, the lovely nineteenth century interiors, the clothes and uniforms.... Yes, this will be remembered. It lends itself wonderfully to colour....'[53]

Colour television – and *Vanity Fair* began the tradition marvellously – brought a revival of interest in classic novels which could be set in luscious locations, classy architecture or rhapsodic landscapes – *Wuthering Heights*, plenty of Jane Austen, *Jane Eyre*, *The Mill on the Floss*, and, most courageously, *War and Peace*. Such were the treats which lay in store for the next decade.

2
The 1970s: Signs of Change

Television in the 1970s was well placed to develop its reputation for dramatising classic novels: television now transmitted in colour. BBC-1 continued to enhance its reputation with the long-established Sunday serials of popular classics (particularly with those considered suitable for younger viewers) and BBC-2 realized its promise in presenting an impressive series of evening serial dramatisations of classic novels, several of which have proved in the long run worthy of a significant place in the history of British television drama. Commercial television also produced fine examples of costume drama, which looked good on colour television. But it was the BBC which still held the field when it came to 'doing the classics'.

BBC classic treatment: the Galsworthy beat

A new age of television drama seemed to open on New Year's Day 1970 with the transmission of the first part of *The Six Wives of Henry VIII*. Bearing in mind BBC classic serial drama's long standing indebtedness to John Galsworthy from the very earliest days of classic novel dramatisations, the comment by BBC-2 Controller, Robin Scott, is revealing. '*The Six Wives of Henry VIII* was an inducement to acquire viewers to BBC-2', he told David Attenborough, as it had what he termed 'Galsworthy beat'.[1] The BBC certainly showed no fear in finding the Galsworthy beat in the most unlikely of texts. It gave the classic treatment to Jean-Paul Sartre's trilogy *The Age of Reason, The Reprieve, Iron in the Soul*, in the 13-episode dramatisation by David Turner *The Roads to Freedom* in 1970 (13 50-minute episodes). This was an in-depth exploration of issues related to personal and political freedom in a world just plunging into chaos as Germany prepared to invade France at the beginning of the Second

31

World War. Mathieu Delarue, the intellectual who needs the support which allegiance would bring him, was played by Michael Bryant, Donald Burton played Brunet, the committed Communist, and Daniel Massey played Daniel the homosexual. This was the first television serial which included real-life historical characters, such as Daladier, Hitler and Chamberlain. The characteristically Sartrian obsessions with philosophical and political ideas proved difficult to work up into acceptable television drama, but this was an extremely adventurous production by David Conroy and directed by James Cellan Jones.

Loyalty to British classics was well maintained with several dramatisations of novels by Thomas Hardy, whose fiction was in the gradual process of being rediscovered. People who know Dorset will testify to a comparative lack of interest in him before the 1970s which strongly contrasts with today's Hardy-obsessed county. The Thomas Hardy Society was not founded until 1967.[2] Even Bournemouth University considered it appropriate to give the name the 'Thomas Hardy Restaurant' to the training restaurant for its catering courses (the 'William Barnes cafeteria' is adjacent to it, by-the-by) – even though the University itself does not boast an English Department and offers no Hardy in any of its academic syllabi. But such confusion is not unusual so far as Hardy's county is concerned: a visit to Dorchester will see the town's post office referring to itself as 'Casterbridge Post Office', while 'Bournemouth' University is itself actually geographically located in Poole. The new recognition of Hardy as being in some way significant to the county after all, and even if it did give rise to such confusions as those noted above, was probably encouraged by the several outstanding BBC television adaptations of the 1970s – *The Woodlanders* (BBC-2, 1970), and *Jude the Obscure* (BBC-2, 1971) followed several years later by *The Mayor of Casterbridge*.

The Mayor of Casterbridge was a BBC TV production in association with Time-Life Films and was broadcast as a seven-part serial between 22 January and 5 March 1978 on BBC-2.[3] The idea for the dramatisation had emanated from the Serials Department of the BBC where script editor Betty Willingale had suggested Dennis Potter's name for the task of transforming the tragic novel into a classic serial for BBC-2.[4] The novel had first been serialised in *The Graphic* in 1886, and tells the story of the rise and fall of Michael Henchard – a man who sells his wife at a fair and by this act brings about his own downfall 20 years later. Henchard is a man deeply affected by powerful, unknown forces in nature and in himself, and Hardy portrays him throughout almost as at a distance, ending as unknowable as he began. Potter took the novel and added to it a close and penetrating analysis of this central character, which eventually saved the production. It was a pioneering work in several respects. *The Mayor of Casterbridge* was the first serial shot entirely on lightweight OB cameras, and the production team clearly had not entirely got the hang of the new technology. The lighting is atrocious in the opening episode, giving the picture quality of a football match (which is what these lightweight cameras had originally been designed to record), with all the variety in camera-work of a tennis match. This did not promise well. But the quality of the acting (Anna Massey turns in a superb performance, looking distinctly anorexic but giving real weight to Lucetta), together with Potter's close observation of Henchard's character saved the enterprise, and it was widely praised by the critics. Christopher Ricks wrote:

> A true dramatisation is one which has an ear for... dramatic ironies and can then refrain from dinning them into our ears... Mr Potter doesn't plod in the novelist's footsteps: he seizes the novel's lines of force, converging on the heart of the book, Henchard's relation to the 'daughter' who does in a way become his daughter.[5]

Potter told Betty Willingale that he saw Henchard as a manic depressive – which arguably tells us more about Potter's psychology than it does about Henchard's,[6] but it was just this exploration of the complexities of Henchard's character which more than made up for deficiencies elsewhere in the production, and it was something of a stroke of genius on Betty Willingale's part to have chosen Potter for the dramatisation in the first place. Many of the novel's themes seem quite obviously to connect with Potter's own, most notably the idea of a single fatal lapse from grace and the 'commodification' of women by men.[7] Any other dramatist may not have been able to rise above the plodding narrative of the original and the technical flaws in the use of the new technology.

The new channel might almost be said to have been showing off, with no less than three dramatisations of major Russian novels. Feodor Dostoyevsky's *The Possessed* (BBC-2, 1970) was dramatised by Lennox Philips, produced by David Conroy and directed by Naomi Capon, starring Keith Bell, Tim Preece, David Collings, Joseph O'Connor, Anne Stallybrass and Rosalie Crutchley. Dostoyevsky's *The Gambler* (BBC-2, 1971) was dramatised by John Hopkins, produced by David Conroy and directed by Michael Ferguson. The cast included Dame Edith Evans, Corin Redgrave, Maurice Roeves, Philip Madoc and John Philips. Tolstoy's *Resurrection* (BBC-2, 1974) which starred Alan Dobie, went almost as far as television adaptations can go in attempting to present the imagining of a creative writer, for Tolstoy's later novel moves more by religious and metaphysical ideas than by strong dramatic situation, and this yielded considerable problems in dramatisation. The novel is the story of an aristocrat who seduces a young woman who then becomes a prostitute. When she is wrongly accused of a crime she did not commit, he moves heaven and earth to achieve a repeal for her, but is shocked when she finally refuses to marry him. For Tolstoy at this stage only redemption through achieving the state of grace offered by the Christian faith is the answer. The pair make their supreme sacrifice by going to Siberia together. Thus inevitably reduced by television dramatisation to its narrative bare-bones Tolstoy's anguished novel seemed to be a fable rather than a mature work of art.

The BBC showed that it could do considerable justice to French classics. *Pere Goriot* by Honore de Balzac (BBC-2, 1971) was one of the earliest examples of the Corporation's newly aroused interest in serious literature prompted by the award of the new channel. Dramatised in four episodes by David Turner, produced by David Conroy, it was directed by Paddy Russell, with Michael Goodliffe (Goriot) and David Dundas (Rastignac). As Balzac himself admitted *Old Goriot* is a novel about what happens to people who insist on keeping up appearances. As a visual medium, television proved unsurprisingly good at showing this in this production. Goriot, a retired merchant, has spent his last sou in paving the way for his two daughters' social advancement, paying their every debt and giving them large dowries, while he lives in squalor in Mme Vauqeur's boarding house. None of the fellow guests will believe his tale that he is the father of the glittering and glamorous baronne Delphine de Nucingen and comtesse Anastasie de Restaund. They, for their part, are too ashamed to acknowledge or to visit him. Rastignac, an ambitious law student, who is his fellow lodger, resolves to rise in society by whatever means are available, and becomes Delphine's lover. Goriot becomes seriously ill after rescuing Anastasie once more. In his last moments he calls for his daughters, but he dies without seeing them. Rastignac sells his watch to pay for the old man's funeral. The adaptation captured the sombre vitriol of Balzac's social vision.

The Corporation's interest continued the next year with their 1972 production of Balzac's *Cousin Bette* (BBC-2 in six episodes). This was dramatised by Ray Lawlor, produced by Martin Lisemore, and directed by Gareth Davies, with Margaret Tyzack (Bette), Thorley Walters (Baron Hulot) and Colin Baker (Steinbock). This was a novel that was possibly not familiar to British readers. The television version went much of the way towards delivering its complex satiric narrative, however. Bette is the poor country cousin of the successful Adeline, of whose social success she is jealous. Adeline is married to the shallow, womanising Baron Hulot. Bette generously takes in and sponsors a poor struggling artist, the Polish refugee Count Wenceslas Steinbock, who repays her generosity by falling in love with Hortense, the Baron's daughter. Bette plans and executes an elaborate scheme of revenge. Knowing exactly where and how to tempt the venal Baron, she sets him up for an affair with the promiscuous young wife of a clerk in the defence ministry, where the Baron holds high office. He sets her up in an apartment and bankrupts himself trying to keep her other lovers away. In trying to recoup his losses he involves his uncle in a scam which goes awry, and the poor relative kills himself. Hulot leaves his son to look after his wife and goes into hiding. He then discovers his son is enjoying his mistress's favours. Bette's plans do not run entirely as she hoped, and she grieves to learn that Hulot's son inherits a fortune. She is taken ill and dies. Adeline dies of shock when she learns that Baron Hulot, anticipating his wife's death, plans to marry a family servant. While none could justifiably claim that the elaborate complexities of Balzac's novel were totally dealt with in this dramatisation, what emerged splendidly was Balzac's portrait of a degenerate, promiscuous and greedy society.

Also in 1972, BBC-2 began broadcasting one of the landmark television classic novel dramatisations – Tolstoy's epic *War and Peace*. It was dramatised by Jack Pulman and transmitted in 20 45-minute episodes (totalling 15 hours) between 28 September 1972 and 8 February 1973. This was certainly a long-term project, three years in the making, and very much influenced by the Russian film directed by Sergei Bondarchuk in 1967.[8] Production involved what was up to that time the most expensive television drama set ever, at £30 000, and about 200 characters with speaking parts.[9] It was produced in association with Time-Life Films Inc. and Yugoslav Films Belgrade, much of it benefiting from filming on location in Yugoslavia, with the Yugoslavian Territorial Army employed as extras.[10] This was an ideal product to demonstrate and justify the BBC Television's recently acquired additional channel, but it earned a mixed reception. To some viewers it seemed too long and reverential, ultimately failing convincingly to render the passion, pathos and complexity of the novel, to others it seemed an uplifting and life enhancing experience.

War and Peace certainly raised the question as to the possibilities of adapting classic novels to the screen – are there some novels which are beyond the scope of television to dramatise? Could it be that Tolstoy's masterpiece is such a literary triumph of the novelist's art, that it defies adaptation? The essence of the problem lies in the very effectiveness of Tolstoy's mastery of narrative, dialogue, monologue and omniscient authorial voice. This problem was accurately focused upon by Clive James, writing in *The Observer*. Tolstoy's creative imagination takes you over completely when you are exposed to it – in much the same way as does Shakespeare's or Dante's – so that you feel that your life is being remade. The aesthetic totality of *War and Peace* is more than just the words on the pages, so there can be no question of:

> ...transposing Tolstoy from the page to the screen, since he is not on the page in the first place.... Universal genius is its own medium and transpositions out of it are impossible – it's one of genius's defining characteristics. That Verdi recreated 'Othello' in music doesn't make Othello a transferable asset. It simply means that Verdi is in Shakespeare's league.[11]

The best BBC Television could do, according to Clive James, was to boil Tolstoy's complexity of dialogue, commentary and revealed action down to a straightforward narrative which faithfully reproduced, yet at the same time, completely betrayed the novel's flow of events. This is an extreme position to take. An effort has to be made to take television drama on its own terms, and in this case it is then possible to see that BBC-2's *War and Peace* was not only a courageous effort, but an aesthetically successful one. It was convincing and moving drama. Its generosity of spirit and capacity to move were by no means dwarfed by its undeniable spectacle – the burning of Moscow and bleak and horrifying retreat across landscape dominated by black woodland and bleak white snow linger in the memory. Some of the novel's most powerful and moving moments are convincingly reproduced in terms of television drama, the sequence during the retreat between Platon Karatayev (Harry Locke) and Pierre (Anthony Hopkins) with its mixture of action, dialogue and Pierre's thoughts in voice-over worked much more effectively than at a simply basic level. The viewer could experience what Tolstoy imagined and wanted us to experience.

In 1973 BBC-2 transmitted a dramatisation of Jane Austen's *Emma*, dramatised by Denis Constanduros, produced by Martin Lisemore, and directed by John Glenister. Emma was played by Doran Godwin, Harriet by Debbie Bowen and Mr Knightley by John Carson. It was loyal, in the BBC Jane Austen tradition, with the convincing classic-serial house style surface quality. The fidelity to Jane Austen's text is marked, but in one important respect, this might be to little avail. There is always the danger of making Emma rather too likeable, when we know the novelist herself declared it had been her intention to create 'a heroine whom no one but myself will much like'. In Doran Godwin's performance she is certainly an interfering little minx, whom it is for the most part quite difficult to like. Mr Knightley's admonishing her is timely and quite enjoyable. Few would relish the thought of being on the receiving end of John Carson's authoritative reproof (in which he draws on strengths previously exhibited to great effect in his creation of Mr Dombey). But it is not here that problems arise as much as from the fact that the effect of *Emma* relies on an awareness that the novelist is deliberately guying and parodying the clichés of the conventional romantic novels of her day. The comic potential of Emma's plans for her little friend Harriet depend entirely on her being the foundling born for better things which Emma supposes her to be. Like Catherine Morland in *Northanger Abbey*, Emma Woodhouse suffers from Don Quixote's similar inability to differentiate fiction from real life. Unless Emma is placed in this frame of reference, then the basic implications of the plot will not make complete sense. *Emma* has a verve and confidence unlike Jane Austen's previous novels. It is no good playing this like *Pride and Prejudice*. Emma is the work of a great novelist who knows what she wants to do and is consciously aware that she can do it. Harold Child's famous remark summarises the situation neatly:

> Jane Austen herself admired Elizabeth Bennett; she loved little Fanny Price; Emma she both loved and admired, without a shade of patronage or a hint of heroine-worship. That Emma should be loved, as she is loved, for her faults as well as for her virtues, is one among Jane Austen's many claims to the rank of greatness in her art.[12]

Somehow in this production that magnitude did not come through. Though well above routine level, this *Emma* just failed to convey that majestic sense of achievement. Considering the supposed values which allegedly dominated life at this time, this production failed to identify or highlight the relevant themes in Jane Austen's *Emma*. Jane Austen is clearly aware of the importance of class and money in the way society works. In her world the aristocracy is modest in size but strong in its assumption of importance. It has survived because of its strict if uncodified rules. This tiny class was enduring the upward thrust of a middle class not only growing but growing in full consciousness of its importance, which was attempting to claim by imitating its display behaviour – manners, snobberies, conspicuous consumption. For many in the more modest reaches of the land-owning gentry economic survival was precarious. It was Emma's secure middle-class position which gave her a position from which she could fantasise about Harriet, and the dominance of the male in Austen's society, backed up with his social position, renders Mr Knightley so big a presence.[13]

British television discovers Henry James

BBC-2 demonstrated its commitment to high culture with an interest in Henry James, who could scarcely be claimed to be a widely read author in Britain. At one stage in his career, James longed for success in the English theatre. But he did not regard his own novels as suitable for dramatisation. Hearing that one had failed on the London stage he was reported to have commented: 'You can't make a sow's ear out of a silk purse.' Neither does it seem highly rated as a fit subject for dramatisation in received television industry wisdom. In *Halliwell's Television Companion* between the entries for 'James, Geraldine, British actress…' and 'James, Sid, crumple-faced South African comic actor…' the name of the distinguished novelist is lacking. Nevertheless, there have been several far from unsuccessful attempts to bring his fiction to the small screen. Colour television may well have contributed towards a characteristically 1970s reawakening of interest in Henry James. Victorian and Edwardian fiction, of course, has always interested media classic serial makers, but James's fascination with European upper-class social mores offered tempting pickings for colour television – handsome clothes for men, beautiful dresses for the ladies, sumptuous, frequently palatial, locations. Television dramamakers' ambitions might well have been spurred by the success of *The Forsyte Saga* to turn attention to James in the early 1970s.

Whatever the reason, the decade was scarcely underway before television declared its interest with *The Spoils of Poynton* (BBC-2, 1971). This was dramatised by Lennox Philips, produced by Martin Lisemore and directed by Peter Sasdy, with June Ellis, Diane Fletcher, Pauline Jameson, Gemma Jones and Ian Oglivy. This four-episode adaptation by Lennox Philips, *The Spoils of Poynton* made a fair fist of dramatising the master for television. And the nature of the task is an interesting one, for the essence of James is the gift of recognizing and unravelling the one simple clue which renders plain some vast complexity of human entanglement. Apparently, *The Spoils of Poynton* was based on the novelist's chance overhearing of a remark concerning a lady in the north of England who was on bad terms with her only son over the ownership of the valuable furniture and other objects in a house which were to come to him by way of his father's will. This was the clue to the labyrinth. Poynton, the house filled with magnificent treasures collected by Mrs Gereth, is the central symbol of the novel. Pauline Jameson was excellent as Mrs Gereth, but Gemma Jones was rather too glamorous for Fleda, whom James created as a rather mousy character. Nevertheless, the adaptation worked by reducing the novel to its basic mechanism and focusing close attention on its workings. A couple of years later this success was repeated with *The Golden Bowl* (BBC-2, 1973). Dramatised by Jack Pulman, produced by Martin Lisemore, directed by James Cellan Jones, with Kathleen Byron, Daniel Massey, Gayle Hunnicutt.

It is a self-evident truth that Henry James's fiction is greatly concerned with the barely concealed tensions between the culture of the New World and the Old World. He shows Americans, often young American women, fascinated on visiting Europe – independent, courageous but often innocent – and coming into conflict with Europeans – wise, cynical but often ethically compromised. *The Golden Bowl*, published in 1904, might be put forward as James's most elaborate treatment of these themes. In Rome, Charlotte Stant, a sophisticated but penniless young woman, has a brief affair with Prince Amerigo, an Italian aristocrat, who has a title but no money. Mutually realising their love could not endure without funds, Charlotte returns to USA. Amerigo then falls in love with Maggie Verver, daughter of wealthy American Adam Verver. They represent those very American virtues so often portrayed by James – moral forthrightness, outward looking, enthusiastic, delicate innocence. Amerigo and Maggie marry. Charlotte and Maggie are friends. Charlotte returns to Europe – to London – and shopping with Amerigo considers buying Maggie a present. It is a golden bowl, perfect except for one invisible flaw. She does not buy it, but it then becomes a symbol of much in the novel – Amerigo's flawed character, as well as the hidden fissures, duplicities and flaws in the various relationships. Maggie begins to realize that, after her marriage to Amerigo, she has lost the close relationship she had with her father. The novel reaches its emotional climax when Maggie buys the golden bowl as a birthday present for her father and on delivering it to the household, the shopkeeper confirms her suspicions as to the relationship between her husband and Charlotte. This is a superbly photogenic moment. Cyril Cusack, as the shopkeeper, is struck by the sight of two photographs. One of Prince Amerigo and another of Charlotte. He casually recalls that four years ago, on the eve of the wedding of Adam and Maggie, Charlotte had called at his shop and nearly bought this very bowl. She would have had it, had it not been cracked. This typically Jamesian moment – a passing remark with the emotional power of high explosives – was fully achieved in this television dramatisation. Maggie's good friend, Fanny Assingham, tells her that her suspicions are as cracked as the bowl and she dramatically smashes it to the floor. Jack Pulman succeeds in translating this novel, whose richness and power lies so much in its themes and ideas, into a powerful television drama. Daniel Massey and Gayle Hunnicutt, as Amerigo and Charlotte, who despite their moral ambiguity, earn our sympathy, and Jill Townsend as Maggie, stays well on the right side of priggishness.

Commercial television recreates the past

Commercial television lavished much that had been learned from the classic serial tradition on various historical costume drama series. Outstanding in this respect was LWT's obvious imitation of Noel Coward's *Cavalcade*, their immensely successful family saga, *Upstairs, Downstairs*, which ran to 13 one-hour episodes between 1971 and 1975, and produced the spin-off series, *Thomas and Sarah* (1979). *The Strauss Family* (ATV, 1972) began with a 90-minute episode and was followed by six one-hour episodes. *The Brontës of Haworth* (Yorkshire TV, 1973) was reverent almost to the point of being doom laden, but this series of three 75-minute serials managed to combine entertainment with education in impressive balance. Literary history was further given media treatment in *Dickens of London* (Yorkshire Television 1976) and *Will Shakespeare* (ATV 1978).

In 1974 Thames presented a curious series, *Napoleon and Love*, with Ian Holm as Bonaparte engaged in a series of amours over nine episodes. Commercial television achieved dazzling success with two royal drama series during the decade, *Edward the Seventh* (ATV 1975) and *Edward and Mrs Simpson* (Thames 1976), and they risked the borderline territory between royal history and royal scandal in *Lillie* (LWT 1978).

Commercial television also broadcast dramatised serial versions of various classic novels with varying success – *Black Arrow* (Southern Television, 1972), *Country Matters* (Granada, 1972), *Father Brown* (ATV, 1974), *South Riding* (Yorkshire, 1974), *The Stars Look Down* (Granada, 1975), *Dick Turpin*, based to some extent on Harrison Ainsworth's

Rookwood (LWT, 1979) and *Kidnapped* (HTV, 1979). Several of these productions were outstanding. Granada's *Country Matters* was a series of 13 50-minute dramas based on fiction by A.E. Coppard and H.E. Bates, and set in rural England. It was voted the best drama series by BAFTA in 1972. Strictly speaking, *Country Matters* was not a classic novel serialisation, but in every respect, it looked like one. Brilliantly devised by Derek Granger, who rightly recognized fashionable British interest in its own rural past at a time when serious economic tensions were beginning to affect the quality of modern British life, and adapted by Hugh Leonard, James Saunders, Jeremy Paul and Hugh Whitemore, these individual stories shared a gift for locating strong characters in dramatic situations set in a credible rural context involving different people and situations, gained a convincing familiar uniformity which awarded the series a quality not unlike a serialised narrative. *South Riding* was dramatised by Stan Barstow in 13 60-minute episodes from Winifrid Holtby's novel. It was produced and directed by James Ormerod, with Dorothy Tutin, Hermione Baddeley and Nigel Davenport. Winifrid Holtby's 1936 James Tait Black prize-winning novel made ideal television serial drama. It was an engrossing mixture of social reforming zeal against poverty and social conditions, with melodramatic elements including seduction, blackmail and a passionate love affair, set in a fictitious South Riding of Yorkshire – a world of natural beauty but made ugly as 'a world besieged by poverty, ugliness, squalor and misfortune'.[14] It was judged by BAFTA as best drama series of 1974.

The BBC continues the classic novel tradition

The Corporation continued to build on its reputation for serious dramatisations of classic novels. Two series of the mid 1970s seemed to affirm the BBC's almost proprietary right to the literary high ground – *The Pallisers* (1974) and *I, Claudius* (1976). *The Pallisers* was clearly from the same stable as *The Forsyte Saga*, and starred Susan Hampshire, Philip Latham, Roland Culver, Fabia Drake, Sonia Dresdel, Sarah Badel and Gary Watson. It took 13 months to shoot the 26 50-minute episodes which were transmitted on BBC-2 between 1 January and 29 June, and 26 October and 2 November 1974. The housestyle was noticeably the same. This lavish saga was dramatised by Simon Raven. In *Box of Delights* it is actually described with anachronistic accuracy as '...a sort of Son of *The Forsyste Saga*.'[15] In terms of surface quality there was much similarity with the BBC's monochrome Galsworthy epic – serious-faced men with ample whiskers and top hats, handsome women exposing acres of shoulder in ample dresses with the dramatic action alternating between intrigue in drawing rooms and galloping with the hunt. But for all its hype and bluster, *The Pallisers* somehow failed to touch the heart of the nation. Trollope believed that the Palliser novels – *The Small House at Allington, Can You Forgive Her? Phineas Finn, Phineas Redux, The Prime Minister* and *The Duke's Children* – would represent his crowning creation, and Galsworthy dearly wanted to be a Trollope for his time. But the magic didn't work. The hype was impressive, however, and a foretaste of what was to come in television programme publicity towards the end of the twentieth century. There was a *Radio Times* Special devoted to the series, which had a glossary, plot synopses, a family tree of the Pallisers, details of the characters, the actors who played them, accounts of the production, and various historical colour pieces including details of Victorian inventions. The publishers Panther marketed the six novels with colour illustrations from the television series. It is interesting to speculate on the series' apparent failure to ignite public interest, as it would appear to have had everything that it required to guarantee a hit. But it is all too easy in retrospect to identify what it lacks – inspiration, to put it simply – but very difficult to analyse and qualify what is meant by the term as applied to this series. One problem is that for all the impression of Trollope's Palliser novels as pounds and pounds of solid meat, examination reveals that huge amounts of the wordage is authorial commentary, and even closer inspection exposes a startling fact – that much of our impression of character, motive and action is in fact delivered by the omnipresent author. Thus, stripping the story down to what happens and who says what, leaves very little with which to fill and ornament the television screen for weeks on end. Writing in *The Listener* Raymond Williams proffered an interesting reason for the series' inability to score a hit with viewers. Unlike the story of the Forsyte family, with whom we could identify to some large extent because it portrayed a bourgeois society to which we still felt some connection, the Pallisers represented a heavily hierarchical and deferential society apparently alien to modern experience, which no amount of design, costume and acting could convincingly bring to life:

> It would be easy to say that this is a machine-made successor to *The Forsyte Saga*, with the ordinary reflex to an earlier, more affluent, more leisured time (that lie that works better than a truth) some such assumption may well have been made. But when you call your

bourgeois family 'Forsyte' you show respect as well as a sense of limitation and postponed, accumulating life. And because this is still a bourgeois society, the adaptation was made and played with a connecting and inner seriousness. The Duke of Omnium and Plantagenet Palliser and Lady Glencora M'Cluskie exact plushy gestures but less reasoned identity, and so characterisation and presentation keep slipping between well-dressed solidarity and late night parody. It may hold at some level, by sheer extent, but it will not be the smoothness of Trollope, who could combine a fascination with the mechanics of power and convenience with a more fundamental, if still edgy, deference than you can now expect from actors and writers and directors. They have after all come in from the streets; they may enjoy the clothes and the mansions and they are professional enough to sketch almost anything; but to take the ideas and the feelings at their full seriousness – that, and it is much to their credit, is beyond them.[16]

Memories of *The Pallisers* were soon to be erased by a drama series whose success probably surpassed the expectations of those who initiated and produced it. This was *I, Claudius*, based on two novels by Robert Graves – *I, Claudius* and *Claudius the God.* (BBC-2, 1976) Dramatised in 13 50-minute episodes by Jack Pulman, produced by Martin Lisemore, directed by Herbert Wise. The cast included George Baker (Tiberius), Brian Blessed (Augustus), Sian Philips (Livia), John Hurt (Caligula), Derek Jacobi (Claudius) and Christopher Biggins (Nero). Biography as a literary genre was a late development in antiquity; its origins may be discerned in dirge and funeral orations and to a greater extent in the character descriptions in the works of the historians such as Thucydides and Xenophon. Plutarch (second century AD) is the first biographer with what we would recognize as a 'modern' approach to writing life stories of the eminent. Suetonius wrote vivid biographies of the twelve Caesars. Robert Graves's *I, Claudius* and *Claudius the God* were based on a very good wheeze – a convincing spoof 'autobiography' by the emperor Claudius – whom it is believed actually wrote an autobiography, now lost.[17] But who would have thought that ancient biography would prove so successful in modern television?

Claudius (Tiberius Claudius Nero Germanicus) was the son of Antonia, daughter of Mark Antony and the elder Drusus, and was an ideal subject for Graves's unusual authorship, because – although his autobiography was not to survive – much historical material remains for the plundering. He lived in such interesting times, full of bloodshed, sex, debauchery, intrigue and politicking; a rich vein of stories simply waiting to be mined. Graves based his work mainly on Suetonius and Tacitus. The period covered, as it were in this eye-witness account, is the history of the early days of the Empire from its establishment under Octavius Caesar (Augustus) through 24 BC to 54 AD, covering the reigns of Tiberius, Caligula, and Claudius – a period of 78 years. Such a set-up and such stories make first-class television serial drama. What we got (and enjoyed) was the ultimate boardroom drama, in Roman togas instead of dark suits. Alistair Cooke commented:

> In this dramatic version, Augustus was seen as a burly, good-natured and baffled target for his wife's unyielding ambition to have her son Tiberius succeed to the throne; as a man barely able to turn around in a court of seething intrigue before he must hatch or stifle another plot and bemoan another murdered. This *I Claudius* was frankly a story about the continuous collisions between the authority of the emperors and the private characters, ambitions, vices, and idiosyncrasies of their families, friends and enemies. Jack Pulman...had the wit and dialogue skill to stay close to the two endowments of Robert Graves...fidelity to his sources...and his brilliant virtuoso idea of having the imperial Romans talk in the familiar idiom of his own generation of British Empire builders.[18]

As Clive James also noted:

> The scenes of dissipation, which earlier in the series tended to recall the Windmill, rose to approximate the standard set by Raymond's RevueBar. Which is probably what the originals were like, when you come to think about it.... A wonderful series, like a sexed up version of *The Brothers*.[19]

Interestingly enough, the series was trimmed and cut for US viewers, who were spared bouncing bare black bosoms when a chorus of African dancing girls helped Augustus celebrate the anniversary of the battle of Actium, a bed scene and the disembowelling of Drusilla, Caligula's sister.

Among the best examples of the dramatisations the BBC continued to make during the 1970s were *Last of the Mohicans* (1971), *Clochermerle* (1972), *War and Peace* (1972), *Madame Bovary* (1975), *David Copperfield* (1974, a passable version with Arthur Lowe, Martin Jarvis and Anthony Andrews), *Our Mutual Friend* (1976), *Count Dracula* (1977), *The Mayor of*

Casterbridge (1978) and *Testament of Youth* (1979). The BBC also pioneered a series of M.R. James ghost stories dramatised for television over the holiday period – *The Stalls of Barchester* (1971), *A Warning to the Curious* (1972), *Lost Hearts* (1973), *The Treasure of Abbot Thomas* (1974) and *The Ash Tree* (1975). In the main, BBC classic novel dramatisations, especially those scheduled for evening transmission, achieved a level certainly better than just the workmanlike. Among the most interesting was *Madam Bovary*, shown on BBC-2 in four episodes. It was dramatised by Giles Cooper, produced by Richard Beynon, directed by Rodney Bennett, with Francesca Annis, Tom Conti, Denis Lill, Brian Stirner.

This production was unusual in that it is one of the very few examples of an adaptation being repeated. The dramatisation, by the great pioneering radio playwright Giles Cooper, was first produced in 1964 with Nyree Dawn Porter in the title role. This new production was equally well cast with Francesca Annis as lead. But the main problem with this otherwise sensitive and well-written dramatisation, was the loss of Flaubert's narrative voice. Flaubert's loathing of bourgeois romanticism comes through in the novel, not just in the characterisation of the silly Madame Bovary and her doomed love affairs, but in the sustained irony of the faultless narrative. What we get on the small screen is an unhappily married young wife of a country doctor in Normandy, who has furtive and sordid love affairs – with a law clerk (Brian Stirner) and a young landowner (Denis Lill) – before committing suicide when her reckless debts catch up with her. The audience receives no explanation for her behaviour – the romantic dream world of Walter Scott and Byronic lovers. One example should make this point. Her suicide, far from being the grand event she obviously hoped for, is sordid. Her great moment in death from arsenic poisoning is spoilt by vomiting, which she had foolishly not taken into account. Even in death she is cheated of the aura of romance she had anticipated. But in her televised death we see precisely (and only) the fact of her dying, while the underlying desires of her psychology are necessarily absent.

In 1971 BBC Scotland began to show the way to a new social awareness in their choice and treatment of classic novel adaptations, focusing on novels which explored the darker side of recent social experience. In retrospect it may look as if the way was opened by the company's sensitive version of Lewis Grassic Gibbon's *Sunset Song* (BBC-2, 1971). These stories dealt with life close to the soil and indeed the breadline in North East Scotland. They were dramatised by Bill Craig, produced by Pharic Mclaren and directed by Moira Armstrong, starring Vivien Heilbron, Paul Young and Andrew Keir. These were followed by two sequels 1982–83. In

1975 BBC and 20th Century Fox combined to produce a five 50-minute episode version of Richard Llewellyn's novel *How Green Was My Valley*, dramatised by Elaine Morgan, produced by Martin Lisemore and directed by Ronald Wilson. It starred Stanley Baker, Sian Philips, Gareth Thomas, Mike Gwilyn and Rhys Powys. The same year Granada Television transmitted Alan Plater's 13 one-hour episode serialised dramatisation of A.J. Cronin's *The Stars Look Down*, which dealt with harsh social conditions and industrial unrest in the North East during the early part of the century. It was produced by Howard Baker and directed by Roland Joffre. The large cast included Avril Elgar, Norman Jones, James Bate, Rod Cuthbertson, Ian Hastings, Alun Armstrong, Basil Dignam and Anne Raitt. These social realist dramas may be seen as an attempt to offset the period charm of costume drama, which had to some extent dominated the early stages of colour television, and were followed by *Fanny by Gaslight* (BBC-1, 1981) and *Fame is the Spur* (BBC-2, 1982).

Dickens redivivus

Dickens, whose works had been such a staple commodity in the early days of the classic serial, might be seen as to be under some kind of eclipse during this decade. *David Copperfield* (BBC–Time-Life) dramatised in six 50-minute episodes by Hugh Whitemore for the Sunday teatime slot was a fairly traditional offering, bordering on the fussy. Although it had several outstanding performances – Anthony Andrews (Steerforth), Martin Jarvis (Heep), David Troughton (Ham) and Arthur Lowe (Micawber) – several major roles were miscast. Patricia Routledge was a rather well-fed and genteel Mrs Micawber, Patience Collier was a sharp and dominant Betsy, with little hint of the warm heart lurking beneath the surface. David Yelland had a good shot at David but lacked that open-hearted warmth all David Copperfields require, while other characters – Traddles, Peggotty, Rosa – just failed to ignite the touch-paper and Ian Hogg struggled with the impossible role of Dan'l Peggotty. Despite every effort the impression of a lot of modern actors dressed up in specially made mid-Victorian costume could not be erased.

Seen in contrast to this is *Hard Times* (Granada, 1977) shown in four 50-minute episodes. This version of a novel (which has not very frequently been adapted)[20] was written by Arthur Hopcraft, who had served a long apprenticeship writing for television, beginning as a sports reporter.[21] The production starred Patrick Allen, Timothy West, Edward Fox, Alan Dobie, Ursula Howells and Jacqueline Tong. Of its many impressive and noticeable qualities, the effectiveness of its design and use of locations, won Roy Stonehouse a BAFTA award. We may now see that its elaborate and authentic locations and studio designs were part of an entirely new way of 'doing' Dickens. Here we had Dickens treated, not in the traditional 'classic serial' way, with an eye mainly on the needs of younger viewers, (and the intention to educate them into a love for the classics), but as an adult novelist with much to say about (and to) the modern world. The work was handled seriously, not solemnly, and adult issues faced in a mature manner – there was no doubt as to Edward Fox's (Harthouse) intentions on Louisa Gradgrind. The tone was wholly free from any sense of condescending to the audience and mercifully in the process of transferring text to screen much of Dickens's tedious didacticism was toned down.[22]

This version of *Hard Times* struck a resoundingly contemporary chord, at the very moment when the air was thick with the fulminations of Keith Joseph, Mrs Thatcher, Paul Johnson and the Duke of Edinburgh as the New Conservatism struggled to be born. The programme was transmitted when the British Prime Minister, James Callaghan, had launched his rather Gradgrindian 'Great Debate' on the need to get schools back to the task of producing a skilled workforce for the manufacturing industries: 'Now, what I want is facts. Teach boys and girls nothing but Facts. Facts alone are wanted in life. Plant nothing else, and root out everything else...' – and so on. At the time Conservative Central Office was lauding the ideal of the self-made man, we had Timothy West as Josiah Bounderby of Coketown, 'a rich man, banker, merchant, manufacturer and whatnot... a man who could never sufficiently vaunt himself a self-made man...' Dickens seems presciently to have anticipated the Aims of Industry, who wailed every time there was a whiff of nationalisation or government intervention that it would kill the golden goose and that all would be ruined:

> The wonder was, it was there at all. It had been ruined so often, that it was amazing that it had born so many shocks.... They were ruined when they were required to send labouring children to school, they were ruined when inspectors were appointed to look into their works, they were ruined when such inspectors considered it doubtful whether they were quite justified in chopping people up with their machinery.
>
> (*Hard Times*, 1854)

This seemed in tune with leading ideas in public debate at the close of the 1970s, a time when state support for industry was falling into disrepute and there was much talk of leaving the running of business, commerce and industry to those who knew how to do it. The English people, Dickens says in *Hard Times*, 'are as hard worked as any people upon whom the sun shines' and are exploited by a dreadful conspiracy between the harsh disciplines of political economy and utilitarianism and the bored, effete upper classes. The Gradgrind party went around recruiting 'and where could they enlist more hopefully than among the fine gentlemen who, having found out everything to be worth nothing, were equally ready for anything?' At a time when it was considered a self-evident truth that the trade unions had too much power and were too ready to hold the country to ransom, here was Dickens with the same message as the *Daily Mail* and *Daily Express*, telling us that time and again the honest English working man was betrayed by the bully boys of the Left. Even the name of the suffering, labouring blackleg, Blackpool, (with all its holiday, conference and working-class associations) seemed prescient, if not redolent. The trade union agitator is despicable in Dickens, less worthy than the men he claims to represent. The dominating ideas of this part of the 1970s were very like those of Thomas Carlyle, to whom *Hard Times* was, in fact, dedicated.

Although Granada's *Hard Times* was a landmark production of a Dickens novel, it is also part of a general revaluation of Dickens. This has been underway since the centenary year of 1970 and the publication of what amounts to a recantation by F.R. Leavis and his wife, Queenie Leavis, of *Dickens the Novelist*. Leavis had little room for Dickens when he was constructing the canon of the great English novelists and novels which was enshrined in his book, *The Great Tradition*. The only novelists worth reading, according to this teaching, were George Eliot, Henry James, Joseph Conrad and D.H. Lawrence. The only work of Dickens to survive his scrutiny (joke intended) was *Hard Times*, so its celebration in this television version of 1977 was, in a sense, appropriate. Dickens's rehabilitation was certainly assisted (only months after Granada's *Hard Times*) by BBC-2's *Our Mutual Friend*, dramatised by Julian Jones and Donald Churchill, in seven 50-minute episodes. It was produced by Martin Lisemore and directed by Peter Hammond, and starred Lesley Dunlop, John McEnery, (John Rokesmith), Leo McKern, (Mr Boffin), Jane Seymour, (Bella Wilfer), Polly James (Jenny Wren). The sense of mood in this production was helped by Carl Davis's beautiful and effective music, subsequently released on cassette – a harbinger of the growing importance of the musical soundtrack in the marketing of television drama series. When *Dombey and Son* was serialised some ten years previously it was supported by well selected passages of music by Sibelius, and

The Onedin Line had sailed out with billowing passages of Khachaturian. But the tendency was now more and more towards television dramas having their own specially-commissioned scores.

Mood is important in *Our Mutual Friend* – a rich and complex novel in which materialism is satirised within a melodramatic narrative. In this television version the melodrama survives successfully intact, but much of the moving imagism of Dickens's imagining is sacrificed. The main metaphor is that of the dustheap, which combines the themes of wealth and rubbish. Dickens had shown an interest in the connections between muck and money as early as *A Christmas Carol*. *Our Mutual Friend* is a monumental satire on a society which worships money, which, Dickens suggests, in itself is worthless. Money is just round bits of metal and pieces of paper, but Dickens shows how modern men and women spend their lives in its thrall. The great metaphor which holds *Our Mutual Friend* together is the vast dustheap which stands for a fortune. These heaps of dust and rubbish were objects of great commercial value. They were bought and sold because of the wealth they might yield – from lost items of valuable property they might contain, and for the marketable material which could be sifted from them – soot used as manure, ashes used in brickmaking, bones and human excrement used in fertiliser. In *Household Words* 13 July 1850 there is an article about the sums of money which could be made out of dustheaps, sometimes as much as between £40 000 and £50 000. Among the frightening sights the last Spirit shows Scrooge is the den of a dealer in urban debris, situated amid streets of filthy, stinking, dank, wretched houses in foul and narrow streets, to which his miserable, grimy possessions are brought after his death:

> ...a low-browed, beetling shop, below a pent-house roof, where iron, old rags, bottles, bones, and greasy offal, were bought. Upon the floor within, were piled up heaps of rusty keys, nails, chains, hinges, files, scales, weights, and refuse of all kinds. Secrets that few would like to scrutinise were bred and hidden in mountains of unseemly rags, masses of corrupted fat, and sepulchres of bones.

As academic attitudes gradually recovered, the rehabilitation of Dickens got underway. In the 1970s there was a marked revival in productions of Dickens novels for BBC Radio Four. Dickens had always been a major element of radio classic serials,[23] but a series of adaptations – variously written by Constance Cox, Barry Campbell and Betty Davies, produced by Jane Morgan – set a consistent standard of style, integrity and dramatic sweep which was new and has subsequently scarcely been equalled. The quality is immediately recognizable, but it is by no means a simple matter to identify the various factors which combined to produce such high production values over a decade, including *Pickwick Papers, Bleak House, Martin Chuzzlewit, Little Dorrit, Our Mutual Friend* and *Dombey and Son*. The casting was immaculate. From such a galaxy of star performances it is unfair to select only a few, but mention must be made of Freddie Jones and Douglas Livingstone – the definitive Pickwick and Sam Weller. Peter Vaughan – cast against type – a convincing and extremely moving William Dorrit, Patricia Hayes immortal as Mrs Gamp, Michael Graham Cox authoritative and touching as Mr Boffin and Robert Lang causing one's flesh to creep as Mr Tulkinghorn. Sylvestre le Touzel delivered an utterly convincing Edith Dombey, which wonderfully combined hauteur, vulnerability and melodrama. The absorbing quality of the narrative was greatly enhanced by extended use of Dickens's narrative voice, by Simon Cadell, (wonderfully darkly modulated in the later tenebrous London-based novels, *Bleak House, Little Dorrit* and *Our Mutual Friend*, but wittily and busily bouncing along in *Pickwick Papers*) and Simon Russell Beale (in *Dombey and Son*) which served not only to hold the complex narrative together, but also to render the experience vastly more Dickensian by bringing home the irresistibly comic, as well as the powerfully demonic, those observations of character, comic asides and ironic observations and casting over the whole the glow of his idiosyncratic imagination.

The fact is that it is not so much the stories Dickens tells us, it is the way Dickens tells us stories. Narrative is a mixture of first and third person. The natural language of moving pictures is third person narrative. The direct narrative voice, first person, voice over, does not really work. In Dickens's case the visual image brings with it the loss of much of the comedy and all of the poetry. Simon Cadell's narrative was always recorded after the rest of the drama, so the authorial voice took its tone from the production, rather than have the actors responding to the voice which guided the story. Imperceptibly this must have supported the coherence of the production style. As this series of productions developed, from *Pickwick Papers* (1974) through *Little Dorrit* and *Bleak House* to *Our Mutual Friend* (1984) and *Dombey and Son* (1996) Jane Morgan became, as it were, an acknowledged exponent of Dickens in much the same way as Beecham with Mozart or Hans Knappertsbusch with Wagner or Kenith Trodd with Dennis Potter. She served a long apprenticeship in radio drama, beginning with several years on the radio soap opera, *The Dales*.[24]

Jane Morgan commented:

> I had done *The Dales* for a period of time, then *The Dales* came off the air. I went to television and worked in television for a bit and when I came back, I think because I'd done rather posh programmes, they realised I knew about books as well as cooking.... It was *Mill on the Floss* which they had to do on very short notice and I did it. I can remember all the people who were in it and it was wonderful actually to have good material to work on.... In some ways the Dickens style comes naturally as I have read all the books since I was a child. I read my first Dickens when I was about twelve for pleasure, so I have got a history of knowing Dickens and loving it. Therefore I have a background and a feeling for it. And I think the other thing is, about the way I do them, it's the result of the fact that I have never believed in just rehearsing and recording a production, for me it's always been a matter of working with an ensemble, a company.[25]

These productions, unfortunately are not all commercially released on audio cassette,[26] became standard versions with an impressive unity of style and consistently excellent ensemble playing.

New technology, new tone

In 1978 BBC-2 transmitted Tolstoy's *Anna Karenina*,[27] dramatised in ten 50-minute episodes by Donald Wilson, and directed by Basil Coleman. This production starred Nicola Pagett (Anna), Eric Porter (Karenin) and Stuart Wilson (Vronsky). Unfortunately it proved a costly demonstration that worthiness and respect for a literary master-piece are alone not a guarantee of success. The result was somewhere between a Russian *Forsyte Saga* and Chekov. Either way, the high moral integrity of Tolstoy's tragic tale of adultery got lost in a display of high production values on the surface of things, but a noticeable hollow-ness beneath. There was no denying the feeling that ten episodes was somehow to tempt high tedium rather than high seriousness. By the end of the decade new technology was making an impact on the making of television drama. In 1978 the BBC created another land-mark television drama series with Dennis Potter's dramatisation of *The Mayor of Casterbridge*, filmed on location using lightweight video recording equipment. This was the BBC's tribute to mark the fiftieth anniversary of Thomas Hardy's death. Obviously the opportunity was taken to make this Thomas Hardy series a lavish tribute to the grandeur and glories of the Dorset landscape using the possibilities of colour video filming on location.

The decade was to end with the BBC transmitting two of the most outstanding classic serials of the decade which demonstrated just what the Corporation was still capable of. The first was Vera Brittain's *Testament of Youth* (1930), one of the key books of the century. It is one of those works which has actually conditioned the very way we regard our century and it affects our perceptions at so many levels. It is Vera Brittain's autobiographical account of her attempt to realise her potential in what was still a man's world. In the telling she renders an account of the social changes brought about by the Great War for Civilisation which contributed to the shaping of the modern world. *Testament of Youth* is the story of an entire generation, and of a world which disappeared forever in that complex of destruction which began in August 1914. Within the narrative there is a dreadful irony. As she struggled to gain her place and competed against the young socially-favoured males of her generation, this generation of young men was being slaughtered in the war. Her father is a manufacturer and has no doubts he is doing the right thing in educating his son, Vera's brother – sending him to public school, Oxford, the lot – while neglecting her. She struggles and eventually manages to secure promise of an Oxford education just as the conflict begins. The war takes her brother, his friends, her friends and the man she hoped to marry. From the irredeemable folly of politics and the terrible destruction of war a new world is born. How was all this to be brought into the sitting room by the small screen? One was inescapably brought to remember Shakespeare's special pleading on behalf of the insufficiencies of the theatre adequately to render the experience of Agincourt. And yet *Testament of Youth* was both convincing and deeply moving. It was dramatised in five 50-minute episodes by Elaine Morgan, produced by Jonathan Powell and directed by Moira Armstrong. It starred Cheryl Campbell, Rosalie Crutchlie, Emrys James, Geoffrey Burridge, Hazel Douglas, Rupert Frazer, Joanna McCallum, Michael Troughton and Peter Woodward. There was a beautiful musical score by Geoffrey Burgon. It might almost be argued that this adaptation was better than the book, simply because it was able to draw on more resources – photography, newsreel, the war poets. We are accustomed to think of the War in terms of old film and photographs and the moving prose and poetry by which people grappled to describe the inexpressible. In this production there were several effective moments when sepia period photography, moving film, words by Sassoon and others, soldiers' letters and so on, took over from Vera Brittain's narrative to tell what she wanted to tell you in ways unique to television. The effect was to tell a period story, but uniquely in terms of a period we could recognize from the medium of television itself. This series won four BAFTA awards. As Philip Purser commented:

> The collision of idealism and carnage in 1914–15 is deftly evoked by the odd bits of archive film, snatches of Rupert Brooke and the echoes of bugles and distant gunfire in Geoffrey Burgon's score. It sounds second-hand, it's not: it is making legitimate use of associations that have been set up over the years by Remembrance Services and Cenotaph ceremonies.[28]

The second was also outstanding, but in some ways a media curiosity. Originally classic serials had been based on novels which were perceived as having been absorbed into the canon of established literary classics, already to belong to that select group of established novels which were passed down from generation to generation to form part of our national culture. But once the classic serial as a genre was established, the process could work the other way – classic status was conferred upon a work of fiction and given the media's accolade by a dramatised serialisation presented with sufficient seriousness. Thus John Le Carre became a classic novelist at the end of the decade when his espionage novel, *Tinker, Tailor, Soldier, Spy* was dramatised in seven 50-minute episodes by BBC-2 in 1979. Written by Arthur Hopcraft and produced by Jonathan Powell, it was directed by John Irvin. It starred Alec Guinness (Smiley), Patrick Stewart, Bernard Hepton, Terence Rigby, Michael Aldridge, Ian Richardson, Alexander Knox, Ian Bannen and Hywell Bennett. In several ways it was a complete television oddity, a kind of drama not possible in any other medium. But it makes a strong point about the way in which a media dramatisation can somehow confer dignity. There was enough plot material in the original novel to make, with effort, about two episodes, but the whole piece was padded-up and gift-wrapped in sumptuous Kings College, Cambridge sort of music which was the final high culture/high camp touch to make it seem much more than it really was. The schoolboy soprano voices bringing with them not only associations of the corrupt English establishment, but also a whiff of heady ambiguous decadence; a full-blown attempt to transform a modern spy novel into a classic novel by means of translating it into an undeniable classic serial. The result is media-literary high camp, a triumph of style over content.

3
The Blockbusters

The new Conservative government elected in 1979 brought a change of climate. The 'winter of discontent', the days of the nanny state, government intervention, trade union power, welfare handouts and so on, were over. Business should be economically run so that debts were met and dividends were paid. Those that could not manage this would be allowed to go to the wall. At the individual level, people should abandon the belief that the world owed them a living and assume responsibility for themselves. Restrictions on enterprise should go. The basic code was survival of the fittest and the leanest, and making ends meet. The state was to be rolled back. Individualism should flourish. Let capitalism thrive. Leave money-making to those who could do it. They would provide jobs for everybody, wealth for the nation and energy for the economy. The benefits would trickle down to the rest of us. Signs of the change were rapid and obvious. Some people did very well, and unemployment increased. Beggars appeared on our streets. People lived in cardboard boxes in city shopdoorways. Every high street sprouted charity shops. Broadcasting was not going to survive without severe change. The BBC soon felt itself under threat. It was a Corporation, part of the very state apparatus that Thatcherism found so uncongenial. Also it had a public service ethos which some of those in high places perceived as tending to liberalism or even anti-conservative. But for the main, the central issue was the manner in which radio and television broadcasting was to be funded. This ultimately was to affect production, how programmes were funded and the kind of programmes which actually got made.

The BBC feels the draught

In 1927 the Charter which brought the BBC into existence represented an interesting and unique compromise between public revenue and government control. The BBC was funded from revenue raised by the system of licences sold to the public. The government granted the Charter to the British Broadcasting Corporation, which was a self governing corporation. Programming policy was left to the Corporation. Consequently the principle of democratic choice was built into the system, for governments are elected by the general public and changes in the Charter could always be negotiated by an elected government. Even after the Act of 1955 had brought commercial television into existence, the IBA had maintained more than a token semblance of the traditional Reithian public service philosophy in its operations. But progressive national economic decline, shortage of public funds, inflation and the mounting costs of broadcasting brought matters to a crisis in the late 1970s. The Labour government had encouraged the BBC to borrow to supplement its income from the licence fee. As long as the BBC continued to service its debts, matters could be maintained and competition with commercial television could be reasonably maintained.

Beginnings of the ratings war

The BBC's comparative ratings with commercial television schedules and programming did not seem to be of much concern, except during the Christmas and New year holiday period, when newspapers carried details of comparative ratings. Matters at this time were seen as some sort of contest and readers' curiosity was aroused as to whether the 'BBC had won the ratings war' over the holiday. When the Keith Joseph/Margaret Thatcher ideology-of-the-market-place was brought to earthlings and turned into economic actuality, broadcasting was among the earliest industries to experience the bracing effects of the change. The income of commercial television was scarcely affected on the same scale as the BBC, which had a more or less fixed income, based on the licence fee. This neither necessarily reflected the industry's costs, nor responded with any appreciable flexibility, to the vagaries of inflation.

The BBC had endured these financial strains for some years, but had eased things by borrowing. The new Conservative government put a tight reign on such slovenly and unhousewifely fecklessness. The Corporation was now to face severe competition in prestige high production values programme output. Signs of the strain were soon to show, and especially in drama.

A temporary eclipse

The BBC's lavish classic serial treatment of John Le Carre's *Tinker, Tailor, Soldier, Spy* in the autumn of 1979 was to be its last glossy, glamorous literary adaptation for several years. Now the long-held belief that British television was the 'best in the world' was to be put to the test. At the very time when the BBC was being told by its paymasters that they should themselves exert the effort to make ends meet by selling their programmes overseas, they were drastically short of the very funding which was needed to put their acclaimed classic drama serials into production. But there was some life in the old dog yet. In March 1980, BBC-2 broadcast Jonathan Powell's production of Zola's *Therese Raquin*, a co-production made with London Film Productions. This was dramatised by Philip Mackie in three episodes, produced by Jonathan Powell and directed by Simon Langton. The impact of this production was vastly more than the sum of its parts – an unforgettably vivid realisation of an extraordinary novel.

The dramatisation unwound this frightening and sordid tale like a tightly-coiled spring. Therese (Kate Nelligan) lives a seething and unfulfilled life with her weak shopkeeper husband, Camille (Kenneth Cranham). Camille's mother, who has set them up in business, lives with them. Therese begins a passionate love affair with Laurent, (Brian Cox) and they decide to kill Camille. He takes some killing, but they finally manage to drown him in a boating 'accident'. But they cannot rid themselves of the feeling of his creepy presence, even though they visit the morgue and see his unmistakable body there, lifeless. This scene was memorably unnerving, and far more chilling than the inevitably rather clumsy attempts to represent the way the guilty partners were haunted by hallucinations of their crime. The sense of nightmare mounts. They believe once they are married, the dreadful visions of Camille will cease, but the corpse seems to haunt them. Camille's paralysed old mother is there, witnessing their guilt, but though she knows, a stroke has rendered her speechless, thus preventing her bringing them to justice. Their love begins to turn to loathing and hate. They finally kill themselves as the terrified old mother sits watching them. This production was a triumph of design, which placed the violent but sordid affair in a dark, greasy social environment you could almost smell, as Clive James commented: '...even in Zola's imagination Paris never looked so tacky. The whole screen is submerged in seaweed soup and liquid sulphur. Somewhere in the middle of the suffocating tedium Therese throbs with "besoin"...'[1]

There was something in this series, in its style, which was new, mature and convincing. There was a boldness in the characterisation and presentation of desire, sexuality and of evil which transcended previous BBC productions. *Madame Bovary* seemed innocent by comparison. It had moments which will always be remembered – the utterly abandoned way the lovers hurl themselves at each other, the recurring moment of Laurent's dreadful death, the moment during cards when the old lady tried to betray their guilt but was unable to communicate except by the terror in her eyes. *Therese Raquin* was one of the BBC's greatest achievements in the classic serial tradition, but its immense promise was not realised for several years.

The BBC's long-held premier position as purveyor of classic literature in terms of television drama was soon to be eclipsed, albeit only briefly. Commercial television suddenly seemed to seize and conquer the high literary territory – so long a treasured part of the BBC's empire – with two spectacularly successful dramatisations. Granada Television's *Brideshead Revisited* and *The Jewel in the Crown* seemed during the opening years of the 1980s to have driven the once unconquerable BBC classic serial from the field. The BBC maintained their connections with the great tradition in a series of dramatisations of the more traditional kind, mainly Trollope, Jane Austen and Dickens, eked out with rather less impressive efforts such as *The Talisman*, *The History of Mr Polly*, *Beau Geste*, (with a sandpit near Wareham in Dorset serving as the desert), *The Invisible Man*, *The Prisoner of Zenda*, *Goodbye Mr Chips*, *Jane Eyre*. There were signs of recovery in *Bleak House* (BBC-2, 1985) and *Tender is the Night* (BBC-1, 1985), but even *Fortunes of War* (based on Olivia Manning's *The Balkan Trilogy*) transmitted on BBC-1 in 1987 did not fully regain something of the Corporation's old form. And there were more threats to the BBC's ownership of the classic serial to come.

1981: the year of Brideshead

Granada launched *Brideshead Revisited* in October 1981. It had originally been estimated in 1980 that this series would cost £3 000 000; the cost rose to £5 000 000 on completion the following year. Production took two-and-a-half years and was plagued by mishaps: matters were seriously delayed in 1979 by ITV industrial action; in 1980 Jeremy Irons (Charles Ryder) was also committed to filming *The French Lieutenant's Woman* and was obliged to go to and from both productions; editing and post-production was beyond everyone's worst fears. Stories leaked to the press with such headlines as

'Bankruptcy Revisited' and 'The Curse That Visited Brideshead'. The production was nevertheless to earn immense critical acclaim. It had an estimated ten million viewers when first transmitted in the UK. It was nominated for 13 BAFTA awards: best actor (Anthony Andrews), best drama series, best design, best make-up, best film sound, best film editing and best costume design.[2] It was sold to 14 countries, including the USA, Canada, Australia and New Zealand, won many awards, including 11 Emmy nominations in 1982. It was the prescience that did it; the series bodied forth values and iconography of the Thatcher revolution – golden days of a wealthy youthful elite, high-class conspicuous consumption, Oxbridge as the backdrop location, a new emphasis on 'heritage' – all of which was to be further exploited in numerous television series as the decade proceeded.

It has been argued that the heritage industry was the only UK industry to thrive under Conservative policies – that modern obsession with finding permanent, solid values in the past, transforming us into diachronic tourists in our own history.[3] History is the parts of the past which are useful to the present. This deep division between the past – the classical, the antique, the ancient – and the modern – the fashionable, trendy, chic, novelty – characterise and animate our culture. The present is the world of the everyday grind, the world of work. Personal memory refreshingly recalls happier, younger days, of a sunny childhood even. But history, the more distant past, is the long summer holidays of our collective past. The past is not so much another country. It is the perfect package holiday. And we have all seen it on TV.

A respect for age: 'Bother', said Pooh

This new age of the longing, lingering look into the past was inaugurated by *Brideshead Revisited*, and brought in its train a massive return to past epochs – the Raj, Edwardian England as constructed by E.M. Forster/Merchant Ivory and Jane Austen country. At the centre of the experience is the haunting emblem of the large country house and there is an impressive list of television dramas set and actually filmed at historic sites up and down the country: *Brideshead Revisited* (Castle Howard, near York), *By The Sword Divided* (Rockingham Castle, Market Harborough, Leicestershire), *Cluedo* (Arley Hall, Arley, Cheshire), *Grace and Favour* (Chavenage House, Tetbury, Gloucestershire), *Poldark* (Botallack Manor, Godolphin House, Doyden Castle, sites in Cornwall), *To the Manor Born* (Cricket St Thomas, Chard, Somerset) and the Inspector Morse series shamelessly traded off the photogenic marvels of the ancient university city of Oxford – the Sheldonian Theatre, Wadham College, Brasenose College, Merton College, Christ Church, Pembroke College and numerous old English-looking pubs where Morse indulges his taste for real ale. *Persuasion* was filmed on location in Bath, as was *Northanger Abbey*. *Pride and Prejudice* used the National Trust village of Laycock, Luckington Court, Wiltshire; Lyme Park on the border of Cheshire and Derbyshire, Sudbury Hall, Derbyshire and Belton House, Lincolnshire and *Sense and Sensibility* used Saltram House at Plymton, Trafalgar House, Salisbury, the Flete Estate, south Devon, Montacute House, Yeovil, Wilton House, Salisbury, Mompesson House, Salisbury and Mothecombe House, London. The costumes of the television sagas are placed on exhibition at country houses – *Sense and Sensibility* at Wilton House, *Pride and Prejudice* at Wimborne Priest's House Museum.

Brideshead Revisited is a key television drama series in several respects. It is interesting that of all the Waugh novels which could have been given the classic novel treatment, choice lighted on *Brideshead*. Much of the appeal of the early parts of the book – and if devotees were honest, they would admit that these are the bits which really pull us – is the demonstration of an unwillingness to grow up, or even of wanting to grow up. Sebastian's teddy bear is a vital symbol here. The 1980s also saw a reawakening of interest in Dickens, (BBC Television serial versions one after another of *Great Expectations, David Copperfield, Dombey and Son, Pickwick Papers, Oliver Twist*) which was much taken with the childish in Dickens, of which there is a great deal. The novels are full of suffering children – the Smikes, Paul Dombeys, Olivers, Davids, Little Nells, Amy Dorrits, Tiny Tims of this world – or insufferably (but delightful) childish adults – such as Pickwick, Captain Cuttle, Mr Dick, Joe Gargery. Concurrently several cultural theorists were advocating the thesis that 'Englishness' was far from being a natural propensity of those who live on these islands, but an artifice, a selected and limited sense of identity put together at the turn of the century in a moment of profound ideological closure which synthesised Elgar, Gilbert and Sullivan, Baden Powell, the public school/Oxbridge ethos, Kipling and all the rest of it.[4]

Infantilism seemed much in vogue at the moment of Granada's *Brideshead*. And the cult of Dickens was part of the craze. It needed to be asked why so many were taken up with little boys and girls. After all, very few of us had to work – like Dickens – in blacking factories as a child or cradled our young sister-in-law as she expired. Yet this mawkish Dickensian infantilism seemed to access a vast reservoir in the national psyche. The sources stem from the construction of childhood during the last century and interesting evidence of the adult–child obsession is to be found in a species of literature, very English and very Victorian, childish but not for children, which was read to children by adults (who probably enjoyed it more than the children did). Kingsley's *The Water Babies* is a good early example, but the key text to the genre is *Alice in Wonderland*. (And isn't it interesting that the so-called *Brideshead* generation at Oxbridge affected a craze for translating *Alice* into Latin?). Strongly implicit throughout *Alice* is the preferable state of summer childhood to autumn and growing up. No doubt the Revd Dodgson had his own reasons for ignoring St Paul's advice about putting away childish things, and indeed his eccentric sexuality and obsession with prepubescent little girls is well documented (in spite of his family's loyal attempts to destroy the evidence). But accounting for Dodgson's predilections is not enough. It does not explain ours. Why prefer this nonsensical childish world to a real grown-up one? It is curious and relevant here that the same period also produced a vast literature of 'nonsense' – passed on to children, but written by adults and relished by an adult readership. Outstanding here is the work of Edward Lear. Lear's nonsense makes a powerful statement.

What comes through the character sketches, limericks and dotty epics is a mixture of anxiety and alienation, faintly disguised in childish gibberish. His verse is a rejection of the daily realities and a search for happy alternatives which we know are beyond realization. It was all grist to a progressively busy English mill – the cult of immaturity. *Peter Rabbit* made his welcome debut in 1902 and *Peter Pan* was premiered in 1904. The British craze for teddy bears took off in 1907. The following year *The Wind in the Willows* appeared, another masterpiece of the childish–adult genre, created by yet another personality of stunted development and sexual immaturity who never wanted to grow up. (It was a favourite of C.S. Lewis's.) And *Winnie the Pooh*, a classic text, was published in 1926, the year Sebastian Flyte was at Oxford with Aloysius. It is all there in our first clues about Sebastian when the Oxford barber tells Charles about the Marquis of Marchmain's second boy: 'Lord Sebastian Flyte. A "most" amusing young gentleman. What do you suppose Lord Sebastian wanted? A pair of hair-brushes for his teddy-bear; it has to be very stiff bristles, not, Lord Sebastian said, to brush him with, but to threaten him with a spanking when he was sulky. He bought a very nice one with an ivory back and he's having "Aloysius" engraved on it – that's the bear's name...' The set of attitudes is neatly caught in Granada's *Brass* parody, where the young Hardacre son, a Catholic priest, (James Saxon) exerts power of blackmail over his mother by threatening: 'I'll have to hit Teddy again!'

These elements home in on a characteristic devotion to the immature, which the nation continues to celebrate – the highly elaborated aimlessness of our 'sports', our child-substitute pets – notice the elaborate anthropomorphic recipes of supermarket pet-food; *Guardian*-readers greeting each other with whimsical childish names on Valentine's Day, and our regular adoration of that supply of choir boy descendants of Earnest Lough – Aled Jones, Anthony Way and whoever is to follow.... These are all symptomatic of particular conditions in British life since the late 1970s which *Brideshead Revisited* was able powerfully to draw on. Like children, we prefer fantasy to reality. Need we comment on the astonishing and lasting success of *The Lord of the Rings*, which BBC Radio 4 was giving the classic serial treatment to at this very time, and which was voted top British book in a Waterstone's event? We expect simple answers to direct questions. We like being told what to do rather than have to think for ourselves – the Ronnie Corbett 'mummy's boy' in the BBC-1 sitcom *Sorry!* which was transmitted the same year as *Brideshead* – was another significant product of Thatcherite Britain.[5] The national nanny at number ten was a long time coming, and was later replaced by a new nanny in the dorm as the Speaker of the House of Commons, Betty Boothroyd. But the signs had been there for years. Mrs Thatcher was an effect rather than a cause. And, no kidding, *Brideshead Revisited* brought with it a boom in the manufacture and sales of teddy bears.

Brideshead Revisited is one of the finest of all classic serials. It was superbly written by John Mortimer, who in realising his task produced a better television drama than *Brideshead Revisited* is a novel.[6] The narrative and the relationships in the dramatisation have more coherence than they do in the book. Waugh could only suggest the nature of the profound attraction and relationship between Charles and Sebastian. Mortimer's script and its production delicately shows us the perfection such liaisons may achieve, however briefly. Mortimer wisely decided to keep much of Waugh's beautiful and precise prose and break all conventions by using considerable voice-over throughout. As this was read by the enchanting voice of Jeremy Irons, the impact was often heart stopping and, frankly, beautiful. Take the brief account of the occasion when Sebastian borrows a car from a fellow student and he and Charles drive out into the country and spend several magical hours together, doing nothing, really, except being together. Mortimer gives this to us exactly as Waugh describes it – every insignificant detail of the drive out of Oxford and into the landscape:

> It was about eleven when Sebastian, without warning, turned the car into a cart track and stopped. It was hot enough now to make us seek the shade. On a sheep-cropped knoll under a clump of elms we ate the strawberries and drank the wine – as Sebastian promised, they were delicious together – and we lit fat, Turkish cigarettes and lay on our backs, Sebastian's eyes on the leaves above him, mine on his profile, while the blue-grey smoke rose, untroubled by any wind, to the blue-green shadows of foliage, and the sweet scent of the tobacco merged with the sweet summer scents around us and the fumes of the sweet, golden wine seemed to lift us a finger's breadth above the turf and hold us suspended.[7]

With Charles's voice providing a gentle commentary, we see them stop the car, get out, eat strawberries, drink some wine, smoke and talk. The camera-work is enchanting, and with the voice-over, the effect is poignant. We are given one of those apparently trivial moments in life in which circumstances raise to the level of paradise. There can be no denying that a large part of the effect of this moment lies in hearing Jeremy Irons's voice giving us Evelyn Waugh's verbal distillation of the moment into the spirit of eternal memory.

> To realise how specific this success was, one needs only to think of the way the idea of Oxford was uniquely called up in the very way Waugh's prose calls it up, giving us an Oxford wholly unlike, say, the Oxford of *Inspector Morse* – Granada Television gave us a city of aquatint, spacious and quiet streets where 'men walked and spoke as they had done in Newman's day', a city of autumnal mists, grey spring time and the rare glory of summer days 'when the chestnut was in flower and the bells rang out high and clear over her gables and cupolas, exhaled the soft airs of centuries of youth...'[8]

The BBC fights back

By way of competition in the year of Brideshead the BBC could only offer *The Borgias*, which was an unsuccessful attempt to recapture the vogue for previous historic costume drama series. It was panned by reviewers. The BBC just about kept their head above the waters with their four-part adaptation of Malcolm Bradbury's *The History Man*, and in the early 1980s trod water as far as the dramatisation of classic novels was concerned. Against *Brideshead Revisited* their offerings seem tame. *Fanny by Gaslight*, Michael Sadleir's quirky atmospheric Victorian melodrama, was dramatised in four 50-minute episodes by Anthony Steven and directed by Peter Jeffries in 1981. In several respects it almost erased memories of Anthony Asquith's 1944 film. Elaine Morgan dramatised Howard Spring's *Fame is the Spur* (eight 50-minute episodes) which was produced by Richard Beynon and directed by David Giles in 1982. Much effort was spent on the social realism of the Manchester scenes which spared nothing in the depiction of grinding poverty, and the production was also noticeable for the fine performance from Tim Piggott-Smith. Only in *The Barchester Chronicles* (1982) did signs of the old BBC confidence remain.

In this seven 55-minute episode dramatisation Alan Plater ran together Trollope's *The Warden* and *Barchester Towers* to make a coherent narrative chronicling the intrigues and politicking of the Barsetshire bishopric. Reduced to its basic anatomy the narrative (like that of *I, Claudius*) resembles a boardroom drama, but here rehoused in an ecclesiastical setting. The story of the Revd Septimus Harding as he attempts to defend himself from the charge, brought by the radical reformer John Bold (and taken up by *The Jupiter* newspaper) of exploiting his position as preceptor of Hiram's Hospital. Much of the drama is injected into the story by the ferocious rivalry between Mrs Proudie, wife of the rather weakwilled Bishop Proudie, and the two-faced careerist, Mr Slope, the Bishop's Chaplain. Concentrating on the aggressive conflicts played for high stakes within closed ecclesiastical doors rather than on the easy charms of life in a Victorian cathedral city, this production eschewed obvious Trollopian charms of Barchester cathedral city old world charm – echoing liturgies, choirs, bells, spires, cawing rooks, gaiters and clerical garb, and the like. Instead, it gave us drama, a drama of conflicts and of tensions. The concentration on action, intrigue and the dramatic clash of character paid off. The casting was inspired. Donald Pleasance, cast against type as Revd Harding, was sincere and deeply moving. Alan Rickman made a wonderful creation of Mr Slope. Bishop Proudie was ideal in the hands of Clive Swift and Geraldine McEwan as Mrs Proudie was the stuff of nightmare. Nigel Hawthorne, as Archdeacon of Barchester and Harding's son-in-law, turned in yet another of his masterly performances which we unjustly seem to take for granted. It was produced by Jonathan Powell and directed by David Giles.

The following year Don Shaw dramatised A.J. Cronin's *The Citadel* in six 50-minute episodes, produced by Ken Riddington and directed by

Peter Jeffries. In most respects this was a worthy, if routine effort, despite the efforts of stars Ben Cross and Clare Higgins, noted for its rather more explicit portrayal of adultery than had been possible in the Robert Donat film version of 1938, but lacking that film's social idealism. *The Citadel* seemed to arouse television drama's interest in bestsellers of yesteryear with medical school associations. Jeremy Paul dramatised Warwick Deeping's *Sorrell and Son* (in six 50-minute episodes 1984, produced and directed by Derek Bennett) for Yorkshire Television. This production, starring Richard Pasco, Stephanie Beacham and John Shrapnel, unfolded the worthy story of a First World War ex-officer working as an hotel porter to send his son through medical school. Another of the genre, Francis Brett Young's *My Brother Jonathan*, the story of a small town physician who yearned to be great surgeon, was serialised in 1985.

The Corporation meanwhile for several years relied on traditional classic serial fare to keep alive (just) its reputation as keepers of the sacred flame of literary high culture. In the main, the choice and treatment exhibited in the Sunday teatime slot was scarcely nourishing, but some protein and high fibre was provided by Jane Austen and Dickens. Although *Pride and Prejudice* (1980), *Mansfield Park* (1986) and *Sense and Sensibility* (1986) were not the work of the same production team, there is an unmistakable family resemblance, if not a factory-line feel about them. Fruit of this regulation standard is the result of the BBC's long standing and harmonious relationship with Jane Austen, a relationship which dates from the earliest days of British broadcasting. At one level, it might well be argued that this is inevitable. If you do a lot of Jane Austen over a fairly short period of time, results of this kind are inevitable. Her works are uniformly set in a limited historical period and within a narrow social milieu. She herself wrote: 'Three or four families in a country village is the very thing to work on'.[9] Her interests are extremely consistent – although this might well be one of her major strengths. Therefore locations, costumes and action cannot be wide ranging. Nevertheless, the style of these production was limited.

In this series of Jane Austen dramatisations, two qualities stand out. For some reason or other, actors achieved a curious way of speaking Jane Austen's dialogue. Words were regarded as highly fragile things. Actors aspired towards a very careful, precise and unemphatic manner of saying the lines as if to ensure that no harm will happen to the words as they leave their lips. This was presumably an attempt at what is considered to be the formality of the late Augustan period; informal contractions are completely avoided, with 'this can NOT be true' being seen as somehow preferable to 'this can't be true' or even 'this cannot be true'. The second impression gleaned from watching these productions is of groups of people living in provincial Regency England who have collectively decided, for some curious reason known only to themselves, to go about their daily business dressed either in brand new clothes or in their Sunday Best (straight back from the cleaners). This unlikely immaculate sartorial display is otherwise at variance with the BBC's reputation for historical accuracy. There seems little point, for example, in the brilliant touch of having the square piano in Mansfield Park felicitously, believably and appropriately out of tune if all the characters flit about dressed as if straight out of the bandbox. This 'whiter-than-white' and 'so-kind-to-coloureds' house style is characteristic of this batch of Jane Austen productions.

Nevertheless, individually viewed these dramatisations were by no means devoid of merit. *Pride and Prejudice* was dramatised by Fay Weldon, produced by Jonathan Powell and directed by Cyril Coke, and starring David Rintoul (d'Arcy), Elizabeth Garvie (Elizabeth Bennett), Natalie Ogle (Lydia), Sabrina Franklin (Jane) and Tessa Peake-Jones (Mary). Considering the feminist credentials of the writer, it might well have been expected that this adaptation would somehow represent what the media would doubtless be tempted to call 'a feminist take' on Jane Austen's masterpiece, but it suffered far less from current-PC than might have been anticipated, perhaps because Fay Weldon wisely chose to incorporate much of the novelist's narrative comments and asides into the dialogue. Alistair Cooke pointed out that Austen presents designers and writers with particular hazards. Designers may easily be tempted into over dressing the performance in Georgian grandeur and Regency elegance. The writer is faced with the technical problem of dealing with a medium which is mainly dialogue: 'this glistening BBC version was so squeaky clean as to suggest at times a doll's house with doll-like emotions. The prettifying confronted the scriptwriter with the extra challenge of giving the story and its characters a verisimilitude beyond their skin-deep elegance.'[10]

The core of the problem in Jane Austen is that the narrator somehow participates in the action of the novel in the very process of narrating it. Fay Weldon bravely attempted to resolve this interesting problem in the novel's dramatisation by having Elizabeth as the central character, using as much of the original dialogue from the book as possible, and supplementing it with direct speech versions of Jane Austen's narrative comments, with sensitive, sparing use of

Elizabeth Bennett in voice-over commentary. This tool of adaptation had two important results. One was that there was no doubt this *Pride and Prejudice* was not a romantic novel but in some shape or form it was a criticism of overtly romantic fiction; the other was to make Mary Bennett, usually a neglected member of the brood, a rather more interesting, and certainly more talkative, member of the family. Elizabeth was cheerful and credibly intelligent, but d'Arcy came through as relentlessly earnest to the point where it was hard to believe in his secret benevolence. His character had been subtly rewritten by Weldon to the extent that one curiously felt towards the end of the dramatisation that Elizabeth really deserved better – which is certainly not the impression given by Austen in the novel. One constantly amusing and satisfying performance was that of Tessa Peake-Jones who made Mary convincing, droll and sympathetic.

The result remains an important example in media history of the adapter's art. Fay Weldon, a distinguished novelist in her own right of course, attempted to solve one of the basic problems in adapting Jane Austen's fiction to drama, namely, how to manage to say what she says in fiction while being obliged to remove the omniscient authorial voice. Her solution was in itself extremely creative and committed without being awkwardly partisan. Some of the glories had to go, such as 'Mr Collins had only to change from Jane to Elizabeth – and it was soon done – done while Mrs Bennet was stirring the fire' or

> Mr Bennet was not of a disposition to seek comfort for the disappointment which his own imprudence had brought on, in any of those pleasures which too often console the unfortunate for their folly or their vice. He was fond of the country and of books; and from these tastes had arisen his principal enjoyments. To his wife he was very little otherwise indebted, than as her ignorance and folly had contributed to his amusement. This is not the sort of happiness which a man would in general wish to owe to his wife; but where other powers of entertainment are wanting, the philosopher will derive benefit from such as are given. (Chapter 19)

Fay Weldon saves as much of Jane Austen's narrative irony and comment as possible by reworking it into dialogue. For much of the time this is scarcely noticeable, except when one recognizes particular gems, such as 'It is a truth universally acknowledged, that a single man in possession of a good fortune, must be in want of a wife.' The way Weldon cunningly works into Mary Bennet's dialogue much of Jane

Austen's more Johnsonian and sententious comments is particularly enjoyable. Although this was a rather housebound production, it was a sharper and more liberated *Pride and Prejudice* than we had seen before. Although the obligations of the happy ending with reconciliation, love and marriage were duly realized, there was nevertheless a feeling that what we were witnessing was not so much perfection as the best that could reasonably be expected, given the social circumstances of the time.

Mansfield Park (BBC-2, 1986) was dramatised by Ken Taylor, produced by Betty Willingale and directed by David Giles. It starred Bernard Hepton, Anna Massey, Angela Pleasance, Nicholas Farrell, Sylvestra Le Touzel and Samantha Bond. This was Jane Austen's third completed novel, published in 1814, a year after *Pride and Prejudice*. It combines two characteristically Austen themes – the impact of social conventions on human behaviour and the erosion of mistaken impressions as a bar to mutual attraction. These themes are held in close focus in a novel which combines contrasting characters and multifarious incidents. Jane Austen uses the staging of a play, the world of make-believe, as a device to connect the narrative threads. Confusions arise from the failure to see matters as they are: 'There is not one in hundred of either sex who is not taken in when they marry. Look where I will, I see that it is so; and I feel that it must be so, when I consider that it is, of all transactions, the one in which people expect most from others, and are least honest themselves.' But another theme underlies this performance – a variant of the Cinderella story. *Mansfield Park* is very much concerned with patience and endurance. Fanny Price, removed from her Portsmouth family at the tender age of ten and transferred to the large, wealthy country house family life, is required to suffer humiliations at the hands of aunts Norris and Bertram, her pretty cousins and, initially, the emotional immaturities of her cousin Edmund. For all her reputation for 'gentle irony' Jane Austen does not mince matters. This is a novel about human vice, cruelty, stupidity and barbarism. Yet Fanny Price survives and shines through it all, her diffidence doing nothing to undermine her strength of character. Edmund at last perceives Fanny's real qualities and – tempered by experience and tested by time – they are united.

In several respects *Mansfield Park* would be the most difficult of Jane Austen's novels to translate on to television, not least because so much happens. It vigorously subverts the assumption that Jane Austen's novels are all, more or less, the same. Less sparkling and racy than *Pride and Prejudice*, more reflective even than *Persuasion*, it is the most sexually daring of them all, and the sections dealing with Fanny's apprehension of Crawford's intentions for her are among Jane Austen's most convincing and effective pages. *Mansfield Park* is full of Austen's awareness of those subtle hints and shadows in which really deep class divisions reveal themselves in social life.

It is a self evident truth that television is more effective in showing what happens than in telling us what people think. Conveying Jane Austen's meaning in television terms must always present a considerable challenge. The danger will always be the risk of rendering clumsily obvious what should really be almost unsaid and scarcely visible. Much that goes on in this novel really goes on in Fanny Price's mind. Another problem, and this would be affected by limitations of the production's actual duration, is that one of Jane Austen's great achievements here is to show how Fanny develops as a result of what happens to her. In the event the various elements of the novel hung together well, but Fanny's sudden transformation from childhood to young womanhood (Sylvestra Le Touzel) while in conversation with a chronologically stable young Edmund Bertram (Nicholas Farrell) was a prestigious television wheeze. Unfortunately it did not work; our viewing perceptions do not easily lend themselves to lapses in verisimilitude within an otherwise wholly verisilitudinous experience. The musical score for this production – traditional melodies for the most part arranged for small ensemble by Derek Bourgeois – was delightful, and matched the mood of the period, and the production, perfectly.

Sense and Sensibility (BBC-1, 1986) was dramatised by Alexander Baron, produced by Barry Letts and directed by Rodney Bennett. The dramatisation was curiously lacking in drama, and this was not entirely down to the novel itself. Even when it is admitted that this is probably her weakest novel; that the comedy (Mrs Jennings, Mr Palmer and Mrs Palmer) is certainly treated as comic relief, rather than integrating the comedic vein so completely into the texture of the novel that we do not notice it is 'comedy'; that the characterisation is rather unconvincing and that the moral message is scarcely hidden if not intoned – the basic set-up is interesting and potentially dramatic. As with all her novels, there is a sensation that we are handling silk, but the fabric is tough and durable. Although here the spirit of Jane Austen has evaporated in the process of television dramatisation and production. The book still reads well. It is full of life, but the best that can be said of this production is that it looks good. This was the dullest of the Jane Austen offerings of the decade, characterised by that curious BBC 'Jane Austen' elocution, immaculate clothes, and Sunday teatime feel. It was loyal to the original novel but unaccountably flat in its impact. It had everything, but nothing of Jane Austen's guts.

Return to the Raj

For a combination of reasons, as part of the ideological shock wave which affected the British with the Falklands war, we experienced a massive nostalgia for the days of the Raj. Granada screened Paul Scott's novel *Staying On* in 1980. This was followed within the next twelve months by the cinema releases of *Gandhi* (Richard Attenborough), *Heat and Dust* (Merchant Ivory) and in 1984 came David Lean's version of *A Passage to India*. Commercial television played an essential role in this wave of imperial nostalgia. Granada Television followed *Staying On* with a stunning serial version of Paul Scott's epic *Jewel in the Crown* (Granada 1984) and in the same year Channel Four screened a serial version of M.M. Kaye's novel *The Far Pavilions*. The last surge of this tide was commercial television's answer to *Gandhi*, the mini-series *Mountbatten, the Last Viceroy* (1985). These years were an extraordinary British experience, of wide ranging and deep intensity, while it lasted.

It is important to realise the lasting cultural depth of this experience. One of its most pronounced symptoms was the renewed craze for curry. The immensely successful and long lasting Curry Club was founded by Pat Chapman in 1984. There were only six Indian Restaurants in Britain in 1950. The die-hard blimps had to trek all the way to London to enjoy a good sweat at Veeraswarmy's. Ten years later there were 300 Indian restaurants. Then came several successive revolutions, including fashions for Tandoori cooking, the introduction of unusual and enterprising ideas for curry dishes (certainly encouraged if not actually initiated by Madhur Jaffrey). Then came Balti. Today there are more curry restaurants in Britain than anywhere else in the world, including India. There are approximately 7000, from John o' Groats to Land's End. There are curry houses in the Shetlands and the Channel Islands. There are more Indian restaurants in London (over 1500) than in Delhi. Perhaps, in fact, there are now too many of them to be supported by the British appetite: although over 2 500 000 customers visit Indian restaurants each week, curry houses are now going bust. The names of the restaurants are frequently redolent of Empire – Khyber Pass, British Raj, Kathmandu, Bengal Lancer, Days of the Raj, Jalalabad, Far Pavilions, Gurka, Jewel in the Crown, Viceroy of India. Curry ingredients and condiments can be bought in most UK supermarkets and sales have grown at an average between 15 per cent to 200 per cent annually since 1982. Ingredient and ready-made sales exceed £600 000 000 a year (ahead of their nearest rival, Chinese, by a considerable distance), as three million households in the UK cook a curry meal at home once a week. The British spend £22 000 000 a year on popadoms for domestic consumption – that is about 440 000 000 popadoms. Films, books and television programmes about British India constitute only one aspect of the vast national indulgence in the days of the Raj.[11]

Granada's *The Jewel in the Crown*, which caught this mood so precisely, was based on Paul Scott's *The Raj Quartet*, and dramatised in 14 episodes (one of two hours, the remaining 13 of one hour each) by Ken Taylor, who had many television dramas to his credit, including *The Seekers* (1964), *The Borgias* (1981) and the BBC's *Mansfield Park*. The series was under the general supervision of Granada Television's Chairman, Sir Denis Forman, produced and directed by Jim O'Brien and Christopher Morahan. The splendid cast included Peggy Ashcroft, Geraldine James, Tim Piggott-Smith, Charles Dance, Rachel Kempson, Saeed Jaffrey, Art Malik, Zia Moyheddin, Eric Porter, Susan Wooldridge. Dramatising Paul Scott's quartet of novels for television serialisation was a formidable challenge. Irene Shubik, who produced Granada's dramatisation of Paul Scott's *Staying On*, drew up the basic plan of *The Jewel in the Crown*, which was then written by Ken Taylor. His task was to reduce four novels, *The Jewel in the Crown*, *The Day of the Scorpion*, *Tower of Silence* and *A Division of the Spoils*, to a consistent epic narrative. The major problem for anyone dramatising these novels is Paul Scott's treatment of time, for the story is not told directly, the narrative is threaded together by third-person narrative, letters, conversations, reports, memories, and the logic of time is jumbled and circular. *The Raj Quartet* constructs its reality by recycling events through various perspectives at various times, in a recurring and multilayered pattern, more like the treatment and variations in traditional Indian music than narrative as experienced in the western European novel. But, as George Brandt convincingly argues, Ken Taylor's dramatisation in some ways significantly echoes Scott's original storytelling techniques, as incident echoes incident.[12] The Quartet deals with events over a five-year period between 1942 and Indian independence, the British leaving India and the slaughter between Hindus and Muslims which followed the partition of the country. But threads of the story go back to the Chilianwallah Barg massacre at Amritsar in 1919, and forwards to some period in the 1960s when the narrator returns to India to ponder on the gathering together of the threads of past, present and future.

The mainspring of the various plot lines is the story of Daphne Manners, the young English girl, who falls in love with Hari Kumar, an English public school-educated Indian, who is thus a fugitive caught between his Indian race and his British cultivation. During the anti-British riots which spread across India in 1942, Daphne (Susan Wooldridge) is raped by Indian peasants in the Bibighar Gardens at Mayapore. Hari Kumar (Art Malik) is arrested as a suspect by the sadistic superintendent of police, Ronald Merrick (Tim Piggott-Smith). Merrick is a repressed homosexual, with pronounced sado-masochistic leanings, and he makes it his duty to ensure that Hari Kumar is severely beaten while held under suspicion. This main story opens out to include other groups of characters and various new storylines which are woven together. The first two novels, *The Jewel in the Crown* (1966) and *The Day of the Scorpion* (1968) are concerned with two acts of violence – the rape of Daphne and the mob attack on Miss Edwina Crane, an elderly English school supervisor – in the period of crisis of 1942 which succeeded the Congress Party's 'Quit India' campaign. Characters initially introduced in the first novel are viewed in the second in harsher light, as we learn more about Ronald Merrick and his treatment of Hari Kumar. Daphne dies in childbirth delivering a daughter. We are introduced to the English Layton family at Mirat, the fortunes of the two Layton daughters, Sarah and Susan, whose lives will become entangled with Ronald Merrick. *The Towers of Silence* (1972), set in the hill station of Pankot, deals with the fortunes of the Layton family and a retired missionary teacher, Barbara Bachelor, who is at the receiving end of the prejudice and snobbery of haughty English wives. The last novel, *A Division of the Spoils* (1974) deals with the two years leading to partition. Events are seen from different perspectives and through the eyes of a new character, Guy Peron (Charles Dance) as the threads of epic are drawn together, Merrick is killed and Guy courts Sarah Layton. These four novels are admired for the richness of their creative life as well as their account of Anglo-Indian history at a particularly eventful time.[13]

In Granada's television version this vast canvas is reduced to a clear (if rich) linear narrative. But its sweep is epic. *The Jewel in the Crown* was a truly epic television drama, and as such it has few rivals. For those who stuck with it from the beginning, it was a magnificent experience. It achieved an average audience of 8 000 000 (*Coronation Street*'s average during the same period was 16 000 000). When it was repeated a year later on Channel Four *The Jewel in the Crown* earned an average audience of 1 732 000. It was largely welcomed by British television reviewers[14] although it did earn some major brickbats, in particular that by Salman Rushdie.[15] It was filmed on location in India and at various locations in the UK and at Granada studios. Wales, as ever, stood in for mountainous parts of India, and the final railway station scene after the massacre was filmed in Buckinghamshire. It was richly-rewarded with honours. The Royal Television Society gave the Writer's Award for an Exceptional Adaptation to Ken Taylor, Dame Peggy Ashcroft received a Performance Award, Vic Symonds and Alan Pickford received Design Awards, and it earned BAFTA awards for Best Drama Serial, Dame Peggy Ashcroft was awarded Best Actress and Tim Piggott-Smith Best Actor. It won an International Emmy Award for Best Drama, the Golden Globe and National Board of Review Award and was voted Programme of the Year by the US Television Critics Association.[16] Granada Television financed the production without recourse to co-production arrangements of any kind, and before the first transmission was barely halfway through the production costs had already been recouped from sales abroad and in the UK. It was shown in Canada, USA, Australia, New Zealand, Jamaica, France, Belgium, Italy, Greece, Holland, Finland, Sweden, Argentina, Israel, Kenya, Morocco, Zimbabwe, Brunei, Sri Lanka, Mauritius, Angola, Nicaragua, Hungary, East and West Germany, Yugoslavia, Poland, India and Bangladesh. This was a production which pushed the potential for literary dramatisation far beyond the home-grown market, and demonstrated just how successful the genre could be.

The new channel

From 1982 the Corporation and commercial television faced a new challenge – Channel Four. This was a recommendation of the Annen Committee: an independent broadcasting channel, which would not itself make programmes but would instead broadcast productions from independent companies. It was operated under the supervision of the IBA. It was partly financed by the ITV companies and was reliant on them for most of its services and much of its contributions. This was an opportunity for previously neglected interests to be served, to buy in productions from overseas, re-run classics from television's past and so on. The new channel has offered some interesting challenges as regards dramatising classic novels or literary fiction. In 1983–84 Channel Four transmitted Little Bird Films/Ulster Television/RTE's production of *The Irish RM*, based on Edith Sommerville and Martin Ross's Anglo-Irish classic, starring Peter Bowles and Bryan Murray. The

26 half-hour episodes were produced by James Mitchell. Whimsy and blarney were reasonably constrained, but a sense of overstaying welcome was difficult to ward off. The channel directly rivalled the major channels in transmitting Julian Bond's dramatisation of M.M. Kaye's novel *The Far Pavilions*, taking the field as a three 90-minute episode mini-series at the height of the return to the 'Raj' craze in 1984. Production values were very high (it cost £8 0000 000) and had a cast including Ben Cross, Amy Irving, Omar Sharif, John Gielgud, Christopher Lee, Rosanno Brazzi, Saeed Jaffrey and Robert Hardy. It was produced by Robert Laing and directed by Peter Duffell. It seemed to have everything, spectacular locations, high Victorian-period colour, Raj setting, romance and massive set-pieces (a vast wedding procession, suttee wife-burning ceremony), but it was style without substance. There was nothing for the viewer to get to grips with. It obviously suffered in comparison with *The Jewel in the Crown*, with which it rubbed shoulders in the schedules.

In January 1985, Channel Four broadcast Barbara Taylor Bradford's irresistible tarradiddle *A Woman of Substance*, dramatised by Lee Langley and produced as a three part mini-series by Portman Artemis Productions. No expense was spared. Stars included Deborah Kerr, Jenny Seagrove, John Mills, Diane Baker, George Baker, Gayle Hunnicutt, Nicola Pagett and Miranda Richardson. This was followed in 1987 by Malcolm Bradbury's charming four 50-minute episode dramatisation of Tom Sharpe's *Porterhouse Blue*, with Picture Partnership Production giving it the full classic serial treatment, which had the effect of bestowing a certain sophistication on its satirical edge. David Jason triumphed as Skullion. The following year Channel Four broadcast Alan Plater's dramatisation of Chris Mullen's disturbing comedy *A Very British Coup* in three 60-minute episodes. This starred a BAFTA winning performance from Ray McAnnally as the Labour Prime Minister Harry Perkins. Production values seemed high (including well chosen Mozart on the soundtrack) giving a classic serial gloss to proceedings.

For a while the BBC seemed unable to rise to the challenge of mounting classic or costume drama appropriate to the hour – Sunday teatime serial versions of *Goodbye Mr Chips*, *The Invisible Man*, *Alice in Wonderland*, *The Prisoner of Zenda* would scarcely, and did not, answer to the purpose – but deep-seated national misgivings seemed to surface in such drama series as *The Monocled Mutineer* (BBC-1, 1986), *Tumbledown* (BBC-2, 1986) and the crisis over Ian Curteis's *Falklands Play*.[17] The Corporation continued calmly to transmit regular wholesome doses of

Jane Austen, Brontë and Dickens, in more or less the same unruffled way as ever, but no longer had its own way so far as dramatisations of the literary classics were concerned.

Despite the exampled originality of approach signalled by Granada Television's treatment of Dickens in *Hard Times* (1977) the Corporation dutifully produced a series of dramatisations of *Great Expectations, Dombey and Son, David Copperfield* and *Oliver Twist* which had a relentless production line-quality about them; one looked very much like another. No top-hatted character could walk down a Dickensian street without obligingly raising his headwear to some passing lady in a bonnet, and no two characters could converse in an interior room without a BBC sound effects Hansom cab trotting by on its regulation hoofs. But there were changes underway in the BBC, changes which would soon bear fruit.

The BBC and the Balkans

The BBC finally rallied with its impressive production in seven parts of *Fortunes of War* (October 1986), dramatised by Alan Plater of Olivia Manning's *The Balkan Trilogy* and *The Levant Trilogy*. That the time was really ripe for change in either the choice or the style of dramatising classic novels was driven home by Granada's cheeky parody of the basic ingredients of so much which had been serialised. The characteristics of the genre had become so marked as to deserve parody, which they got in good measure in *Brass* (Granada 1983–84). This was a satisfying mixture of cliché characters and well worn storylines lifted mainly from Galsworthy and the 'trouble at t'mill' school of industrial drama, vigorously laced with lashings of D.H. Lawrence, *Wuthering Heights*, A.E. Coppard, the Brontës, Daphne Du Maurier, *Brideshead Revisited*, Mary Webb, H.E. Bates, *Cold Comfort Farm* and the rest of them. The series was dominated by the magnificent performance of Timothy West as Bradley Hardacre, a pantomime version of the traditional wicked mill-owner, (whose origins go back to Josiah Bounderby of Coketown and beyond). He has a drunken wife, a problem family, and devotes his energies to working for the fortune he knows is to be made from manufacturing a silent explosive. The series left no respected media classic novel unscathed.[18]

By the time any genre has become the fit subject for parody, it is fair to guess that things are ready for a change, and, seeking for the first signs of the undeniable shift which was to change the whole style of the BBC classic novel dramatisation, two 1985 productions stand out as the earliest clear manifestations of the revolution. F. Scott

Fitzgerald's novel *Tender is the Night* was dramatised by Dennis Potter in six 55-minute episodes and directed by Robert Knights. It starred Peter Strauss, Mary Steenbergen, John Heard, Sean Young and Edward Asner. It was vastly professional, beautifully written and very dramatic. The main impression was extremely well dressed, manicured, polished, and parted down the middle – Peter Strauss never had a hair out of place and was dressed like a model. This was nevertheless serious adult drama, with high production values obviously committed to the service of 'great literature'.

This was a very popular production, with an average audience of 8 700 00 (cf *EastEnders* 24 000 000), and the Corporation was obviously flexing its muscle and showing what it could do. When this is compared with the average audience of *Yes, Prime Minister*, (7 500 000) transmitted the same year, we can see how popular serious literature can be.[19] Then, in the autumn, came *Bleak House*.

Despite its strong melodramatic plot and multiplicity of vivid characters, *Bleak House* had not previously proved a favourite for television dramatisation. This may possibly be a result of the (mistaken) assumption of early broadcasters that Dickens was particularly suitable for younger audiences. The novel was dramatised and transmitted by BBC Television in 1954 in twelve 30-minute episodes in a version written by Constance Cox. The version written by Arthur Hopcraft, transmitted in 1985, although not immediately perceived as such at the time, was a significant development in the classic serial tradition. Hopcraft's previous Dickens dramatisation, *Hard Times* (Granada 1977) pointed a way which a few followed, but with this *Bleak House* new vistas came to view. There was as ever a tension between the claims made for Dickens's unique suitability for film and television treatment, and the quality of the actual realisations on screen. The problem lie in the vast difference between Dickens's literary artistry – which excelled in the comedic grotesque, the sentimental and the melodramatic – and the accepted mode of naturalism and realism which was the dominant fashion of modern filmmaking and broadcasting. The best solution to this fundamental problem until recently had been sought in casting: either using character actors in those roles seen as comic or grotesque, and traditional straight actors in the rest; or by toning down the grotesque to a more moderate level. The results had hardly been satisfactory, given either the WC Fields/Freddie Bartholemew casting, or the attempt by Bernard Miles to render Joe Gargery as an everyday rural bloke of modest eccentricity. In *Hard Times*, and even more in *Bleak House*, actors were cast who played the roles neither for laughs nor terrors. Instead, they took the simple acting line of playing them for all they were worth, thereby discovering new and convincing depths.

Produced for BBC Television by John Harris and Betty Willingale, designed by Tim Harvey and directed by Ross Devenish, this was the first Dickens dramatisation for television to be shot entirely on film. It cost £2 800 000 to make. The fog and confusion of London, which in the novel is a larger metaphor for the tenebrous confusion of the law, was presented realistically, and it worked. The grime, squalor and – yes – the stink of Victorian London was all there, on screen. The serious problem of the authorial voice was largely solved in action and dialogue, and the sonorous voice-over at Joe the Crossing Sweeper's death was seamlessly (and effectively) transposed to John Jarndyce (Denholm Elliott): 'Dead! Dead, your Majesty. Dead, my lords and gentlemen. Dead, Right Reverends and Wrong Reverends of every order. Dead, men and women, born with Heavenly compassion in your hearts. And dying thus around us every day.' The power and authority of this production stem largely from the quality of its acting. The casting could not have been faulted. It is possibly unfair to single out just a few for mention, with Diana Rigg setting a standard against which all subsequent Lady Dedlocks must be judged. She had the perfect mixture of hauteur, vulnerability and sex appeal. Bernard Hepton (Krook) and Peter Vaughan (Tulkinghorn) gave immortal performances. Faith to the genius of Dickens seems to have paid off here, and Arthur Hopcraft's gift for preserving the essence of Dickens in a television script was a great incentive to the actors.

Peter Vaughan (Tulkinghorn) commented that he came to playing the classics through the work he has done, not through an academic education: 'Most of my classical knowledge has come through the work that I have done. I didn't have a university education or anything of that nature. I was just a grammar school boy and started acting when I was sixteen. So what I have come across has been as a result of the accidents of a career...'.[20] He gets all the evidence he needs, not from accumulated received traditional ideas about the various character parts, but from the script:

> Some actors have a trick or two for getting into a character. I don't work in that way at all. I get all the evidence from the script. When I did Tulkinghorn in *Bleak House*, there was this superb description in the book about Tulkinghorn and his walk and so on. You know – that he's like a huge bird walking about – and so that's the

evidence use. I became a bird, like him.... What one has to do is really find the man, as I call it, my phrase for it, finding the man, and until you've done that you can't really play a character.... It is not a question of thinking 'Victorian' or thinking 'modern' when you play a character. There was a similarity in the process: ... it's just that your evidence is different. I mean obviously if you're thinking 'Victorian' and of the way of life of that time and the social mores and social conditions – all of those things have to be taken into account and sort of integrated. They're usually on a subconscious level. All they do is help you believe. You have to believe in the man you play. If you believe in the man you're playing, the audience will as well. If you don't believe, there's no hope that the audience will believe.[21]

With this transmission the days of quaint old BBC 'Dickensian' Dickens were quietly but firmly laid to rest, only a couple of years before the Sunday serial tradition finally hit the buffers. As far as the BBC Sunday teatime tradition was concerned, little fuss was made of its quiet demise. Its last major production, *Vanity Fair* (1987) was produced by Terrance Dicks and starred Eve Matheson as Becky, Rebecca Saire as Amelia, James Saxon as Joseph and Jack Klaaf as Rawden. This was traditional BBC fare and the fact that it was scheduled for the traditional Sunday audience probably prevented it benefiting from the sexual honesty socially achieved in the past few decades – the nature of Becky's actual relationship with Lord Steyne (a rather miscast Clive Swift) remained unclear. The suggestion that Becky first insured and then poisoned Joseph was interestingly cynical and worldly.[22] After a fair to middling version of *The Franchise Affair* the Sunday serial slot quietly shut-up shop.

The Dickens-for-the-young tradition the BBC had originated was kept briefly flickering by commercial television. In 1989 ITV transmitted *Great Expectations*, dramatised in six 50-minute episodes by John Goldsmith, produced by Greg Smith and directed by Kevin Connor – a Primetime production for the Disney Channel in association with HTV and Tesauro Television (Spain). This production cost £4 million and it looked pretty good. The casting was very interesting with Martin Harvey as young Pip and Anthony Calf as the mature Pip, Kim Thomson as Estelle, Anthony Hopkins as Magwitch, Jean Simmons as Miss Havisham, John Rhys-Davies as Joe Gargery and Ray McAnally as Jaggers. Much of the very effective location shooting was done in Chatham and Rochester. However, the production was not twee free. The Gargergy's house was surprisingly spacious for a rural blacksmith and the furniture far too recently-purchased. The little swinging sign outside saying 'The Forge' was reminiscent of 'Ye Olde Tea Shoppe' and young Pip was never seen without his spanking Sunday best on. Although not fair-haired and blue-eyed as Dickens so carefully described him, John Rhys-Davies looked and acted like a blacksmith, and combined gentleness of spirit with the strength of an ox. Scenes between him and young Pip were as tender as could be wished and certainly the right side of syrupy; you could believe he loved Pip as his own child. His response to Jaggers's offers of money was magnificent and worthy of Dickens's imagination. His behaviour at the funeral of Pip's sister was believable and moving. Trabbs and his wonderful Boy were retained to excellent effect and it was touching to have Jean Simmons, David Lean's original Estelle, as Miss Havisham. Ray McAnally's Jaggers was fine, with bushy eyebrows and wagging finger. Much of the detail was retained to good effect – the pins in the bread and butter, the conversation at the Gargerey's Christmas lunch, the whole saga of Orlick – but some additions were unfortunate, Biddy's frightful carol singing brats, for example, were unforgivable. Anthony Hopkins made a good job of Magwitch, especially after his illicit return to London. But somehow this is processed Dickens, sanitised, deodorised, smoothed out.

In the mid-1980s BBC television drama showed undoubted evidence of creative life elsewhere. Among the outstanding offerings were Andrew Davies's surrealistic drama of modern university life, *A Very Peculiar Practice* (May/July 1986, with a second series February/March 1988); Alan Bleasdale's controversial First World War socio-political drama, *The Monocled Mutineer*, (August/September 1986) Dennis Potter's masterpiece, *The Singing Detective* (November/December 1986) and Alan Plater's beautiful dramatisation of Olivia Manning's *Balkan Trilogy* and *The Levant Trilogy*,[23] in seven one-hour episodes, *Fortunes of War*, shown on BBC-1 between 11 October and 22 November 1987. The novelist was married to R.D. Smith, then a British official working in the Balkans, which gave her experiences of Romania before the outbreak of the Second World War, the Russian invasion and escaping to Greece, and on which these novels are based.[24] The production values were very high and in some ways this may be seen as a long overdue but nevertheless reassuring answer to the challenge of commercial television drama's *Brideshead Revisited* and *The Jewel in the Crown*. Guy and Harriet Pringle, the characters based on R.D. Smith and herself, Olivia Manning, were appropriately taken by Kenneth

Branagh and Emma Thompson, with Ronald Pickup as the emigre aristocrat Prince Yakimov. Alan Bennet provided a delightful cameo as the aristocratic academic, Professor Lord Pinkrose.

Towards the end of the decade there was little evidence of strong life as far as dramatised versions of classic novels were concerned. LWT made an interesting but toothless serial drama, *The Charmer* (six one-hour episodes) using characters and situations from Patrick Hamilton's classically seedy and creepy yarns *The West Pier* (1951), *Mr Stimpson and Mr Gorse* (1953) and *Unknown Assailant* (1955). It was written by Allan Prior, produced by Philip Hinchcliffe and directed by Alan Gibson. Watching it was a curious experience as one was conscious of being distantly reminded of something else. With effort one could identify the original, but this only brought home the odd way in which matters somehow had been rendered into a more homely intrigue and murder story, with all the satiric edge blunted. Nevertheless, Nigel Havers (Gorse) and Bernard Hepton (Stimpson) turned in sound performances. An alcohol-free *Hangover Square* cannot now be an impossibility. The expertise and devotion formerly expended on dramatising the classics was now spent on the hit series of the time, *Inspector Morse* (Central Television) based on the novels by Colin Dexter, starring John Thaw and Kevin Whately, which began transmission in 1987. Television viewers' taste for the style and mores of bygone years had to make do with 1930s upper-class crime novels in BBC-1's *Miss Marple* (1984–92, which starred Joan Hickson), Agatha Christie's *Poirot* (LWT-Carnival Films), and BBC-1 series of Margery Allingham's *Campion* (1989, adapted by John Hopkins). Toff detectives seemed the closest we were now to get to classic novels served up as costume drama. We had reached the end of an epoch. The BBC had quietly closed the classic serial unit. No one could have guessed what a renaissance in the classic serial tradition lay in waiting for the next decade.

4
The 1990s: Renaissance of the Classic Serial

Current imperatives: economic and technical developments

Before the arrival of the commercial channel, the BBC had enjoyed the monopoly which Lord Reith had considered essential to good broadcasting. Then it faced competition with ITV. For a while, ratings seemed of little account, but in due course it became an accepted principle that the BBC really should not simply expect its licence fee without demonstrably having striven to provide a service which the public supported. The competition for ratings was then to be pursued in earnest.

The BBC found itself beleaguered in the early 1980s. Its self confidence had been severely shaken during the period of high inflation in the 1970s when the real value of its licence fee revenue was eroded. The Callaghan government had encouraged the Corporation to borrow to make ends meet, pending the eventual granting of an increased licence fee. The new government elected in 1979 did not take such a charitable and long suffering view. The Corporation was soon to find its independence and monopoly challenged by Thatcherism, which viewed it as a rather indulged publicly funded corporation operating under a traditionally rather liberal philosophy. Other factors contributed to its jitters. The Sound Broadcasting Act (1972) had ended the BBC's monopoly of radio broadcasting by setting up commercial radio in the United Kingdom, which began broadcasting the following year. This may now be seen as the thin edge of a very significant wedge. Six years after this Act, the Annan Report on the future of broadcasting was published. A fourth television channel was to be added to BBC 1, BBC 2 and the commercial channel. Channel Four was to broadcast a national service under the IBA, financed by advertising and government grants and was destined to supply educational and minority interests not already catered for. Channel Four began broadcasting in 1982. The following year the Cable Authority was established to supervise cable networks. Until 1982 the BBC had been in a strong position. Running two channels with competition only from a single commercial channel, it usually earned fifty per cent of the ratings. Then in 1982 Channel Four appeared, and the BBC could no longer take for granted that it would earn 50 per cent of the ratings.[1] The BBC was well aware that the licence fee was up for renewal in 1985, yet nevertheless had spent considerable sums attempting to compete with ITV's breakfast television.

If good ratings would incline government to award a generous increase to their £46 licence fee, then the Corporation might well have considered they had got it right in 1984 with *The Thornbirds*, a seven-part American drama series, bought from ABC/Warner, based on the best-selling novel by Colleen McCulloch, starring Richard Chamberlain. It was shown on Monday evenings, necessitating the removal of *Panorama* for its accommodation. It achieved good ratings but offended taste in high places. Additionally it had the misfortune to coincide with Granada's immensely prestigious *The Jewel in the Crown*. Douglas Hurd, then a junior minister at the Home Office, made no bones about his low opinion of *The Thornbirds* and of the BBC's judgment in screening it. Such was the heated debate in the quality papers that many were made to feel uncomfortable for having enjoyed a drama in which a handsome priest had put his vows aside and had sexual intercourse with a young girl.[2] The new politics also found itself ill at ease with the apparent independence of the BBC, particularly as far as news and current affairs were concerned, finding serious fault with BBC coverage of Northern Ireland and the Falklands war.[3] Additionally, interesting evidence of ideological tensions surfaced in the controversy aroused by such dramas as *Boys From the Blackstuff, The Singing Detective, The Monocled Mutineer, The Falklands Play*. It was perceived that the Corporation's free spirit was essentially the result of its funding, as the licence fee made it independent of commercial pressure. Government control of its funding was seen as a way of shortening its lead and bringing it to heel, and therefore the pressure to increase its license fee in line with inflation was resisted. In 1986 the Peacock Committee published its deliberations, and the BBC was spared the worst. The introduction of advertising to the BBC was rejected, but the Peacock Committee recommended wider choice for consumers in television output and an increase in supply from outside production companies. This would develop the BBC's role as a publisher rather than simply a maker of programmes.

The Conservative government resisted pressure to increase the Corporation's funding from the public purse, continued its attacks on what were perceived as the BBC's irresponsibilities, and attempted as far as it was able indirectly to interfere with BBC programmes. For example, in 1987 the Conservative government successfully forced the BBC to cease production of a programme on the Zircon spy satellite. The BBC's answer to these pressures was twofold; internal economies and the extensive marketing of its products. And the consequences of these pressures on British television broadcasting as a whole have been considerable. The Corporation's efforts have been Homeric. The new economic imperatives may be sensed in the change of tone of the BBC's annual published reports. In 1985–86 the BBC reported generally on a good year's sales, accounting for 7 per cent of BBC Enterprise's total income. Among the best selling drama series in the USA were *The Borgias, Tenko, The Father, The Invisible Man* and *Doctor Who*. No sign of a boom in classic novels.[4] By 1997 their television programme sales and distribution business had grown by 20 per cent. The sale of television programmes by BBC Worldwide Commercial Activities in 1996–97 was £354 million, four per cent higher than 1995–96.[5] In the following year BBC Worldwide made an operating profit of £9 million, £4 million lower than the previous year, reflecting the high level of investment in new services. Sales to the USA increased by 25 per cent. Additionally they licensed 31 431 hours of programming to 70 other countries.[6] This policy of concentrating effort to such an extent on overseas sales has led to a revival of classic novel serials, and to the survival of the big boys (both the public Corporation as well as the commercial companies) in this particular area of the market. Dramatisations of classic novels, somehow seen as characteristic of British media high culture, were rapidly identified as ideal products to make at home and sell abroad. The major companies, and the BBC above all, were seen as most likely to produce quality goods of this kind.

Government sensitivity and attempts at direct intervention continued. In 1988 live broadcasting of IRA spokespersons was banned, and in film reports actors' voices had to be dubbed to replace IRA personnel. The Thames Television programme about the shooting of three IRA gunmen in Gibraltar, *Death on the Rock*, raised vociferous protests. Additional unwelcome competition for the BBC came in 1989 when Rupert Murdoch's satellite television transmissions began with

Sky TV. In April the following year British Satellite Broadcasting (BSB) began transmission. In November it merged to form BSkyB. Further deregulation was signalled in the 1990 Broadcasting Act which licensed Channel 3, Channel Four and a new Channel 5, as well as cable and satellite broadcasting. At least 25 per cent of television output in future was to be bought from independent production companies. A new system of auctioning the franchises for the commercial television companies was introduced. A new Radio Authority was established to allocate up to three national commercial radio stations. These were to be awarded by competitive tender. The nature of the on-going debate as to the comparative merits of government deregulation and the continuation of the BBC as a free-standing corporation was demonstrated in 1992 in the government publication, *The Future of the BBC* and the BBC's own publication, *Extending Choice*. The resignations of several of the highest-level executives in television drama production, Michael Wearing, Charles Denton, Jonathan Powell, demonstrated the seriousness of the battle being waged by the BBC to maintain its lead in quality television drama production.

This is the context within which the impressive revival of the classic serial should be examined. The 1990s seemed likely to be troubled waters for television broadcasting in the UK. The government seemed determined that existing institutions should be subject to challenge and more open competition, and the ripples of uncertainty were to affect both the Corporation and commercial channels. The 1991 Broadcasting Act unsettled commercial television as it introduced the award of the ITV franchises by means of a bidding procedure. Also both the BBC and ITV were obliged to commission a quarter of their programmes from independent companies. With the BBC's Charter up for renewal in 1996 the Corporation had to be seen to be rationalising its procedures, cutting its costs and improving its revenues. Several top ranking resignations had signalled the strains under the new management. Rating figures and programme sales grew in importance. Cop shows, medical dramas, soap operas thrived. This was scarcely the soil in which we might have expected a sudden flowering of the classics. But that is just what happened.

It would not be correct to describe what was happening in television during the early 1990s as going down-market, so much as uncertainty. Ratings were important and soap operas were good for ratings. There has been considerable discussion as to the causes of this situation. Sustained concentration on one storyline was no longer tenable. Viewers seemed to like the variety of several stories interchanging as they unfolded, multi-layered narrative as pioneered in such American products as *Lou Grant* and *Hill Street Blues*.[7] This narrative format was well-established in soap opera and consequently it was no accident that this genre thrived, with *Coronation Street* revamping itself, jettisoning much of its traditional north country working-class 'social realism' and appearing four evenings a week during the next decade, to the direct benefit of its ratings. The BBC had triumphed with *EastEnders*, so why not try again? The answer was *Eldorado*, a soap and sangria saga set in Spain. Ten million pounds, and a custom-built village set later, it flopped. Yorkshire Television's *The Darling Buds of May* became a national institution. The BBC's attempt to answer this with *A Year in Provence* sank without trace. However, political comedies such as Andrew Davies's dramatisation of Michael Dobbs's *House of Cards* (1990), *To Play the King* (1993) and *The Final Cut* (1995) for the BBC touched the nation's funny bone. Here we had a success repeated twice over. *Oranges Are Not the Only Fruit* (BBC-2, 1990) was deeply convincing and moving, and probably unrepeatable. Alan Bleasdale's *GBH* (1991) for Channel Four is probably charitably best forgotten. But Lynda La Plante (an astonishing one-woman television drama industry) created a winning formula with Helen Mirren in *Prime Suspect* as Inspector Tennison. Central Television led the popular drama series parade from 1991 on with Lucy Gannon's *Soldier, Soldier* which survived for four seasons, with leading members of the cast deserving campaign medals.

It might well have seemed as if the British had forgotten all about dramatised classics. And then, out of the blue, came David Nokes's dramatisation of one of the glories of the national literary heritage, Samuel Richardson's *Clarissa*. Had we but known it at the time, this was no shooting star, but a portent of things to come. *Clarissa*, dramatised by David Nokes and Janet Barron, produced by Kevin Loader (executive producer, Michael Wearing) and directed by Robert Bierman, was transmitted in three one-hour instalments on BBC-2 in 1991. It had a budget of £2 million and the production was beautifully designed by Gerry Scott and costumed by Ken Trew. Much of it resembled eighteenth-century paintings miraculously brought to life – a mixture of Joseph Highmore, Francis Hayman and William Hogarth.[8] Among the specially-constructed Georgian items were a three storey house, a coaching inn and a London street market paved with cobbles.

Samuel Richardson's epistolary novel *Clarissa, or, the History of a Young Lady* (1747–48), presented and explored the beginning stages of a new Puritanism in social morality. The early Georgian period, under the shrewd management of Robert Walpole and his successors, witnessed the increasing prosperity of the merchant and trading classes, (the sense of New Money behind Clarissa's family fortunes was subtly but firmly indicated) combined with what Louis Cazamian has identified as 'a new spirit of probity and fervour'.[9] Methodism and a sentimental reaction would contribute to an eventual romantic revival, and Richardson's masterpiece is usually identified as a key expression of these themes. The villain Lovelace with his cunning stratagems to ensnare the pious Clarissa carries strong echoes of the Restoration rake (and even of Milton's Satan), but in his relish for evil he foreshadows much that is Byronic: 'I love, when I dig a pit, to have my prey tumble in with secure feet and open eyes: then a man can look down upon her, with an "O-ho, charmer! How came you there?".' Clarissa, an austere Christian, resists the blandishments of the very devil in preserving her virtue against overwhelming odds, supported only by her trust in heavenly reward.

Clarissa is the virtuous daughter of good family. She is pursued by her sister's former beaux, Lovelace, who, as a systematic amorist, regards the conquest of her virtue as a challenge. Clarissa's family are resolved that she should marry the wealthy Solmes, who is repugnant to her. In escaping the tyranny of her family she is lured into the clutches of Lovelace who drugs and then rapes her. She dies in shame and grief. Putting aside its length – this novel at a million words is the longest in the language – on the face of it, it hardly seems a tale designed to appeal to audiences of television drama in the 1990s. But its adapters described it in *Radio Times* as 'one of the most powerful fictional explorations of sexual politics in English'. Its significance as an outstanding study of sexual obsession and identity has been strongly reasserted in the present decade. Among its several impressive achievements was the fact that it made excellent drama. As its star, Saskia Wickham commented:

'I think what *Clarissa* did was say, you can make costume dramas and they're not all about people sitting around drinking cups of tea with their fingers cocked out. They're actually quite exciting and they're quite relevant and they're timeless.'[10] At the first audition the director asked Saskia Wickham what she thought of the character. She answered that their biggest job would be making the audience like her, because she would come across as quite annoying. It was absolutely essential that we should feel for her. Letters from numerous viewers assured her that she succeeded.

As David Nokes admits, the major problem faced in adapting a literary text from the past is having to confront those shifts of sensibility and cultural assumptions that make the idioms of one age strange to another. In the case of Richardson's Clarissa Harlowe, it is not as if we are actually lost on the language of Christianity, but that its role as a cultural signifier has experienced vast change in the past 200 years. Now, Clarissa herself is explicitly presented as a Christian heroine, and her vocabulary is stuffed with scriptural allusions. When she can spare the time from writing those copious epistles, her favourite recreation is reading her Bible. As David Nokes puts it:

> Such a character poses problems for modern viewers to whom such insistent demonstration of piety, suggests not an honest and virtuous idealism, but the obsessive rituals of a zealot. It was a problem we were forced to confront.... Had we opted to remain strictly 'faithful' to her pious vocabulary, we would have risked alienating an audience for whom such language is not the natural expression of moral conviction, but the private language of a sect. Believing strongly in the powerful modernity of Richardson's psychological study of family violence, intimidation, seduction and rape, I chose to secularise some – but by no means all – of Clarissa's moral vocabulary in order to maximise its dramatic appeal. This, it might be argued, was misrepresenting the text. I prefer to think that it would have been a greater mis-representation to have made a popular best seller of its own day into an exclusive religious icon of ours.[11]

The writers distilled into three television episodes the very essence of Richardson's prolix novel. The actors, indeed the production team as a whole, concentrated their efforts on realizing the script, not on a misguided concept of loyalty to the original novel. Their collective and combined aim was to do justice to the script. Saskia Wickham admits never having read the book in its entirety. But when she saw the script it was love at first sight. She knew immediately that she deeply wanted to do it:

> I remember when I got the part, I went into Waterstone's, floating with happiness, and said, have you got *Clarissa* by Samuel Richardson? – longing to say, 'Because I've just been offered the lead and I'm playing it on the BBC....' And he looked at me and said: 'Golly! You don't want to read that, do you? I think I might have a copy of it wedging a door open somewhere...'. I used the book, and referred to it a lot and found it enormously helpful, but

I had to play the script, I couldn't think of the book all the time. It can be very confusing if you read the book too closely when you're doing it....

Her identification with the role and with the production was complete:

I don't think I'll ever do anything as wonderful again. There's a shot, actually right at the beginning of the film, where they're about to read the will, and Clarissa walks down the staircase and past all the servants and they all curtsied and I did that and I thought: I'm in heaven. I have got the best job in the whole world. I can't believe I'm being paid to do this. It felt so wonderful. And a word about getting the period feel. I would often feel, because the places we filmed were so accurate, especially the Harwood's house (which was actually in Shropshire) which had all the original details and they even had beautiful paintings from that period that they let us use. The people who were on the film crew were the people who looked out of place. They looked as though they were wrong. And we looked and felt as if we were right. I felt as if I lived in that house and wore those clothes. There was a very specific time, I remember, actually we were filming in the Inns of Court, and Sean and I (Sean Bean, who played Lovelace) were riding up in a carriage, and they'd covered the whole of the Inns of Court is a sort of sawdusty sand to make it look period and anything modern had been covered up or disguised. Honestly, you looked at passers-by in their modern clothes, and you thought: 'What are you doing here?' The designer built wonderful convincing sets in Ealing Studios. We had a chef who made 18th century food. And the director was equally determined, he said: 'I want you to look as though you've worn those clothes all your life. You mustn't look as if you're in fancy dress costume.' And I never felt like that. I really felt at home. Living in my own time.

The reviews were unanimously favourable. Among the most perceptive was Richard Last, writing in the *Daily Telegraph*, who commented that it was not only superbly literate but was above all:

...embedded deep in the property conscious mores of the 18th century upper class, and their rigid notions of behaviour proper to the sexes... for the purposes of a television serial, Richardson's million word novel is a tale of richly drawn individuals locked within these constraints. His unconventional heroine is a strong willed, intelligent, over-pious girl faced with an unacceptable arranged marriage... If the BBC took a risk in committing two years and £2 million to a costume piece never before attempted on celluloid, they took an even greater risk in casting an unknown in the title role. Whoever chose Saskia Wickham, a twenty-four-year-old actress with no previous television experience, knew what they were about. She invests Clarrissa with an astonishingly mature blend of dignity, feminine resolution and – as her complex response to Lovelace's advances progresses – latent sexuality.

Even the fact of her softly appealing features are just short of obvious beauty gives her an advantage. When she smiles, which in the circumstances is not often, the screen is illuminated.[12]

Why the BBC did not make this available to purchase in video form remains a mystery.

Clarissa signalled the revival of the television classic serial as serious adult drama, with a vigorous future as an internationally marketable commodity – a harbinger of the age of *Middlemarch, Pride and Prejudice* and *Vanity Fair.*

In October 1993 BBC-1 transmitted Stephen Lowe's three 50-minute episode dramatisation of Stendhal's *Scarlet and Black*, produced by Rosalind Wolfes and directed by Ben Bolt. This was a courageous undertaking as Stendhal's masterpiece is complex both in terms of the ideas it engages and in the method of its narrative. It is subtitled *A chronicle of the 19th century* and that is certainly how its author regarded it. To its contemporaries it would have seemed a discussion of the post-Napoleonic struggle between liberal republicans who would have regarded Napoleon as the 'great liberator' and the Royalists who supported the monarchy under Charles X. Julian Sorel, the hero, a carpenter's son, personifies the upwardly mobile ambitious young man who sees the way to the top has been freed up by Napoleon's destruction of the *ancien régime*. He seeks to satisfy professional ambitions in the military and then in the church, making dangerous sexual liaisons in the process for which he is persecuted by the very state in which he had hoped to succeed. He is employed as tutor to the children of M. de Renal, Mayor of Verrieres, and has an affair with Mme de Renal. He then returns to the seminary where his success leads him to the post of secretary to the Marquis de la Mole, whose daughter he seduces. To avoid scandal the Marquis arranges for him to be ennobled and given a promotion in the army. Mme de Renal threatens to expose him. He attempts her death. He has lost his contest with destiny, but goes bravely to the scaffold. The historic moment between the revolution and the abdication of Napoleon, which removed the glass ceiling of class and allowed men of ambition to realize themselves, has gone. Stendhal drives home his theme by having his hero more or less in discourse with Napoleon. How to do this in television terms? Well, in this production Napoleon frequently appears recognizably in person and converses with Ewan McGregor (our hero). Did it work? It was a bit stagey for some, but others accepted it at a Brechtian level. It might have been better to have jettisoned all hopes of delivering the ideological goods and go for the drama of Julien's complex amorous and professional career moves, in the hope that the themes would be self evident. In the event, the result was felt by many to be stodgy, but with some very good moments provided by the brilliant acting of T.P. McKenna, Lisa Coleman, Rachel Weisz and Stratford Johns.

In January the following year the new age of classic novel dramatisations was confirmed with the transmission on BBC-2 of Andrew Davies's six-episode version of *Middlemarch*. Peter Waymark, writing in *The Times*, rightly regarded it as a challenge, ceding also that the challenge had been met: 'George Eliot's great novel *Middlemarch* is often regarded as the finest in the English language, to be compared in scope and subtlety with *Anna Karenina* or *War and Peace*. For television it is one of the ultimate challenges.'[13] A very great deal was riding on this BBC production. It had been internally resolved that the reception of *Middlemarch* would decide whether or not the Corporation was to continue with classic novel dramatisations. They sank £6 000 000 in this venture. As Lynne Truss wrote at the time, with the BBC having let it be known that if the series was not a huge critical success, they threatened to give up adapting proper books altogether: 'one felt more than slightly blackmailed – rather like the infants at *Peter Pan* when told that if they do not clap their hands very, very loudly, poor little Tink will die.'[14] In the event, they had nothing to worry about. It earned good reviews, arousing considerable positive comment. It was shown in Australia, Belgium, Bosnia, Brunei, Bulgaria, Croatia, Denmark, Egypt, Eire, Finland, Germany, Holland, Hong Kong, Hungary, Iceland, Israel, Jordan, Malta, Mexico, New Zealand, Norway, Pakistan, Poland, Romania, Singapore, Slovenia, South Africa, Spain, Sweden and Thailand. Overseas sales earned the BBC one million pounds.[15] This production demonstrably brought off a very difficult trick. It was an acclaimed and popular drama series, yet at the same time satisfied traditional élitist cultural tastes, earning warm support from the likes of Roy Hattersley and A.S. Byatt. The production repackaged culture as nostalgia which could be consumed in several ways.[16]

Libby Purves put her finger on it when she wrote:

> There will be howls of anguish .... from ageing Eng. Lit. graduates,
> as they see yet another of their cherished bastions of exclusivity
> thrown open to the idle and vulgar herd, for *Middlemarch* – the book
> which Virginia Woolf so ominously called 'one of the few English
> novels written for grown-up people' – *Middlemarch*, by the alarm-
> ingly serious Ms George Eliot, most difficult, discursive, reflective
> and effortful of 19th century novelists; *Middlemarch* which has kept
> many a poor undergraduate up all night with a wet towel round her
> head – has come at last to television.
>
> What is more... appears so faithful to plot, spirit and character
> that it will be impossible to tell who read the book and who took it
> in effortlessly from the screen. Eliot, who believed in effort, reflec-
> tion and self-improvement by deep private study, would be
> disgusted at the easy way we live now.[17]

In this respect, Andrew Davies was an ideal writer to dramatize
Middlemarch for television as he combined several loyalties. He started
professional life as a teacher, progressing from school teaching,
through teacher training to lecturing at Warwick University, and was
committed to English literature in the traditional, dare one say it,
Leavisite manner. He became a writer, novelist, screenwriter and television dramatist. He says that he did not go from one to the other – he
continues to write both fiction and drama. He was offered his first
adaptation in the late 1970s, R.F. Delderfield's *To Serve Them All My
Days*, produced by the BBC in 1980. He served a long apprenticeship
writing television drama with successes in original drama series, such
as *A Very Peculiar Practice* 1986 and 1988, and dramatisations such as
House of Cards (1990) behind him. But as well as this highly developed
media professionalism, he brought with him a continued commitment
to classical literature and to teaching. He admits this when he says that
dramatising the classics for television is a bit like translating them
from one language into another and adds:

> I also think of it in some ways related to what I used to do when I
> used to lecture on them. It's like saying 'This is the way I read this
> book and this is what I think it is really about and look at this bit,
> isn't it good?' and sometimes, on occasions, don't you wish she had
> done this instead of what she did do.[18]

The style of television drama, he believes has changed, 'partly as the pace of life generally has changed, and the general pace of film and television drama tends to spell things out less and I suppose they move from image to image, and scenes tend to be shorter than they used to and more points made with just a visual image rather than two pages of dialogue.' He feels that with a Victorian novelist like George Eliot, there is a fair amount of baggage to carry, and it is rather like a person carrying suitcases on a railway station with no porter:

> You carry as much as you can, and then go back and get the rest, and then go on. In dramatising a close packed novel like *Middlemarch*, you have to make sure you carry the goods from scene to scene, sequence to sequence. But... televising a novel in no way violates its sanctity... because there the book still is. And if you say Oh – you've spoilt it for me the person who says that must have had a very weak grip of the book to start with, if they could have it taken away just by seeing somebody else's dramatisation of it. It's like going to the school pantomime, say, *Little Red Riding Hood*, and saying, I shall never enjoy *Little Red Riding Hood* again because the infant's school production of it was so bad.[19]

Andrew Davies's television dramatisation of *Middlemarch* provides generous evidence of these principles. Over and above everything, there is a sincere commitment to the serious purpose of this great novel. The characters and plot are faithfully reproduced. The narrative is wholly coherent and the work may be followed and understood whether or not one is familiar with the original. But it is a translation into a completely different language. It can be read at the level of any modern quality television drama – take the scene at the Vincy's breakfast table and the banter between Ros and Fred – which could be between any middle-class adolescent brother and sister. Only the costume places it in the late 1820s. Yet at the same time, it is true to George Eliot. The same can be said of Lydgate's proposal to Ros Vincy. We are well prepared for this, we already sense how dangerously magnetic Lydgate finds her sexuality – and Ros's interest in him is well conveyed. The novelist takes pages of text to explain that Tertius had no need, really, to go to the Vincy's house. He knew that Mr Vincy, for whom he had a message, was at work. But for a variety of reasons, he went. Ros misunderstands his unexpected appearance. It is beautifully, sensitively, maturely written by a novelist at the height of her considerable powers. It takes a few moments of film, but all we need to know is there, in word, gesture, facial expression. And, true to its traditions, as the couple fondly embrace, the music wells up and the credits roll. But every time we see it, it works. We understand why Lydgate acted as he did. It resembles a similar moment in Puccini's *La Boheme* as Rudolpho touches Mimi's hand and is utterly gone. There can be no half measures at such moments. At one moment we are safe and free. The next totally encaptured. George Eliot wrote of this moment: 'In half an hour he left the house an engaged man, whose soul was not his own, but the woman's to whom he had bound himself.' Andrew Davies wanted to portray the pretty, shallow but immensely powerful personality of Ros, who is able so wholly to dominate the intellectually highly-developed Tertius Lydgate. Davies has the courage to create this in a brief scene – not in the book – of Lydgate gently undressing Ros, unfastening her underclothes, lovingly calling her his 'little bird'. Yet Andrew Davies is also loyal to the larger themes of *Middlemarch* – one of the very finest 'Condition of England' novels. He says:

> The book feels very modern even though it's a nineteenth century book. It's set in a time of recession, it's got people who are very much constrained by society, money, the limits on their own ambition. It's also very modern in terms of the psychological relationships between the characters, the importance it puts on love, sexuality, energy.[20]

George Eliot subtitled the novel *A Study of Provincial Life* but she used a sequence of linked stories of life in middle England at the turn of the 1820s and 1830s emblematicallty to stand for those fundamental changes in British life which collectively gave rise what is now termed the 'Condition of England Question'. She set her novel in a period of vast and comparatively sudden change as we developed from a mainly agricultural and trading nation to an industrial and commercial nation. The country lived through the agitation for the great Reform Bill and its enactment by parliament, which seemed to break a logjam and precipitate all manner of possible changes in society. The significance of the times lay not so much in what the Reform Act achieved (not all that much, in fact) but in what the passing of the Act demonstrated beyond any shadow of doubt, that change was possible. Old England was yielding place to the new. This is given us in the BBC's *Middlemarch* which opens with images of grazing sheep, a herdsman, a stage coach and the building of the new railway lines.[21] Economic and political change was inextricably mixed with social change. The ambi-

tions for reform had been building in the country for several generations to reach a peak during the agitation for the Reform Bill in 1832
and its immediate aftermath. John Morley characterises these years in
his biography of Richard Cobden. The spirit of reform was now
released:

> A great wave of humanity, of benevolence, of desire for improve-
> ment – a great wave of social sentiment in short – poured itself
> among all who had the faculty of large and disinterested thinking.
> The political spirit was abroad in its most comprehensive form.[22]

These are the very changes talked over by Dorothea and her uncle at
the opening of *Middlemarch*. She draws plans to rehouse the poor, he
talks of land and agricultural reform and stands for parliament. She is
idealistically committed to change. He just cannot help going along
with it. They live in an age when change was in the air. The opposition of stagecoach and railway was fundamental in the thinking of so
many contemporaries, who felt they were living in a time of very
rapid change, symbolised in the decay of horse transport and triumph
of steam.

The majority of Victorians who could recall an age before the rail-
road felt they had lived in two separate worlds. The railway is a
recurring image in Victorian writing as a metaphor for those great
changes which cut modern times off from the 'Good Old Days.'[23]
Thomas Hughes invited readers of his vastly popular novel, *Tom
Brown's School Days* (1857)[24] to look out of the railway carriage
window and see for themselves how matters stood. Thackeray drew a
line dividing those days before the railways from the rapidly changing
modern and modernising days he lived in:

> It was only yesterday, but what a gulf between now and then! Then
> was the old world. Stage-coaches .... riding horses, pack-horses,
> highwaymen, knights in armour, Norman invaders, Roman
> legions, Druids, Ancient Britons painted blue.... All these belong
> to the old period.... But your railroad starts the new era, and we
> of a certain age belong to the new time and the old one.... We are
> of the age of steam.[25]

It is all there in the opening moments of Andrew Davies's dramatisation. Tertius Lydgate, the young ambitious university educated medico
arrives in Middlemarch by stagecoach (its bodywork surprisingly clean

considering how many hundreds of miles it has travelled) passing *en route* the railways then under construction. We have a lingering shot of the railworks and the locomotive seen as the coach passengers would have seen it. 'Look!' Lydgate observes, – the Future!'. The stage rolls into Middlemarch, but we have glimpsed the future.

One of the most effective features of the production was the convincing sense of location. We believed in a real place called Middlemarch, where Bulstrode ran the bank, Vincy ran a textile company, Lydgate had ambitions for the hospital, Mrs Cadwallader gossiped and nearby Brooke and Chetham ran farms. This was mainly as a result of using the ancient market town of Stamford, Lincolnshire, which remains almost unspoilt by the industrial revolution and retains much of its eighteenth-century character. It was therefore ideal to stand in for a pre-industrial town immediately prior to Victorian expansion. Watching *Middlemarch* we definitely had the sense of observing everyday life unfolding in a modest township in which the high drama of particular lives was situated in the humdrummeries of ordinary life. As Brian Tufano, director of photography in this production, commented:

> The best way of making use of a location is to make the location tell the story. It is another character, it is another subject. All those locations we used were chosen with great care, because they say something about the characters that actually live in those houses.[26]

The casting and acting was faultless. Newcomer Juliet Aubrey played Dorothea and set her own mark, bringing no associations from previous roles. Caroline Harker played her sister Celia as a Sloane Ranger. This was neatly done. Robert Hardy as Arthur Brooke created his definitive fogey role. Patrick Malahide as Revd Edward Casaubon was absolutely convincing. Douglas Hodge and newcomer Trevyn McDowell were happily cast as Lydgate and Rosamond. This beautiful production of *Middlemarch* attested the BBC's almost proprietorial right to the genre of the classic novel dramatisation, which for some years had quietly and modestly slumbered and might almost have been in danger of mossing over. Once more there was a name and a reputation to live up to, and it might well have been hoped that the transmission of David Lodge's six episode dramatisation[27] of Dickens's *Martin Chuzzlewit*, (BBC-2 with WGBH Boston) in November 1994, produced by Chris Parr and directed by Pedr James, would put matters beyond any dispute. In the event this *Chuzzlewit* was a mixed blessing.

The work is seldom considered one of Dickens's finest novels, although it contains some of his finest characterizations, comic situations and pages of brilliant writing. The weakness in *Martin Chuzzlewit* is that the very strength of the novelist's invention seems to break out from under his control, to wander at will and refuse all attempts to contain it. The theme Dickens proposed to handle was selfishness. The balance and emphasis of the story changed as he began to develop it. But in essence the novel is a study of what money does to people, and what people will do for money. The novel is made up of two parts. Old Martin Chuzzlewit (Paul Scofield) has learned to distrust humanity as a result of his family's obvious attempts to lay hands on his fortune. He distrusts his grandson, Martin, (Ben Walden), who is in love with his ward, Mary Graham. Young Martin is a pupil of the architect, Seth Pecksniff, an oily hypocrite, who has designs on Mary Graham. To test young Martin, his grandfather causes his dismissal. Martin then seeks his fortune in America, but returns a sadder but a wiser man. Reconciled with Old Martin, he marries Mary. The second plot concerns Martin's brother, Anthony, and his scoundrel son, Jonas. Jonas marries Mercy, one of Pecksniff's daughters, and bullies her vilely. He murders his father and also murders Montagu Tigg, a swindler who is blackmailing him. He poisons himself rather than face trial. Opportunities for Dickens's penchant for melodrama, morbid psychology and surreal comedy abound.

Characters took on a life of their own (much as this may still be relished and enjoyed in reading the novel) to the detriment of sound construction. Any attempt to reduce this bursting saga to the confines of six-episode television drama serial will show signs of the struggle. The interlacing of the storylines coherently over six episodes was achieved at the cost of much trimming, but the whole of the American episode was more or less jettisoned. Dickens believed the strength of this work lay in its sound construction, although few readers would agree. It is among the creakiest sentimental melodramas he ever evolved. But his tireless invention was exerted elsewhere in this performance. *Martin Chuzzlewit* has earned lasting admiration for its consistently dazzling characterisation and vigorous comedy – not so much in the action, as in the fancy and dynamism of its prose and dialogue, which frequently attains a sublime dottyness bordering on phantasmagoria. This works on the page, but how much of it was brought to the television screen? Seth Pecksniff is one of the great characterisations of literature, as a portrait of hypocrisy he has few rivals. He is consistently presented in masterly prose which invariably serves to sharpen the satirical edge. Time and again he is handed to us garnished with prose of utter genius:

> It was once said of him by a homely admirer, that he had a Fortunatus's purse of good sentiments in his insides. In this particular he was like the girl in the fairy tale, except that if they were not actual diamonds which fell from his lips, they were the very brightest paste, and shone prodigiously.

The moment of Pecksniff's unmasking at the close of the novel, when old Martin knocks him to the ground with a blow of his stick, ascends to heights of ridiculous melodrama which surpass anything Dickens had yet written. He puts words in Pecksniff's mouth of sublime comicality:

> I have been struck this day... with a walking stick, which I have every reason to believe has knobs upon it: on that delicate and exquisite portion of the human anatomy, the brain. Several blows have been inflicted, Sir, without a walking-stick, upon that tenderer portion of my frame: my heart.... And if you ever contemplate the silent tomb, Sir, which you will excuse me for entertaining some doubt of your doing, after the conduct which you have allowed yourself to be betrayed this day; if you ever contemplate the silent tomb, Sir, think of me. If you find yourself approaching to the silent tomb, Sir, think of me. If you should wish to have anything inscribed upon your silent tomb, Sir, let it be, that I – ah, my remorseful Sir! that I – the humble individual who has now the honour of reproaching you, forgave you. That I forgave you when my injuries were fresh, and when my bosom was newly wrung. It may be bitterness to you to hear it now, Sir, but you will live to seek a consolation in it...

On screen we have only Pecksniff's actions and words, the genius of Dickens's narrative prose is absent. The best that could be done to make Pecksniff comic is to deploy slapstick, knockabout and pratfalls. We cannot share Jonas's thoughts and feelings as we do in the book. In fact we get the story, extremely well performed. Tom Wilkinson's Pecksniff was an immensely comic creation, Tigg (Pete Postlethwaite), Jonas (Keith Allen), Mrs Gamp (Elizabeth Spriggs), and Maggie Steed (Mrs Todgers) were magnificent and in any just world would have earned a clutch of BAFTAs for their individual performances, but there was something muddled at the core of this series.

Martin Chuzzlewit is not a gloomy book, (though it is aware of the darker side of human nature); it is no *Hard Times* or *Bleak House*. That darkening vision was to come later. But the production designers decided to go for a murky dark quality. The London scenes were filmed at King's Lynn, which was significantly and effectively given a make-over for the task. But the effect was stylistic dislocation. This was early Dickens treated like *Our Mutual Friend*. It was also burdened with a political slant alien to its real nature. The director, Pedr James, admitted to his attempts to create something akin to post-Thatcherite England, when the last utility has been privatised and poverty took to the streets.[28] This point highlights a serious problem in this production which, in turn, raises issues endemic to media attempts in translating classic novels from the printed page into radio or moving pictures – the creation of appropriate style and ultimate authorial control. It seems that all was not harmony between writer and director in this BBC production and the strains showed most seriously in the conclusion. Pedr James tended to see this novel in terms of a Dickensian social satire which he firmly set in a Dickensian Victorian city location – labyrinthine streets, mud, muck, jostling humanity, poverty, filth, fog, murk, deprivation, and human indifference. The *Radio Times* assured us before transmission that:

> The BBC's stunning new adaptation ... aims to capture the filth and flavour of Victorian London.... The atmosphere has been laid on with a trowel, and the red mud – actually, sterile mushroom compost with the fibrous quality of horsedung – is thick on the cobbles. The costumes look frayed.... The BBC promises viewers Victorian London at its rheumatic and choleric best, and no self respecting card manufacturer would want it featuring in his Christmas range.[29]

Such endeavours show the tendency to plaster *Chuzzlewit* with qualities associated with the gloomy parts of *Oliver Twist*, *Bleak House*, *Our Mutual Friend*. They were anxious, in the light of *Middlemarch*, to avoid the accusation of creating something with that exquisite heritage feel. Jeremy Turner, *Chuzzlewit*'s costume designer, commented:

> I'm not interested in making people look gorgeous. Costume is there to tell you something about their character. If anything, the costumes in *Middlemarch* were too beautiful. We certainly won't be using that approach. In *Martin Chuzzlewit* you'll be able to smell the sweat.[30]

These are all qualities associated with social realism, believed to be the invention of nineteenth-century novelists. Hippolyte Taine's theories of literature based on Darwinian scientific principles (*Histoire de la litterature anglaise* 1864; *La Philosophie de l'art* 1869) gave birth to Naturalism in fiction. Taine's literary philosophy was that it was the duty of creative literature to portray human society as objectively as scientists observed nature. Naturalism absorbed the biological theories of Darwin and the economic determinism of Marx. Romantic subjectivism was firmly shown the door. Stendhal, Balzac and Flaubert were in some way precursors of the movement, but in Daudet, Maupassant and above all in Zola the doctrines found their most powerful expression. Emile Zola was particularly responsive to Taine's ideas and concentrated on a meticulous accuracy of detail and detached observation. These works were widely read in Britain, and whether we are aware of it or not became the ideological basis from which the cause of social realism has always been argued. David Lodge, however, sees Dickens as a 'dramatist manqué' and asserts that:

> In an earlier century he would have been writing plays, and in ours would have been writing for film and television. He loved the theatre... and ended his life... giving charismatic public readings from his novels. The innately theatrical quality of his imagination is very evident in *Chuzzlewit*. We don't need an authorial voice to tell us what the characters are feeling or thinking. They reveal themselves by their actions and, above all, by their language.[31]

During the last week of *Martin Chuzzlewit*'s transmission David Lodge published an article in *The Independent* in which he revealed something of the conflict of wills within the context of which the final version of the script was created. The first drafts of scripts, he admitted, are usually written in collaboration with a producer and a script editor and 'disagreements between writer and director are not uncommon'.[32] The producer, Chris Parr, had encouraged Lodge to adapt the novel pretty freely, but the director, Pedr James, wanted him to restore much of what he had cut. The script editor, Nell Denton, suggested to David Lodge ending the serial with a double wedding (Martin and Mary, and his friend John Westlock to Ruth, Tom Pinch's sister). This appealed greatly to Lodge's conception of the essential theatricality of Dickens's work: 'The idea appealed to me as a background to the final credits and I developed it into a multiple wedding – incorporating the union of Mark Tapley and Mrs Lupin, and taking the liberty of marrying Mrs Todgers off to Mr Jinkins at the same time.'

It seems clear from this evidence that Lodge thinks that if Dickens were working today he would not just be writing television drama, but commercial television soap opera. Pedr James hated it. 'He felt it was a soft-soapy, feel-good ending that undermined the seriousness and pathos of the novel's conclusion.' After some debate and filming different variants of the conclusion, Pedr James's version was used. Lodge comments: 'The moral of the story is, I suppose, that you can lead a director to water but you can't make him drink.'[33] This exposed matters usually kept hidden in production, several issues in classic novel adaptation about fidelity to a novelist's work and the authorial/power relationship between writer, director and producer. The dramatisation of Dickens's *Hard Times* transmitted by BBC-2 at Christmas time 1994 develops those issues further. This was certainly not in the ancient BBC tradition of the classic serial. Ostensibly made for BBC Schools Broadcasting it was a highly idiosyncratically didactic version/vision of the text, billed as 'Peter Barnes's Film of *Hard Times*'. It was dramatised and directed by Peter Barnes and produced by Richard Langridge, and starred Bob Peck and Alan Bates. In style it was an homogenisation of Brecht, German Expressionism and the comedy of the highly wrought mechanical type associated with Ben Jonson and Terence. But it seriously distorted the original. The grotesque comicality was gone, replaced by a grim Cabinet of Doctor Caligari tone. Trade unionism, lampooned and distrusted by Dickens, is given sympathetic treatment. The circus scenes lacked any sense of attractive fun. The barmy exaggeration into the grotesque which renders Gradgrind and Bounderby laughable but loathsome at the same time is wholly lacking. Dickensian mischief is completely obliterated, leaving nothing but the sterility of parable, enlightening what Macaulay actually meant when he said: 'I read Dickens's *Hard Times*. One excessively touching, heart-breaking passage, and the rest sullen socialism. The evils he attacks he caricatures grossly, and with little humour.'[34] Schoolchildren would have been left with the probably indelible impression that Dickens is a very glum writer. Its contribution to the Christmas spirit in 1994 is less certain.

February 1995 was considerably cheered by BBC-1's transmission of Maggie Wadey's five-part dramatisation of Edith Wharton's unfinished novel *The Buccaneers*, co-produced with WBGH Boston, produced and directed by Philip Saville. English interest in Edith Wharton had been aroused by the release in 1993 of Scorsese's film of *The Age of Innocence*, which spread the useful rumour that Edith Wharton was like Henry

James without the tedium. Yet another recycling of the Jamesian myth of New World innocence coming to terms with Old World decadence, *The Buccaneers* made delightful television. It was a lively tale, a sound mixture of wit and melodrama, which played the sexual scale from flirtation to rape, and offered boundless opportunities for sunshine, landscape, country house living, horses and carriages, splendid dresses and saucy décolletage. The straightforward narrative of four American young charmers let loose on the hunt for husbands in England at the end of the century might have been made for colour television. It starred Carla Gugino, Alison Elliott, Mira Sorvino and Rya Kihlstedt as the four New York belles with Cheri Lunghi, Dinsdale Landen, Rosemary Leach, Jenny Agutter and Connie Booth supporting. Scarcely was this treat over, when on Easter Day 1995 BBC-2 transmitted a dramatisation by Nick Dear of Jane Austen's *Persuasion*.[35] This new BBC version was watched by 3.8 million viewers. It was repeated on BBC-2 on Christmas Day. Charles Denton, BBC's Head of Drama, commented that Jane Austen 'was the Quentin Tarantino of the middle classes'.[36] This was initially budgeted as a BBC Screen Two production at £750 000, but additional funding was raised by making it a co-production with WGBH Boston for cinema release in USA, as well as French television involvement from Millesime. The American and French involvement resulted in some interesting adjustments in scripting and editing. It was rebudgetted to be shot on 35mm and the BBC upped their funding to £1 000 000.[37] In USA it was given cinema release and took $56 000 (£37 000) in its first week in New York and grossed $150 000 in Los Angeles.[38] It was produced by Fiona Finlay and directed by Roger Mitchell. Fiona Finlay had been interested in making a film of *Persuasion* for several years and attempted to get writer Nick Dear onboard. He was not keen and preferred to do either *Sense and Sensibility* or *Pride and Prejudice*. But he agreed at least to read *Persuasion* and revised his thinking, having realized *Persuasion* was a much more mature work. He was to spend two years on the script.

Persuasion, a compressed and complex work, has always been a favourite with radio and television. It was screened on BBC television in 1969, written by Julian Mitchell, starring Ann Firbank and Bryan Marshall, filmed in Dorset and Somerset. This new 1995 BBC-2/WGBH version was fairly faithful to the plot, though some additions were curious. Sir Walter Elliott, a snobbish feckless baronet, (Corin Redgrave) is compelled to let Kellynch Hall to Admiral Croft (John Woodvine) and his wife. He has three daughters – Elizabeth (Phoebe Nicholls) who has much of her father's hauteur, Anne (Amanda Root) who was persuaded to end her engagement to Mrs Croft's brother,

Captain Frederick Wentworth, (Ciaran Hinds) on grounds of his lack of social standing and Mary, married to Charles Musgrove, heir to a local family. The central interest lay in the relationship between Anne and Frederick, and this production rightly focused on this. It is usually assumed that the heroine has many of Jane Austen's qualities. She is no longer a young girl, being in her late twenties, and – like Jane – she has loved and lost. In foregoing Frederick, a young naval officer, she has bowed to family pressure. She is reticent and long suffering. Often turned to for comfort and advice, she is so placed that she cannot resolve her own problems. The arrangement with the Crofts brings her into Frederick's company once more and his love for her gradually revives. Although a direct contemporary of the Romantics, Jane Austen was not, on the face of it, a romantic. (There are some neat satiric asides about Byron and co. in this performance.) Not for her rapturous landscapes, mountains, forests, castles, torrents, tempests, winds and streams. Nevertheless, she effectively delineates the complexities of human feelings, and her account in this novel of the stirrings of affection and the growth of passion between man and woman has no equal in her work. Anne and Frederick are reconciled, but their path is by no means clear. He is initially attracted by Charles Musgrave's sisters, Louisa and Henrietta. Louisa is badly hurt in a fall at Lyme Regis, which is handsomely filmed on location. This occurs when his love for Anne is reawakening. Louisa makes him feel responsible for her and consequently his affection is compromised. Mercifully, Louisa is then attracted to another naval officer, Captain Benwick. Frederick renews his courtship of Anne, whose family has now removed to Bath.

The most effective scenes in the production are located in the magnificent Georgian city. As Corin Redgrave – in the person of Sir Walter Elliott says – 'Bath is incomparable!' and this production proves his aesthetic judgment faultless. Exterior and interior sequences were equally rhapsodically filmed with Old Masterish effect. The main impressions are of brownish-reddish autumnal tints in Bath street scenes and golden candlelight indoors. The photography under Julian Daly's direction is nothing short of handsome. At Bath Anne is vigorously pursued by William Elliott, her cousin, (Samuel West) who is expected to inherit the Kellynch estate. This match would have family approval, but Anne learns that William is also involved with another young woman. Anne has resisted overtures made to her and throughout remained loyal to Frederick. Her upright behaviour further endears her to Frederick who now renews his offer of marriage, and is accepted. Jane Austen's under-

standing of human motive and richness of characterisation trans-
forms this simple tale into a complex novel of quiet humour and
sensitive observation. The closing moments when Wentworth
contrives in a letter to reveal his feelings to Anne is superbly done
in ways particularly suited to television drama, with Anne reading
the letter as she hears Wentworth's voice. The change of emotional
gear was well prepared by Robert Glenister (as Captain Harveille)
revealing that men have feelings of sentiment and love as well as
women. Not as compact as *Pride and Prejudice*, or as wide in its scope
as *Mansfield Park*, *Persuasion* is Jane Austen's most characteristic novel.
Here she exhibits insights into the deeper recesses of human behaviour. There are moments here which are so vivid and convincing they
become almost part of our own experience. Anne is an immortal
creation, to whom our hearts go out. She is also a rarity in literature
– a saintly character who is not a bore.

The production has a unifying and coherent style. They have obviously resolved to go against the existing tradition for Jane Austen of
Quality Street-National Trust village-Empire line and aimed for a kind
of historically back projected social realism. The keynote is struck from
the very opening scenes, showing a labourer scything the grass at
Kellynch Hall and the rough life on board with the Royal Navy in
Napoleon's time. The costumes designed by Alexandra Byrne look
lived-in and the production design by William Dudley is certainly
plain and straightforward but for the most part authentic and
convincing. The American company who had invested in filming gave
the BBC detailed notes which were incorporated in the script. They
were not happy about some of the casting, hoping especially that a
well known star would have taken the role played by Amanda Root,
but were satisfied with her screen test. Millesime wanted the entire
Lyme Regis sequence removed as too boring. Nick Dear's version
required a brief opening sequence on board a Royal Naval vessel of the
period. The only authentic one available was HMS *Victory*, which was
busy entertaining tourists and, therefore, only available for limited
periods. Getting Admiral John Woodvine aboard from a small boat
involved hiding the modern city visible from on board with a glass
matte and an edited sequence from the 1984 Dino de Laurentis release,
The Bounty. A shot from *The Bounty*, showing the vessel romantically
riding the waves at sunset, was used at the end of *Persuasion* to indicate the romance of Anne Elliott's and Captain Wentworth's final
union. Even more curious to traditional Janeines must be the
moments after Anne has read Wentworth's letter and follows him into

the streets of Bath. The novelist has her in command of her senses, although overwhelmingly happy, fending off all offers of a sedan chair or whatever, and determinedly going on a 'quiet, solitary progress up the town' during which she was sure she would meet him. She is accompanied by Charles Musgrave as she steps into the street. They have got as far as Union Street when they meet Wentworth. Charles leaves them when they reach his house, and the two proceed to Belmont. They walk together oblivious to those who pass by them:

> where the power of conversation would make the present hour a blessing indeed; and prepare for it all the immortality which the happiest recollections of their own future lives could bestow. There they exchanged again those feelings and those promises which had once before seemed to secure everything, but which had been followed by so many, many years of division and estrangement.[39]

Thus the reader experiences the long-delayed reconciliation of hero and heroine. But the television viewer of 1995 was treated to the astonishing spectacle of Anne's trotting into the street, recognizing Wentworth, a passionate and lengthy kiss between the two while – and can you credit this? – an Italian circus procession goes by complete with jugglers, a brass band, fire-eater, and a barker on stilts!

None knew it at the time, but the system was cranking itself up for Austen-mania. There were cinema releases of *Sense and Sensibility* and *Emma*; television transmissions of *Pride and Prejudice*, and *Emma* just around the corner. BBC-1's production of *Pride and Prejudice* was simultaneously underway with *Persuasion*. It was as if the old production-line was reasserting itself: props and costumes needed for filming were frequently commandeered for *Pride and Prejudice*, and the *Persuasion* team had to send to Italy and Australia for replacements.[40]

5
The 'Pride and Prejudice Factor'

Andrew Davies's six-part adaptation of Jane Austen's *Pride and Prejudice*, produced by Sue Birtwistle and directed by Simon Langton, was transmitted on BBC-1 during the autumn of 1995.[1] The germ of this production was planted in 1986 at a preview of *Northanger Abbey*. Andrew Davies and Sue Birtwistle were sitting together. She turned to him and said:

> I know what I'd like to do: *Pride and Prejudice* and make it look like a fresh, lively story about real people. And make it clear that, though it's about many things, it's principally about sex and it's about money: those are the driving motives of the plot. Would you like to adapt it?

It was a favourite novel of Andrew Davies and he agreed to do it. The results certainly realized the promise of that moment – more fully than was suspected at the time.[2] But Sue Birtwhistle's identification of what she wanted the novel and its dramatisation to be about – sex and money – illustrates just how far the dramatisation process has moved on. What she had done was to isolate two issues guaranteed to make an impact with a particular telly-watching audience.

What did this production have which contributed to that impact? It stuck to the story fairly closely, with some effective additions (not as risqué as pre-transmission publicity had suggested). But above all it looked handsome, sexy, polished, and moneyed. And it was lively, animated, witty and moving. A major contribution to its quality, striking from its beginning, was the way it actually looked – the locations, costumes, light and colour and the wonderful airy, outdoor nature of this production. The production team had several basic assumptions to work from. One was to ensure that the various houses: the Bennet's house, Longbourn, Darcy's grand house, Pemberley, Catherine de Bourgh's house, Rosings Park, and Netherfield, the house Bingley rents – were all real, substantial places and that they appropriately represented those who lived there, and, even, those in the audience who would have liked to live there. Luckington Court stood in for the Bennets' house and reflected Mr Bennet's social standing. Lyme Park, on the Cheshire/Derbyshire border, stood in for the Darcy's stately Georgian pile, Pemberley (interiors at Pemberley had to be filmed at Sudbury Hall, Derbyshire, and this caused considerable problems for continuity). Rosings was represented by Belton House in Lincolnshire, a Restoration house with appropriately stiff formal gardens. For Netherfield they used a country house near Banbury. These all provided solid, believable locations which carried the right messages for the exterior and interior filming. The National Trust village of Lacock in Wiltshire stood in for Meryton. Then there was its brightness and clarity as a television product. This was partly as a result of the considerable recent developments in filming television drama and partly as a result of the way it was written. Simon Langton, its director, commented that there is now a complete change in the way things are done:

> Now virtually every expensive drama is done on film, as opposed to being done on tape, and so a whole generation of people, who have grown up entirely weaned on all film productions, will not stand for the more limited standards of tape – the sort of tape you associate with soap-operas and things like that, even though some of them are terribly good in the way they use them now. I remember thinking back – when I was asked to do this new *Pride and Prejudice* – to the last one the BBC did in 1981. This was typical of production at that time. They had exterior shots, and they'd go away to Norfolk or wherever it was and shoot the exterior sequences on film and marry them up later to the rest of the video footage. Well, I looked at it to refresh my memory and my partner's daughter, who was about thirteen or fourteen at the time, just sort of walked through the room and glanced at it and went 'Ugh!' and I said, 'Well, why did you go like that?' And she said, 'It's all artificial' – and that's all I got. Then she went out. She was right. It was artificial, because the colours of the lighting, which was all artificial, coming from a single direction, and the way the furniture was juggled around and the way the walls juggled every time a door was

shut – elements like that were par for the course in those days. These were the conventions of the time, and one accepted them. But not today. Things have changed and people are far more particular about the look of things. And I think actors, personally, perform better in the real place and they feel better and you actually can do a shot and you look through the window and you see the gardens outside and you can get character and depth into whatever you're doing and there's similitude to whatever you're doing.[3]

Jane Austen's contemporaries would have known how to read the story of Wickham and Lydia, delicately sketched in *Pride and Prejudice*. They would be able to flesh out the details with the support of the basic assumptions and social mythology of the day. As presented in the novel, it is a briefly told but terrible story of the callous seduction of a silly and selfish girl by a calculating systematic amorist followed by economic manipulation. Lydia is only 15 and the novelist makes sure we know that. We are told that she was young and silly and could only think of having a good time. Although not apparent to us until we learn – as Elizabeth Bennet learns from Darcy – that Wickham has tried it on before with Darcy's young sister. The key to the novel (if not the whole of Jane Austen) lies here. The immutable custom was succession through the male. A woman could own property so long as she was single. When she married, all property went to her husband. The age of consent – and had been since the thirteenth century – was twelve.[4] It was a man's world. Inevitably in propertied families the males were educated for the professions, the first born got the title (if there was one) and the estate. The females were educated or trained to attract worthwhile husbands. They must be beautiful, graceful, accomplished and pure.[5] Even so, things may not perfectly work out – one thinks (as the novelist wants one to think) of Charlotte Lucas and Revd Collins. If a young woman should fail in the marriage market, then she would face a dreary living as a governess (at best) or a spinsterhood spent in the family home. If a young woman were courted and yielded to seductive blandishments, she was ruined as far as the marriage market was concerned. Rumour, gossip and lateral communication would see to that. No eligible male could accept soiled goods. A life of quiet shame at home or economic survival on the streets was all that would be on offer.

The exposition of *Pride and Prejudice* puts the set-up before us – the Bennet family is dominated by one overwhelming problem. The estate can only descend to the males in the family. They have gallantly tried to produce a male, but only managed Jane, Elizabeth, Kitty, Mary and Lydia. The estate will go to Revd Collins, the nearest male relative. The best hope for the daughters is a sound marriage. Then Bingley and Darcy turn up, followed by the soldiers and Wickham. The first two we recognize as representatives of the famous truth universally acknowledged – the bachelor in possession of a good fortune inevitably in search of a wife. Wickham would equally be recognized as a character type. He is the archetypal vicious seducer, a well known figure in social mythology and writings of the day. This story is given the full treatment in Samuel Richardson's *Clarissa* (1747–48) which Jane Austen certainly knew. Dr Johnson published a celebrated essay on seduced maidens for *The Rambler*, which was reprinted in *The Gentleman's Magazine* in 1751.[6] Oliver Goldsmith's immortal novel, *The Vicar of Wakefield* (1766) – one of the most well known and popular of the age – tells the tale of a daughter seduced by a squire who is finally able to rejoin her family only after being snapped up by a young baronet. The ultimate version of the story was realized by Henry Mackenzie in *The Man of Feeling* (1771), which was the summation of all tales of seduction, abandonment and prostitution. The prototype was a young girl of good family who is idle (Lydia has a vacant mind) and prefers dreaming about a dizzy social life and luxury instead of applying herself to her needle – a sure sign of insufficient moral fibre. The second ingredient is a charming young man from the upper classes, who is determined to push his cause. Wickham fits the bill exactly. Readers in Jane Austen's day would be aware of an additional important detail which is not widely realized today, that clothing of the period rendered a young woman's virtue fairly easy of physical access.[7]

At the end of the eigthteenth-century females did not cover the lower part of their anatomy with separate garments. In essence they were clothed in long skirts, petticoats, corset and linen chemise worn against the skin. The French Revolution simplified dress. Women wore high-waisted, Grecian style dresses of soft muslin. Even when pantaloons (made of light stockinet and reaching to the knees or even lower) were first introduced in the early 1800s they were only considered suitable for the more saucy or racy females. It was not until the 1820s they became the regular wear of duchesses. Between 1820 and 1850 'pantalets' – (loose drawers with frills at the bottom of each leg) were worn by children and young women. But it was not until the mid century that all classes had adopted under garments.[8] It would be an interesting application of the sociological imagination to attempt to establish who at Meryton would be likely to wear such underwear.

The age old story was told yet again by the Revd William Dodd in *Magdalen, or History of the First Penitent Prostitute Received into the Charitable Asylum* (1799). This tells the story of a vicar's daughter seduced and abandoned by a young man of good family, and eventually reduced to prostitution. Such a story represents the collision between the naive and the worldly, innocence and cynicism. *The Gentleman's Magazine* (which we may be sure Mr Bennet read) satirically commented about the art of seduction: 'Why, such a plan, no doubt would have been disgraceful and infamous to have attempted upon a woman of Rank and Fashion! – but to an ordinary girl, and below one's rank, Lord! where's the harm?'[9] It is interesting to note that ideas of Protestant tolerance behind the establishing of homes for 'fallen women' required the fallen woman to be of a lower social status than the seducer, and Jane Austen's story accords with this – Wickham is of a higher class than Lydia. He was educated at a good school and was at Cambridge. All this was paid for by the Darcy family. He is a predatory young buck, who regards young women he meets as fair game, knowing that a girl's parents will either hide a disgraced daughter, or pay him to do the decent thing and marry her. Either way, he is on to a winner. Such careers are well documented and they started while the lads were still at school. Take the example of George Hangar, fourth Baron Coleraine, who served in the army during the American War, and succeeded his brother in the peerage in 1814. He was educated at Eton, and records of his schooldays:

> I was a very idle boy... but after I went to Eton I became a very tolerable Latin scholar, and could construe most books with sufficient readiness. But I took a most decided aversion to the Greek language, and never would learn it. My studies, however, after some time, had a different direction; for, from the moment I came into the fifth form, I studied everything but my book. My hours out of school in the day were employed in the sports of the field.... By night game of another kind engrossed my whole attention. At that very early period I had a most decided preference for female society, and passed as much time in the company of women as I have ever done since. A carpenter's wife was the first object of my affections; nor can I well express the nature of my obligations to her. Frequently have I risked breaking my neck in getting over the roof of my boarding house at night, to pass a few hours with some grizette of Windsor. During the latter part of my time at Eton, to perfect my education, I became attached to, and was much enamoured of the daughter of a vendor of cabbages. Ovid's *Epistles*

were totally laid aside for his *Art of Love*, in which I made a very considerable progress. The big boys had a very wicked custom every Sunday of resorting to Castle prayers at Windsor, not to seek the Lord, but to seek the enamoratas who constantly and diligently attended to receive our attentions.[10]

Then there was William Hickey, who left detailed accounts of his sexual initiation with a young servant girl while he was a schoolboy. While a pupil at Westminster he knocked about with young military and naval officers:

> ...with all of whom I, as a fine forward youth, was in high favour, and many a bumper of champagne and claret have I drank in the society of this set, at taverns and brothels, accompanied by the most lovely women of the metropolis, and this before I had completed by fourteenth year.[11]

While at boarding academy at Streatham, Hickey passed his time in debauchery with the servant girls, spending all free time away from classes pursuing sexual conquests in London. All this before he left school at sixteen.

This was the way of the world and it is implicit in the social scene Jane Austen portrays. It is a world where men were a cross between God and Sir Galahad. They ran the world and they could do as they liked. There was in this world a double morality. Men could play the field, enjoy whatever they could find. But they all expected (and demanded) to marry virgins:

> It is essential to recognise the superiority of your husband simply as a man... in the character of a noble, enlightened, and truly good man, there is a power and a sublimity so nearly approaching what we believe to be the nature and capacity of angels, that ... no language can describe the degree of admiration and respect which the contemplation of such a character must excite.... To be admitted to his heart – to share his counsels, and to be the chosen companion of his joys and sorrows! It is difficult to say whether humility or gratitude should preponderate in the feelings of the woman thus distinguished and thus blest.[12]

A girl once seduced, gossip and reputation being what it is, was unlikely to have much chance in the marriage market. The usual pattern was the promise of marriage, then elopement, followed by abandonment of the young woman by the man once he had enjoyed her. She was then too ashamed to come home to her family, as a creature with no academic or professional attainments, she was stuck for a means of earning her living except through prostitution. Prostitution was therefore endemic in such a society. It initiated and trained the young males of the tribe and it offered employment to those who were irreparably damaged by the system. The theme is constant by implication in Jane Austen in Willoughby's story in *Sense and Sensibility*, the potential seduction by Harry Crawford of Maria Bertram during the family absence in *Mansfield Park* and the behaviour of William Elliot in *Persuasion*. Elizabeth Bennet is convinced that Wickham had little intention of marrying Lydia, as he would be sure there was no hope of his marrying for money as far as the Bennet family was concerned. In Elizabeth's eyes it is a matter of her sister's silliness and Wickham's lubricious wickedness:

> How Lydia could ever have attached him, had appeared incomprehensible. But now it was all too natural. For such an attachment as this, she might have sufficient charms; and though she did not suppose Lydia to be deliberately engaging in an elopement, without intention of marriage, she had no difficulty in believing that neither her virtue nor her understanding would preserve her from falling an easy prey.[13]

The moralistic attitude to such situations is satirised by the presentation of Mary Bennet at her most sententiously Johnsonian. On hearing of her younger sister Lydia's seduction Mary says:

> This is a most unfortunate affair; and will probably be much talked of. But we must stem the tide of malice, and pour into the wounded bosoms of each other, the balm of sisterly consolation.... Unhappy as the event must be for Lydia, we must draw from it this useful lesson; that loss of virtue in a female is irretrievable – that one false step involves her in endless ruin – that her reputation is no less brittle than it is beautiful, and that she cannot be too much guarded in her behaviour towards the undeserving of the other sex.[14]

The theme is frequently echoed in Dickens. This is the mainspring of *Oliver Twist*, as Oliver's mother is a very nice middle-class young lady who is seduced and abandoned by a young Naval officer (echo of

Jane Austen?). Alice in *Dombey and Son* is seduced and then abandoned by Carker, then forced into a life on the streets. Little Em'ly in *David Copperfield* is abandoned by Steerforth, and liable to lapse into prostitution, as etched in by Martha's story. This, potentially, is the story of Lydia and Wickham, had matters not been resolved by Darcy's paying of the couple's debts and his gift of £1000 to set them up in married life. Andrew Davies constructed the drama so that the plot unwound like a coiled spring. He sees the novel as much a comedy as a love story, and many of the gags actually come off the pages, but he added a few laughs along the way just for good measure. One was the Revd Collins's being shocked at accidentally seeing Lydia's display of bosom while he was staying with the Bennet family, and the immaculate timing which allowed him to be halfway down the stairs before we heard the Bennet girls' collective giggles as Lydia returned to the bedroom and told them what had happened. Davies has an absolute gift for transcending the conventions of television drama at the same time as conforming to them. This dramatisation ended with a wedding, not found in Jane Austen's novel, but definitely required in television drama. But he writes the scene using the words of the marriage ceremony for appropriate comment. As the camera pans across the faces and lights on Wickham and Lydia we hear the officiating prelate's voice saying that matrimony was ordained: '...for a remedy against sin, and to avoid fornication; that such persons as have not the gift of continency might marry and keep themselves undefiled members of Christ's body.'[15]

Much of the energy and animation of this production are the result of its outdoor quality which features not only the beauty of the landscape and impressive stately architecture, but footage of movement, horseriding, dancing, music, coaches, carriages and wonderful shots of Jennifer Ehle, as Elizabeth Bennet, running about the countryside overflowing with good spirits and obviously glad to be alive, animation which innocently suggested a lively sexual energy. The other enjoyable and impressive source of this *Pride and Prejudice*'s animation was the centrality of dancing in the culture Jane Austen describes. The English country dance tradition was an integral part of society's lubrication, a reflection of the network of social alliances and connections which held the varying elements of society together. French society had traditionally been dominated by the powerful metropolitan élite – fashions, taste and style dictated by Paris and Versailles – hence the vigorous discipline of Baroque dancing. But England was very much a rural and country house culture, run by English country families with their stately country houses, where you had regular dances at town and village assembly halls, and the lavish balls held in aristocratic and landowning country houses. This is what kept English country dancing going. It is this tradition which Jane Austen chronicles. (Note the scenes at the Assembly Rooms in Bath in *Northanger Abbey* and *Persuasion*). *Pride and Prejudice* is full of references to dances and dancing, and so are Jane Austen's letters. She would have imbibed all her expertise about country dancing at the Basingstoke Assemblies between 1792 and 1801, when she was old enough for dancing, and when the Austens left Hampshire. During this time some 50 balls would have been held at Basingstoke Town Hall during the winter months. Such occasions were family social events – the older to gossip, play cards, socialise, and the younger to meet, flirt and play the marriage market. Just as at Meryton, local gentry, well-to-do families, middle classes (of several descending orders) attended and mixed. And no doubt, as in *Price and Prejudice*, relationships grew snobbish and prickly.[16]

The dance sequences were a noticeable feature of this production, and an important part of its narrative and style. Simon Langton, the director commented:

They were scripted in, but in fact we enlarged them. It became a cumulative process. I got together with the producer and the choreographer, Jane Gibson, and the composer Carl Davis, and we weren't absolutely sure what we were going to use, but when we actually sat down and wrote down the number of dances that were needed in all six hours, it was something like twenty two dances. And some were very long, and some were quite short. Some were just background. But they were there because they were such an absolutely essential part of life at that time. The whole business of the assembly hall in a community was vital to the social life. Of course, the assembly halls were the equivalent of the weekend dance hall or whatever, and then of course, you had the grand balls which were given by the local squires. These were grander affairs altogether. The assembly halls were the most important, because you had very big ones such as the ones in Bath, but others could go to the village hall, but nevertheless they were the highspot of the social life of the day. Jane, our choreographer, had this wonderful book from Jane Austen's time that has all these Country Dances and with instructions how to do them. It's called *The Apted Book of Country Dancing* which was rediscovered at the turn of the century. It had been lost for about a hundred years – I think the reason it's called that is because it was found in somebody's house, who was called Apted – it has nearly forty dances, several with the music and very elaborate plans for particular dances. Jane could translate all these and we sat down and went through them on the piano and chose the ones we wanted. They had wonderful English names like 'The Shrewsbury Lasses', 'A Trip to Highgate' and 'Mr Beveridge's Maggot'. I think all this worked well in the production, but some people said those dances were interminable. But they all had a particular reason and a particular point. The big one we did was obviously quite difficult. We had about eight pages of dialogue while they were actually dancing. I can't tell you how complicated that was to do on film, because you can't do it all the way through. You have to split it up. And then that led to continuity problems and the timing thing was difficult. But they managed it. Jane is not only a marvellous choreographer, but she takes the entire cast and teaches them from scratch, so even if you were tone deaf you would learn how to dance in a couple of days. She specialised in using extras who were not necessarily dancers, because they all stand out and do very elegant things with their arms which, of course, you wouldn't get if you had Mr and Mrs Bloggs having a dance at the assembly hall. So she managed to get people and train them. That's how we got that, sort of truthfulness, we were aiming at. Not some special period feature, but the kind of social event typical of the day.[17]

Carl Davis's music for *Pride and Prejudice* certainly contributed towards its quality as drama and gave this production individual colour, cohesion and character. This pushed music for television a whole stage further in its development. For so long in the British experience of television, although we turned out seemingly endless miles of Quality-Street costume drama with a reputation for historical authenticity, the music was seldom period music. There are one or two significant exceptions, of course, such as David Munrow's mock-Tudor *Henry VIII* score. But in the main British television music models itself on lush late-Hollywood romantic idioms, played by smallish instrumental ensembles.

So we can see this is a comparatively recent development in television dramas. Initially the need for music in television drama was supplied, as it was in early radio dramas days, with carefully selected, appropriate excerpts from the standard symphonic repertory. Robert

Louis Stevenson's *The Master of Ballantrae*, serialised on BBC television in 1961, used sections of Dvorak's *New World Symphony*. *Dombey and Son* on BBC-1 in 1968 was very well served by Sibelius. As late as 1974 *The Onedin Line* put to sea laden with Khachaturian. Not now. All modern television series require their own branding. To make them appealing, and to render them a recognizable individual product, they have their own music, as a kind of cook-in sauce. But the sauce is as important as the meat it enhances, let there be no mistake about that. It actually gives the product its character, rendering it palatable and digestible. This process has become more efficient, more customary and routine than ever before. And, as always, the craftsman negotiates a rewarding deal with the system, but genius transcends it. Such a musician is Carl Davis. It is an easy matter to scan his impressive credits without paying due regard to the creativity at play. He is one of the most in-demand writers of film and television music, having provided scores for *The World at War*, *All Our Working Lives*, *The Naked Civil Servant*, *Anne Frank Remembered*, *Hollywood*, *Silas Marner*, *Scandal*, *Far Pavilions*, *Hotel du Lac*, *The French Lieutenant's Woman*, *A Year in Provence*, and the restored version of the Abel Gance silent classic, *Napoleon*. And he provided a superb score for BBC Television's *Pride and Prejudice*. Here Carl Davis solved a fundamental problem in current television drama productions with a bold stroke. Budget restrictions may limit the instrumental resources available to a composer, but he exploited the limitations of these resources to create something historically appropriate – a musical score that was in period for the action of Jane Austen's masterpiece. He commented:

> I'm almost part of the script.... Just as producers select a costume or a prop, I select certain sounds that help the audience understand and feel what's going on. I choose an orchestra that offers me the sound colours of the period and have it play the kind of music that reflects the character of each scene.... The theme is going to be listened to as a piece of music, with no dialogue or sound effects over the top. That minute is the composer's chance to make his statement – the theme is the moment of glory.[18]

Jane Austen's novel was published in 1813. Carl Davis's score was written for a small instrumental ensemble in the manner of Schubert or Weber. The sound texture and style of the epoch are well captured, and on first hearing, one might genuinely mistake the music for an instrumental ensemble by an early nineteenth-century Viennese or

German composer. The affinity with Beethoven's *Septet* and the Rondeau of Mozart's Piano Concerto Number 9, K271, is obvious enough. But the subtle way this basic source material is used in television terms is outstanding.

The theme music which introduced the series is delightfully melodic, and perfectly located the viewer every week. The incidental music deftly supports and underlines action, speaking in a period tone. The featured music – domestic recitals, dance and ball scenes – is tuneful and appropriately played in careful, but not obtrusive, period style. The shots of the band revealed natural horns, nineteenth-century strings and woodwind, including a serpent. There was one moment when featured music was combined with incidental music to superb effect. This moment in particular may serve to illustrate the value of music in television drama, the moment when while playing the piano, Elizabeth's eyes meet Darcy's and they realise they are falling in love. At that moment the music gradually modulates meltingly into what seems a dreamy slow movement of Beethoven. Acting, filming, editing and music are all creatively and collaboratively working together to create a dramatic moment full of meaning. Carl Davis explains:

I try to work within the period. As soon as you actually have period costumes and props and period dialogue, it's my tendency to work within that and not fight it and not leap beyond the period too much. I try and view music as one of the elements that make up a film. Of course, music has a much deeper power of suggestion, because it can operate on both an emotional and a philosophical level and I think it adds more than people suspect. There's that party at Pemberley. When Elizabeth's and Darcy's eyes meet she is playing Beethoven's *Andante Favori*. That moment was very carefully written and planned. I recorded the Beethoven before they shot it, because obviously Elizabeth doesn't actually play it. They had to have music ahead and then plan the shot and the editing. You didn't see any close-ups of hands playing or anything. You saw her at the keyboard and a movement of her shoulders perhaps. Then the director planned the shot and did it and then when it was edited together, he suggested the moment their eyes met and we added the orchestra to the existing track. It kind of grew a bit at a time. Then Darcy goes out into the dark and watches the carriage go down the drive. At that point I reprise the Mozart she was playing before that scene – 'Voi Che Sapete' from *The Marriage of Figaro* – and she goes and he is left alone with his thoughts and I reprise that orchestrally.[19]

The pastiche historical score and playing were a highly commendable part of the series, and together with pre-publicity, orchestrated media public relations, articles in *Radio Times* about the cuisine featured in the series and so on, all constituted an important element in this production and in its marketing. The CD of Carl Davis's *Pride and Prejudice* music was available in shops even before the series had run its course.

No one could have foreseen its public impact nor its effect on British television drama production. It was sensationally successful and seemed to strike a resounding chord in the national consciousness, reminiscent of the effect of previous literary works, such as Goethe's *Die Leiden des Jungen Werthers* (1774), which had made Goethe famous all over Europe. This novel made it *de rigeur* for young men to wear blue coats and yellow breeches, with suicide enjoying a brief fashion.[20] It was parodied a year later by Friedrich Nicolai as *Die Freuden des Jungen Werthers* and by other writers (including Thackeray). *Pickwick Papers*,[21] whose monthly parts sold 40 000 an issue and had five theatricals on stage before its completion brought on a literary craze. It gave rise to Pickwick hats, gaiters, ornaments, songbooks, joke books, cigars, toasters and to the name 'Pickwickian syndrome' to a form of hyperventilation.[22] BBC-1's Sunday evening transmission of *Pride and Prejudice* in autumn 1995 summoned to itself several important elements then current in cultural discourse – including what amounted to a possibly accidental but nevertheless noticeable interest in Jane Austen – and gave rise to what was fairly soon dubbed the '*Pride and Prejudice* Factor'. The ensuing craze for dramatisations of classic novels was to turn Jane Austen into what Professor David Nokes identified as a 'market leader' which offered:

> ...what film makers like best, a formula; her novels define an identifiable territory, and her style, visually translated into production values as a world of lace bonnets, low-cut dresses, English gardens and stately homes, has the readily marketable appeal of a nostalgic cult. Even that distinctive voice, however edited into one liners, diffused among different characters or used to cue in comic cameos, seems to nourish some hunger for wholemeal dialogue among an audience jaded with junk-food slang.[23]

And these endeavours survive in the context of highly competitive economic and commercial context in remarkably good shape.

The evidence is there to be seen in the *Radio Times*. On the face of it, things have changed considerably since the earlier days of Reith's BBC.

1 *The Mayor of Casterbridge* (BBC-2 1978), dramatised by Dennis Potter. This featured effective location work. It was the first serial filmed by lightweight outside-broadcast cameras, and signalled the revival of the classic serial.

2 *Brideshead Revisited* (Granada Television 1981), dramatised by John Mortimer. Evelyn Waugh's loving recreation of Oxford's golden generation of the twenties.

3 *The Jewel in the Crown* (Granada Television 1984), dramatised by Ken Taylor. This was triumphantly launched at the high tide of the UK's Raj mania. The UK has more Indian restaurants than there are in India.

4 *Clarissa* (BBC-2 1991), dramatised in three episodes by David Nokes and Janet Barron. Starring Saskia Wickham, this was an adaptation of Samuel Richardson's million-word masterpiece.

5 *Middlemarch*: Rufus Sewell, Juliet Aubrey and Robert Hardy.

6 *The Buccaneers* (BBC-1), dramatised by Maggie Wadey. Four young American charmers are let loose in the hunt for husbands in Edwardian England in this adaptation of Edith Wharton's unfinished novel.

The *Radio Times* in the 1940s and 1950s was black and white and printed on utility paper. The front page invariably featured some great composer, or writer or dramatist set within a seriously arty design by Eric Fraser. High days and holidays might find the pages adorned with designs by Norman Mansbridge, but the general tone was invariably dutiful, worthy and tactfully uplifting. The *Radio Times* in the 1990s, as befits post-modernist days of commercial competition and privatisation, is highly glossy, coloured and lavishly designed and illustrated – a true emblem of the world it serves – which is more than likely to be adorned with pictures of Chris Evans, Lily Savage, Steve Coogan or Julian Clary or even an unclothed Helen Mirren. Its pages are so glossy the print is not easy to read. Nevertheless there, tucked within this meretricious gallimaufry, you will find *Middlemarch*, *Clarissa*, *Pride and Prejudice* and *Nostromo* among the listings. The *Radio Times* even featured a pin-up portrait of Fitzwilliam Darcy (Colin Firth), suitably enhanced with a gold frame – sex and money, as it were. As *Radio Times* duly recorded, Jane Austen was wholly and completely absorbed into the media world. The classic-costume-novel-television-drama is now seen simply as a commodity (albeit a classy one) in the schedules:

> Jane Austen as hot Hollywood scriptwriter? Potential American backers of *Pride and Prejudice* wanted to know whether the author would do book signings. And if that sounds unbelievable, then the picture of her on the Internet, lounging by a pool, complete with bonnet, mobile and laptop, is even more bizarre. But you get the point: in media terms, Austen has gone global.[24]

Signs of a Jane Austen revival had been indicated in the favourable press reception of the BBC's Easter 1995 transmission of *Persuasion*. But nothing could have prepared us for the autumn triumph of *Pride and Prejudice*. This series brought in its a wake not only a flurry of adulation from the critical press, but numerous media spin-offs. There was an irrepressible tide of Jane Austen revivalism, affecting several areas of cultural production and consumption – 'the *Pride and Prejudice* Factor'. The moment of *Pride and Prejudice*'s emergence needs exploring. The impact of this production confirmed the significance of BBC's recent *Middlemarch* and the promise of *Clarissa*. These had positive reviews in the quality press, and got talked about in BBC-2's *The Late Show*. The cultural significance of the BBC's *Middlemarch* may also be assessed from the fact that Roy Hattersley found himself obliged to deliver himself of portentous *Guardian* column inches on the glories of

George Eliot and her contribution to the 'Condition of England' debate. But there was more to it even than chattering class approval. *Middlemarch* marked a major development in the classic serial tradition. It is now even possible to surmise that a great deal was riding on this *Middlemarch* that *Pride and Prejudice* confirmed. The Sunday teatime classic serial had definitely been driven into the ground by the mid-1980s. A tedious sameness, a factoryline uniformity had overtaken productions, which appeared to merge seamlessly into each other as a Brontë modulated almost imperceptibly into yet another Dickens and was followed by *Beau Geste, Alice in Wonderland, The Prisoner of Zenda...* who cared?

Then, with no funeral rites at all, it was finally laid to rest. No one was really aware of precisely when it drew its last breath, and nobody seemed particularly to care. It had indeed been in poor health for some time. But the days of the family Sunday serial, of entertainment and uplift in easy weekly instalments were finally over. Granada's 1977 *Hard Times* and the BBC's attempt to repeat its success in buying the production team and transmitting *Bleak House* in 1985 were now not to be seen as wonders, as isolated aberrations, but as signs, as portents. The television classic serial had moved into serious adult drama, which sought to appeal to the same audiences who watched Dennis Potter, *Oranges Are Not the Only Fruit, Edge of Darkness, Inspector Morse* and Alan Bleasdale.[25] Concurrently, adult costume drama was identified as one of the products that British television was good at and that could be made profitably to sell abroad. If *Middlemarch* succeeded then classic novel dramatisations might take on a new kind of life, healthily competing in the global market with other television products. Recent changes in the commercial television companies' franchise arrangements, and the severe budget restrictions within which the BBC was now forced to operate, had brought about severe changes in television scheduling and programming policies. In the old days, the BBC was able to operate its Reithian doctrines of public service broadcasting with an almost god-like indifference to the mundane matters of audience ratings. Recent changes have resulted in the Corporation's need to accommodate far more of an accountant's perceptions to the quality of its broadcasting.

The BBC has to maintain rather more than respectable ratings in order to justify its licence fee and to safeguard its interests longer term against the constant threat of dismemberment. In addition it is now common for the Corporation to secure at pre-production stage co-production funding from overseas – usually the USA – to underwrite budget costs. This is especially the case with drama productions, one-off plays and costume dramas especially. Consequently, the BBC is no longer able to embark on drama production in a spirit of free market aesthetic or cultural do-gooding. In drama productions today there has to be a built-in awareness of wide audience appeal over a wide international cultural range. Television drama productions are part of an international cultural commodity market. Drama series have perforce to bear American audiences in mind. The inroads of feminism and other forms of political and economic correctness must be taken into consideration. Drama productions are launched with a greater awareness of the importance of publicity and marketing, together with quite an array of additional merchandise: videos of the production, television tie-in paperbacks, books on how the production was made, cassettes and CDs of the soundtrack, travelling exhibitions of the costumes and so on. The consequences of these influences in the making and marketing of classic novel dramatisations will be considerable. This may, in part, help us to understand the apparent sea change in public taste which seems to indicate an interest in Jane Austen, for a while even replacing Dickens as the philosopher's stone in the alchemy required to turn old-fashioned novels into popular new television dramas.

While it would be an exaggeration to say that it has to have an international appeal, it is nevertheless reasonable to argue that television drama, to justify its funding, has to satisfy audience expectations and appetites both sides of the Atlantic. Several of the proclaimed victories of political correctness may be slight or of short duration, others pay little more than lip service to social change, but few would doubt the durable change that feminism has wrought in American and British realisations and expectations. Socially and professionally women expect recognition and fulfilment. There is a whole new audience of socially, sexually and politically enfranchised women whose tastes must be satisfied. This has obviously had an impact on consumer marketing, and, given the economic bases of broadcasting, has affected television drama. The transmission of the series on Sunday evenings was a crucial and interesting decision. Research reveals that this is prime time as far as this new liberated female audience should be watching television. The slow but sure adjustment of the gender balance soon showed its impact. There was the introduction of women newsreaders, presenters, weather forecasters. All male situation-comedies such as *Dad's Army* and *All Gas and Gaiters* became a thing of the past and hit shows with leading women characters took over: *The*

Good Life, To the Manor Born, Keeping Up Appearances, Absolutely Fabulous, Birds of a Feather, The Vicar of Dibley. Women starred in major drama series such as *Miss Marple, Widows, She's Out, Prime Suspect,* and *Hetty Wainthrop.*

Several prestigious television dramas created with an eye to the young(ish) upwardly mobile professional woman were scheduled for transmission on Sunday evenings from the earliest days when the ratings rivalry between the Corporation and the commercial television companies became a game played in earnest – *The Ginger Tree, A Piece of Cake, Wish Me Luck, Band of Gold, The Governor, The Buccaneers, Playing the Field.* And it cannot be accidental that after many years of media neglect, David Nokes's dramatisation of Samuel Richardson's *Clarissa* (BBC-2 1991) was such a success. Andrew Davies's dramatisation of *Middlemarch* for the BBC had again put forward a strong leading female character, whose story dealt with issues of concern to today's women. There was a move away from Dickens, who appeals stongly to the male perspective and constantly presents two female character types – either pliable and saintly heroines, (Nell, Dora, Amy, Esther) or over-powering older types (Betsy, Mrs Clennam, Mrs Joe). *Clarissa* was followed by a flood of television classic novels featuring strong female leads, *The Buccaneers, Pride and Prejudice, Emma, Tenant of Wildfell Hall,* Charlotte Brontë, *Moll Flanders, Wuthering Heights, Tess of the d'Urbervilles,* and *Far From the Madding Crowd.*

The phenomenon termed the 'Pride and Prejudice factor' and the strength of the following which *Pride and Prejudice* drew to itself is demonstrated by the ratings. It was estimated that BBC's *Panorama* interview with Princess Diana on 20 November 1995 earned 21.1 million viewers. This is an estimated 83 per cent share of the total television audience. (Compare this with the 7.7 million who watched Jonathan Dimbleby's interview with Prince Charles and the 27 million in 1987 who watched the episode of *Coronation Street* in which Alan Bradley attempted to murder Rita Fairclough.)[26]

We may gain some sense of the size of these viewing figures by comparing them with other successes. The episode of *EastEnders* in December 1986 which dealt with the split between Den and Angie attracted 30 million viewers (but that included repeat showings) and the Sharongate story in *EastEnders* in October earned 25.3 million (including repeats). Torvil and Dean got 23.9 million in February 1989. The National Lottery Launch in November 1994 got 17.9 million. *Elizabeth R* (documentary about Queen Elizabeth II) shown in February 1992 achieved 17.9 million. And then we turn to *Pride and Prejudice*. There are really revealing figures for Sunday 22 October 1995. Up to this stage, *Pride and Prejudice* was achieving an average figure of 10 million on Sunday evenings at 9 p.m. There were difficulties with scheduling the opening 75-minute episode of the final series of Granada Television's immensely popular *Cracker*, which was originally scheduled for Monday 23 October. *Cracker* was to be shown, as it always had been, in the prime time slot of Monday evening at 9 p.m. However, this would have meant putting the news back by fifteen minutes. The Independent Television Commission refused to allow ITN's *News at Ten* to be rescheduled a quarter-of-an-hour later. Consequently, *Cracker* was rescheduled to be transmitted at 9 p.m. on the preceding Sunday evening. An interesting (and revealing) situation was thus created. ITV's impressively popular psycho-crime drama, starring Robbie Coltrane, was to compete directly against the BBC's popular classic novel drama series. Well, what happened? *Pride and Prejudice* did not seem to lose a single viewer. It maintained its audience (8.6 million viewers) against *Cracker*'s 14.5 million. It was estimated that one million viewers video recorded both shows. The newspapers' verdict was that *Pride and Prejudice* took on *Cracker* and held it to a draw.

This dramatisation of Jane Austen's ever popular novel shows some very interesting signs of change in the style and tone of the television classic serial. There is much more emphasis on female experience. The sexual and social opportunities of all the Bennett girls, not just Jane and Elizabeth, are explored as never previously. Darcy's dark, brooding sexual magnetism is more fully suggested than ever before. The actual pool where he was famously filmed taking a dip and wrapping his body in a towel which revealed his masculinity has become an object of tourist pilgrimage. The sorrowful destiny of Charlotte Lucas and the likely fate of Kate and Mary Bennett is more sympathetically revealed than in the last adaptation.[27] Dickens had always dominated the BBC classic serial tradition. It is true that *The Forsyte Saga*, shown in the evening schedules, pre-figured a break from the 'family' Sunday afternoon classic serial,[28] and that the inception of BBC-2 introduced a goodly number of adult classic novel dramatisations shown in the evening schedules – *War and Peace, Madam Bovary, Sentimental Education, Germinal, Anna of the Five Towns, Therese Raquin* – but nevertheless for decades Dickens's fiction really was the bread and butter of the Sunday teatime classic serial. This was appropriate. John Reith's BBC was a patriarchy, the tone of the BBC easily lapsed into the patronising. Dickens' work is very male-centred, his perspective is liberal in a rather genteel manner, his view of the world is very much from the masculine position. No matter how the Marxists attempted to appropriate Boz as one of their own, he was far from a revolutionary. There were major changes in broadcast culture. These were characterised by a move away from male domination and patriarchy, a growing pluralism (including the loss of the BBC's monopoly over broadcasting), a seeming decline in Dickens's absolute dominion over the classic serial, and an increasing interest in female writers and women's perspectives. The tendency was to give us Miss Marple, Inspector Tennison, Bramwell, Hetty Wainthrop, strong female women characters in *Peak Practice* and *Casualty*, Zoe Ball, Anna Ford, Jill Dando, Winifrid Robinson, Philippa Thomas, Sophie Raworth, Juliet Morris, Vanessa Feltz, as well as leading female characters in situation comedies such as *Absolutely Fabulous*, *Birds of a Feather*, *Keeping Up Appearances*. The fashion for Jane Austen, which was to peak with the '*Pride and Prejudice* effect' is part of much larger cultural currents.

Consequently the eclipse of Dickens as a broadcasting staple takes on the nature of a *coup d'état*. Not only have we had serials such as *Clarissa*, *Middlemarch* and *The Buccaneers*, all of which give full focus to women's experience, but we have the new approach to Jane Austen so well evidenced in the 1995 version of *Pride and Prejudice*. Sue Birtwhistle was right to insist that the focus of the production should be on money and sex, because she knew this would appeal to a particular viewing audience: an audience with time on their hands, money in their pockets, liberated sexuality and desires, who wanted a touch of the classics because they were classics, but who also wanted them reduced into neat dollops of sweetness for easy consumption. When Darcy emerges from his swim in his wet shirt the fantasy is complete: sex and money made easy and wrapped in the respectable cloak of a classic. This was a new phenomenon.

Persuasion on BBC-2, (given a very successful cinema release in the USA), the cinema release of *Sense and Sensibility*, BBC-1's serialisation of *Pride and Prejudice*, Meridian Broadcasting's *Emma* and the Miramax film release of *Emma*[29] seemed all of a piece, a kind of cultural sea change. The phenomenon involved far more than just the films and television dramatisation. *Pride and Prejudice*, shown in USA, Australia, Belgium, Bosnia, Canada, China, Croatia, Cyprus, Czech Republic, Denmark, Eire, Finland, France, Germany, Greece, Holland, Hong Kong, Iceland, Israel, Italy, Ivory Coast, Japan, Kuwait, Lebanon, Malaysia, Malta, Norway, Oman, Poland, Portugal, Romania, Russia, Singapore, Slovenia, South Africa, Spain, Sweden, Switzerland, Thailand, Turkey and Yugoslavia – has earned the BBC £1 620 225.[30] The BBC/Penguin Books, *The Making of Pride and Prejudice* became a bestseller. The novel remained in the paperback bestseller lists for months. By November 1995 it had sold over 150 000 copies in the Penguin/BBC tie-in version alone. The VHS video was a bestselling item for months, by the beginning of November the home video had sold 150 000 copies, and we had modern authors writing continuations of Austen's novels,[31] together with a Jane Austen industry which produced books on a variety of topics but with few convincing direct connections with Jane Austen the novelist. Among the articles of merchandise were biographies of varying depth and merit, volumes devoted to the Jane Austen Christmas, food of the period, the world of Jane Austen, domestic music of the period, country dancing. There were Jane Austen diaries, calendars and trinkets of all kinds. The retail chain Pastimes offered customers their Jane Austen Promotion, which included a night gown. Sales of bespoke corsets boomed, somewhat reminiscent of the craze for Werther's yellow boots. Film locations became tourist attractions. Much was made of the fact that commercial television's *Emma* was actually shot at the National Trust village of Lacock. An enterprising company marketed Jane Austen bed linen: 'inspired by the Regency period in which Emma lived and loved... a beautiful range of bed linen and bedroom accessories created from original documentation housed at the Victoria and Albert Museum.' It was available at such quaint little old-world village shops as House of Fraser, Debenham's and Sainsbury's DIY store, Homebase.[32] The costumes from BBC Television's *Pride and Prejudice* went on exhibition at appropriate stately homes. You could return to relive those genteel and peaceful times. *Radio Times* addressed its readers during the serialisation of *Pride and Prejudice*: 'You've seen the sumptuous spreads in BBC-1's adaptation of the Austen classic – now you can lay on an authentic period feast, with a menu devised by series' chef, Colin Capon.' The '*Pride and Prejudice* factor' assumed the characteristics of a saint's cult, complete with hagiography, shrines for pilgrims to visit, scriptures, habits, effigies and holy relics.[33]

Pride and Prejudice arrived at just the right moment to touch precisely the right buttons. Elizabeth Bennett and Mr Darcy had been so completely absorbed into our popular culture that by August 1998 BBC Television was able successfully to use clips from the serial, with suitably dubbed dialogue, as part of their public advertising campaign for television licence renewal. Darcy paid ostentatiously by credit card. But Mrs Bennett, as befitted her class, saved up to pay with stamps.

6
The *'Pride and Prejudice* Effect': a Promising Future for the Past

For a combination of reasons, variously suggested to be insecurity about the present, the undermining of national identity as a consequence of the European union, economic decline, the craze for devolution, the British seem to be taken up with their own past. Television's fascination for costume drama at the close of the 1980s intensified during the 1990s. With tourism such an expanding industry we seem in danger of turning the country into a vast theme park. We have the New Conservatism initiated by Thatcherism to thank for this state of affairs. Not only did this encourage a politically nostalgic nationalism, but it legislated out the regulation of the media industries and thereby encouraged free market factors in media production. The BBC felt under threat, and among its various endeavours to compete in the ratings game with the commercial channels, it reverted to one of the areas in which it had always excelled – the classic novel dramatisation. The BBC's success was fairly immediate, and its ratings were impressive. An average of 10 million viewers on a Sunday evening loyally consumed *Pride and Prejudice*, producing what became known as the *'Pride and Prejudice* effect'. It was plain for all to see, the BBC was demonstrably earning its right to the licence fee by giving audiences what they wanted. Translate this into the terms used in the commercial sector of the television industry and we have been delivering audiences regularly to advertisers. The point about a successful drama series is that it regularly delivers target audiences to those who want to give them messages about products. This direct competition between the Corporation and the commercial channels was a new situation in British broadcasting, and commercial television sought to emulate the BBC's success.

As the BBC made more and more such dramas, commercial television went all out for ratings. *Coronation Street* was put in the hands of a new producer, several members of the cast culled, new blood and story ideas introduced, and the whole show revamped and rescheduled for five evenings a week with numerous new characters, sex and violence. The importance of soap operas in the ratings war was demonstrated by the establishment of the British Soap Awards, first held in May 1999. Additionally, the companies went for sure-fire winners such as cop shows, medical dramas, safe costumers (the Catherine Cookson factor?), intensified the search for such ratings-bait as game and quiz shows (*Who Wants to be a Millionaire?*, winner of BAFTA for Light Entertainment Programme or Series 1999) and drama series based on winning formulae – (for example *Inspector Morse*, *Prime Suspect*, *Cracker*, *Soldier, Soldier*, *Kavanagh QC*, *Peak Practice*). By the end of the decade ITV had eased out *News At Ten*, so as to free up the weekday evening schedules to make room for what were perceived to be major two part dramas or mini series. ITV's foray into classic novels dramatisations should be seen in this wider context of direct competition with the Corporation. While this was a new departure in television and gives some indication of the wide-ranging activities covered by the term '*Pride and Prejudice* factor', it led to a particular kind of interest in the past. Indeed, it led to media and consumerist constructions of a very particular kind of past, for this is what audiences wanted to see.

This became obvious both here in the UK and – as overseas sales and co-productions became more and more important to the British television industry – ever more abroad. In an almost forgotten novel published in 1946, *Yes, Farewell*, by Michael Burn, a young man named Simon has such a fascination with the past that he talks of historical characters as if they were friends and acquaintances. Simon tries to encourage friends to share his enthusiasms: 'What are you reading?... I love biographies. I have just been sent the most delightful book. It's about Lady Caroline Lamb. You know, the one Byron was crazy about. You must read it.... It's simply enchanting.' Michael Burn comments: 'Simon knew all the small talk of dramatic periods. He talked about Mary Queen of Scots, Rasputin, Ludwig of Bavaria, as if they were still alive and intimate friends of his, putting on his confidential air and dropping his voice to a whisper...'. 'You know what they say about Marie Antoinette... I wonder... I've always thought her so attractive...' Burns adds 'He knew the names of the Prince Regent's mistresses and would have liked to live under the Regency. I adore the whole idea, don't you? Bath, I mean, and Brighton, and everyone so witty and well dressed... Simon loved memoirs, diaries, scandalous private journals. History was a gigantic gossip column.' Could the

British turn into a nation of Simons? The *'Pride and Prejudice* factor' of the mid 1990s was only one set of symptoms present in a general state of high fever, well diagnosed by Professor David Nokes (who dramatised *Clarissa* for BBC-2) when he hailed the transmission of *Gulliver's Travels* in 1996:

> ...Channel 4's spectacular Easter Version of *Gulliver's Travels* is the latest in the current wave of literary adaptations for the screen. As film makers and television executives sense a waning public appetite for Tarantino violence and raunchy Rambo-clones, the mob rush to plunder the library shelves for bankable literary classics has become almost a stampede. When Martin Scorcese takes a detour from his familiar mean streets to revisit the elegant mansions of Edith Wharton, we know some kind of cultural shift is taking place. Currently almost every self respecting dead white author, from Daniel Defoe to Thomas Hardy, is under contract to some major studio...[1]

It takes some time, years in many cases, to get major television projects from initiation to schedules, and productions such as *Gulliver's Travels* had been in planning and production many months before the *'Pride and Prejudice* factor'. Nevertheless as far as consumers of television programming were concerned there really did seem to be something of a fashion for classic novel adaptations, for after the hullabaloo of *Pride and Prejudice* in autumn 1995 they were listed in the schedules more frequently than any one could remember. It was reported that Andrew Davies was doing two classic novel adaptations for the commercial channel – *Moll Flanders* and *Emma*. Michael Wearing, then Head of BBC's drama serials, retorted that there was not a boom in the classics on the box. The BBC, he claimed, had always been active in this area, and what was happening was that ITV was trying to muscle in:

> It's a myth that costume drama is enjoying a resurgence. It's always been popular. Just in the past few years, the BBC has made, *The Buccaneers, Scarlet and Black, Persuasion, Clarissa, The House of Elliott* as well as *Pride and Prejudice*. ITV has discovered costume drama after a long time. The success of *Pride and Prejudice*, which they decided not to make, has led them again to look at classic adaptations. The truth of the matter is that the advertisers would like that audience profile, which historically belongs to the BBC.[2]

In fact both BBC and commercial television companies were working on productions of *Jane Eyre* and *Emma* at the same time and the BBC put their plans on hold. The BBC had *Ivanhoe* and *Nostromo* in production and various commercial television productions included *Rebecca*, *Ebb Tide* and *Far From the Madding Crowd*.

Gulliver's Travels was shown on Channel Four during Easter 1996. It was produced by Duncan Kenworthy, (*Four Weddings and a Funeral*) for RHI Entertainment Inc., Channel Four Television/Jim Henson Productions and directed by Charles Sturridge (director of *Brideshead Revisited*). This £13 million seven-years-in-the-making production came to screen in Britain with its reputation to some extent already made. It had been shown in USA the previous February where it had drawn recordbreaking audiences of 56 million viewers, attracted mainly by the well publicised special effects. It starred Ted Danson (*Cheers*) and Mary Steenburgen with James Fox, Peter O'Toole, Geraldine Chaplin, Ned Beatty, Sir John Gielgud, Robert Hardy, Sashi Kapoor, Omar Sharif and Edward Woodward. Unlike so many previous 'adaptations' of *Gulliver's Travels*, this version really did attempt to go the whole hog. Up to now we have had to be content with versions either just of his voyage to Lilliput or at best, to Lilliput and Brobdingnag. But here Simon Moore, who wrote this version, and Tim Webber, who supervised the visual effects, together with Roger Hall, who designed the production, have given us the flying island of Laputa as well as Yahoos and talking horses. As Dr Johnson famously opined, once you had thought of big men and little men, the job was as good as done. On the face of it, this production – give or take a few million dollars worth of special effects – proves him right. But it is not as simple as that. Yes, we can now convincingly show you Gulliver among tiny men, and dwarfed by big men, but there was always more to it than that. Swift's presentation of the creatures of Brobdingnag was more than just bigness. It was grossness he was obsessed with, and that was not realised on screen here. Those who have not read it, have been spared. Those who have may well have forgotten. But we might be grateful for the mercy shown us in this production. The nurse giving suck to the infant, for example:

> ...no object ever disgusted me so much as the sight of her monstrous breast, which I cannot tell what to compare with so much as to give the curious reader an idea of its bulk, shape, and colour. It stood prominent six foot, and could not be less than sixteen in circumference. The nipple was about half the bigness of

my head, and the hue both of that and the dug so varified with spots, pimples, and freckles that nothing could appear more nauseous...[3]

This is nothing compared to Swift's description of various deformities observed in such magnitude, as well as the vermin crawling on people's flesh and his exact account of a criminal's beheading with the head bouncing and blood spurting as much as forty feet in the air.

So all claims as to the completeness of this dramatization must be discounted. But we were compensated for the loss by the addition of much that Swift had not thought of – such as Mrs Gulliver (Mary Steenburgen). But given the ability to swallow the rather self conscious, crude and often implausible narrative additions, there is much impressive about this production. Watching it from the beginning, one who knows Swift's original might well wonder where they are and what is going on. The tale has been recast in a narrative frame. Gulliver returns to find his wife (Mary Steenburgen) and son Tom in the machinations of crafty Dr Bates (James Fox). Gulliver has a struggle on his hands to regain Mrs Gulliver and his child and also to prove that he is sane. Swift's accounts of Gulliver's voyages are retold by Gulliver to his family, Dr Bates and to various others who he is trying to convince of his sanity. This results in the narrative thread of the adventures constantly being interrupted by cutting back to the returned Gulliver telling the story. The effect of this way of dealing with Swift's work means that the various incidents are never given a chance to establish their validity. They remain jumbled bits of Gulliver's recollections. Consequently the stories of his voyages certainly do seem the stuff of fantasy, from his discovery on the beach at Lilliput by the eighteenth century's answer to *Steptoe and Son*, to his account of the Yahoos and the Hounynms – travellers' tales. But the interpolated narrative apparatus adds considerable material, scene after scene, to *Gulliver's Travels*, the book Swift actually wrote. So much so that it would require considerable semantic elasticity to term this an adaptation or dramatisation. It is a couple of stages removed from the original, to which it bears striking resemblance. Nevertheless, at the time, to viewers at home, it seemed to be part of the resurrection of media interest in classic novels.

Then, in the autumn, ITV transmitted a version of *Moll Flanders*, made by Granada Television. Written by Andrew Davies in four one-hour episodes, produced by David Lascelles and directed by David Attwood, Moll was played by Alex Kingston, Jemmy by Daniel Craig and Mrs Golightly by Diana Rigg. This might well have been made in the wake of the *'Pride and Prejudice* factor' for costume dramas, but with a sure eye on the ratings:

> ...Granada Television did not simply want to adapt another nine-teenth century novel, which has become the fashion.... *Moll Flanders* gave Granada the recipe for a historical costume drama cum saucy romp, four hours of television filled with beautiful costumes and locations, and the story of a spirited orphan who is seduced at an early age and marries five times, before entering a life of crime that leads to the gallows. The producer... and adapter... also saw many parallels between *Moll Flanders*... and modern day Britain, with divisions in society forcing those at the lower end to make very stark choices...[4]

It has always been recognized as a ramshackle sort of novel, but a very interesting one. Andrew Davies adapted it with Brechtian alienation effect, with Moll telling her story directly to camera, addressing the viewer in an almost Mother Courage manner. But in this, as in the economic philosophy by which Moll lives, he is fully realizing what is there in Defoe's novel, for one of the charms of the work is Moll's constant direct address to the reader and the ideology which motivates her:

> ...my heart would sink within me at the inevitable approach of misery and want. O let none read this part without seriously reflecting on the circumstances of a desolate state, and how they would grapple with want of friends and want of bread; and it will certainly make them think not of sparing what they have only, but of looking up to heaven for support, and of the wise man's prayer, 'Give me not poverty, lest I steal'. Let them remember that a time of distress is a time of dreadful temptation, and all the strength to resist is taken away; poverty presses, the soul is made desperate by distress, and what can be done?...[5]

Davies considered the Restoration as jolly, with London enjoying a free and easy period when Puritanism was on the run, theatres opened, there was social mixing and plenty of sex:

> ...you get all these actresses and prostitutes and semi-prostitutes, and there were beggars on the streets. I was trying to find parallels

between that century and this. It was very much to do with the rise of capitalism and the merchant classes, and the general expectation that if you wanted to get on you had to look out for yourself...[6]

He sees Moll Flanders as a self reliant, enterprising sort of person, who has seen social deprivation and wanted no part of it. For her virtue is by no means its own reward. Andrew Davies commented:

> ...the book in a way did have a terrific number of modern reso-nances. It was an early Thatcherite novel... because it seems it was saying you've got to look after yourself in this world because nobody else is going to and they're going to put you down and you've got to look and see what you've got and what you can sell and what your assets are and you've got to trade them for the biggest price you can... and all that kind of thing. And it just fitted in with all that. I hadn't really thought of it as particularly feminist, except that it was very pleasant to have a female character who was so resourceful. And another thing that I liked, or found interesting about the Defoe novel is that in a way it poses a bit of a challenge to the very idea of character as we've absorbed it through the 19th century novel and Freud and things like that, because Moll, in one sense, doesn't really have a character, she adapts to the given circumstances. You know, when she's in a Puritan family, she tries to be a Puritan. And when it's be a thief or starve, she's a thief. In a way, Defoe is saying we'd all be like that, which is why I have her keeping on turning to the camera at crucial moments to say 'what would you do?'[7]

The series was the story of a social survivor, who goes from one adventure to another through a series of liaisons providing the oppor-tunity for splendid locations (both lavish and sordid), plenty of travel (to the New World and back) and a wide variety of characters of all shades. Where Defoe failed to oblige, Davies boldly invented, including Lucy Diver, a composite top pickpocket and thief based on several Defoe characters rolled into one (played by Nicola Walter). As if crime, bigamy, prostitution were not enough, for good late twentieth-century measure, Davies adds lesbianism. (Not too far fetched, as it happens, for Defoe had more than hinted that his other tarty heroine, Roxana, had a relationship with her maid, Amy.) Pulling things further out of Defoe's time, the director admits he was much influenced by *The Wild Bunch*. There may be reservations about the cavalier treatment of the story, the engrafting of contemporary attitudes, and the romps with an eye to the ratings – but *Moll Flanders* had an outstanding quality – it looked good. It was not just the concentration of lavish costume, but of the locations, so well chosen by Stephen Fineren – Smiths Hall, near Bolton, streets in Lacock, Packwood House, Warwickshire, Castle Lodge, Ludlow, Tatton Park, Cheshire, Astley Hall, Chorley, the George Inn, Norton St Philip (near Bath), Turnaware Point, on the River Fal, in Cornwall, the Red Hall, and Grimsthorpe Castle, Bourne in Lincolnshire, Little Moreton Hall, Congleton, Cheshire, Hadden Hall, Bakewell, in Derbyshire and superbly constructed studio locations of seventeenth-century London streets and Newgate Prison (at a cost of £250 000) built at Spectrum Arena, Warrington. The brave, some might say reckless treatment of the novel by its adapter, the almost outrageous style of its acting, its sumptuous costumes and handsome locations all combined to give this series style, a consistent style of its own – which is rare enough in classic serials. Its overt sexiness made it much talked about. Ice was used to enable Alex Kingston's nipples to stand out during filming. It is said to have 17 sex scenes.[8] It was also popular in USA. When screened on American Public Service Broadcasting it earned the channel its highest ratings ever – 4 600 000. In the UK it attracted an average audience of 13 million, 3 million more than *Pride and Prejudice*. This was an effect which surpassed its cause.

In November 1995 ITV transmitted Andrew Davies's dramatisation of Jane Austen's *Emma*, made by Meridian Broadcasting in association with Chestermead Ltd. and A&E Network It was produced by Sue Birtwistle and directed by Diarmuid Lawrence. It starred Samantha Morton (Harriet), Kate Beckensale (Emma), Mark Strong (Knightley), Bernard Hepton (Mr Woodhouse), James Hazeldine (Mr Weston), Prunella Scales (Miss Bates), Dominic Rowan (Mr Elton), Raymond Coulthard (Frank Churchill) and Olivia Williams (Jane Fairfax). It looked like the old firm of Birtwistle and Davies again, who brought us *Pride and Prejudice*. Once again, Lacock served its turn as the Jane Austen country town, Highbury in *Emma*, and the other locations were handsome to look at: Trafalgar Park, near Salisbury was Hartfield, Donwell Abbey was impersonated by Broughton Castle, near Banbury, and Sudley Castle, Gloucestershire and Dorney Court, Windsor, stood in for Randalls. The production, it seemed, was also blessed with the most beautifully appropriate filming weather which brought an extremely attractive light and summery feel to most of the proceedings. The dramatisation carried some highly characteristic fingerprints, although apparently not as many as he wanted. 'I wanted a bedroom scene, but nobody else would stand for it. I raged, I tried tears, threats, persuasion, but I couldn't talk them round, so I think they were probably right' he says.[9] He believes there is a bit of a question mark about Emma's character, and a bedroom scene would have resolved it: '...She cheerfully tries to arrange everyone else's love life, but you do sort of wonder whether she's grasped what all this boys and girls stuff is about....' As he points out, there is a rather darker side to Knightley's attraction to Emma, which we seldom actually think about: 'There's this huge gap between them – well, not disgustingly so, but he's known her since she was a baby. At one point in the novel he says he thinks he's been in love with her since she was about thirteen, and you think 'hello, hello', because he would have been a bloke of about thirty then....'[10] This idea was completely abandoned, as in the event, the Meridian Mr Knightley only looked a year or so older than Emma, even though at one stage he does mumble some claim about cradling Emma in his arms when she was a baby.

Davies confesses to hating Frank Churchill, whom he sees as a villain who has never known love and only learned to manipulate women. He believes that Frank probably seduced Jane Fairfax at Weymouth and that she remained sexually enthralled by him. Knightley, he thinks, could have lost his virginity while on the Grand Tour. Nevertheless, Andrew Davies keeps these theories on a strong leash in this dramatisation. But it shows evidence of his touch. An obvious example which demonstrates Andrew Davies's ability to use the language of television drama to tell us what Jane Austen wanted to tell us, resulting in excellent television which is at the same time true to the book, may be found in his treatment of the Emma/Knightley relationship. When Knightley (Mark Strong) admonishes Emma (Kate Beckinsale) after her cruel humiliation of Miss Bates (Prunella Scales) we see things as Emma sees them, with a close up of Knightley's serious disapproval:

> How could you be so unfeeling to Miss Bates? So insolent in your wit to a woman of her age, and of her situation! ... When you were a little girl, it was an honour for you to be noticed by Miss Bates. Now it is the other way round; she is poor, she has sunk from the comforts she was born to – and you choose to humble her, to laugh at her, openly, in company? Her situation should secure your compassion, not your ridicule. It was badly done, Emma, badly done, indeed![11]

Knightley cannot see that she weeps. When, a few scenes later, she reflects on her feelings for him, and realizes that she has always loved him, and that is why his reproof wounded her so much, we see what she remembers – his face. When described, it sounds corny, but seen in sequence in the television drama, it works superbly.

Another example of his skill in deploying modern media resources to do justice to a classic novel is in the conclusion he provides for his dramatisation of *Emma*. The ending of the novel is extended, its threads gradually falling into place and gathered together. This is highly suitable and reads well, but is not the stuff of television drama. Davies solution was an invented harvest supper, bringing main characters and plot lines together in a credible and dramatic manner. This works well, as this dramatisation goes to some lengths to establish and locate the action of the drama firmly in the context of an agricultural based economy. We are conscious, in watching this *Emma*, not just on the stately home side of things, but of country life and country living. As Andrew Davies says:

> The resolution of the plot is very lengthy in the book, and, in parts, I don't think it is all that brilliant. For example, getting Robert Martin and Harriet Smith together seems unnecessarily complicated.... And in the book there are a number of little scenes after the engagement of Knightley and Emma which would take up a lot of screen time. So we would have gone from a big scene – the proposal – to a series of rather little scenes.... So I wondered if it wouldn't be possible to think of some kind event, other than a wedding, which would bring all the characters together and tie up all the loose ends. I then imagined a kind of harvest supper, like in Hardy's or Tolstoy's novels – all that lovely stuff of bringing the harvest home and the haymakers and the good gentleman farmer...[12]

This was a time when the whole community worked together, and Davies was able to show Knightley as an ideal old fashioned landowner who rewarded his workers and shared the success of the harvest with them. Andrew Davies intended this to contrast with the Eltons, who feel rather superior to their workers. England didn't have a revolution, he says, though it must have been a close thing. Our landowners were not decadent aristocrats living in luxury miles removed for their tenants. 'They were actually there managing their estates. It's like old fashioned conservatism, really.'[13] Thus a harvest home event with Knightley at its centre would make a plausible conclusion to this dramatisation of Emma. Historically it made good sense. Although we naturally tend to associate such scenes more easily with the world of Thomas Hardy, it would accord with the kind of community which Jane Austen portrays.[14] And it worked well. But if there is one thing which will make this otherwise reasonable but certainly not outstanding dramatization worth remembering, it is Prunella Scales definitive performance of the immortal Miss Bates, a wonderful combination of the silly and the pathetic, created with that kind of histrionic professionalism, rendered with an excellence it is easy to take for granted.

Significant evidence of just how profoundly the *'Pride and Prejudice* factor' had penetrated our cultural consciousness was demonstrated within months of this transmission. On Saturday 6 September 1997, in the wake of that terrible accident in the Paris underpass, when it befitted us to bear our hearts in grief, and our whole kingdom to be contracted in one brow of woe, Michael Fish, the BBC Weatherman, who usually appears before us sporting one of a wide range of colourful jackets, wore a sombre suit. The commercial television channels demonstrated their sense of responsibility by a repeat transmission of Meridian Broadcasting's version of Jane Austen's *Emma*: '...brought to you by the team which initiated *Pride and Prejudice* (Sue Birtwhistle and Andrew Davies).'[15] Both sombre suit[16] and costume drama reveal much about our culture's value systems. Even though our national uniform of shell suits and trainers might proclaim the ultimate triumph of informality, we still have sobersides garb stored in the wardrobe. Despite the Jonathan Miller-led assault on film and television versions of classic novels,[17] a dramatised television version of an Eng. Lit. masterpiece is regarded as sufficiently high cultural and high-minded a product to be transmitted to a nation in mourning at the death of a dearly beloved young Princess.

The BBC's autumn serial, which began in November 1996, was Anne Brontë's *The Tenant of Wildfell Hall*. It was dramatised by David Nokes and Janet Barron (who had written Richardson's *Clarissa* for BBC-2). This was a BBC Production, with the Canadian Broadcasting Corporation and WBGH Boston, produced by Suzan Harrison and directed by Mike Barker. This novel, the second from the young novelist who died before she was 30 years old, was published in 1847. It is a characteristic Brontë performance, a melodrama with a central dominating mystery and an interesting leading female character, plenty of false clues, mistaken identities set in wild landscapes and a corrupting city environment with plenty of symbolic apparatus *à la* Byron, Wordsworth and the high romantics. All this would argue its case well as a television series for the 1990s, although time has blunted what might originally have been its shocking portrait of the treatment of women in marriage and the realities of social bigotry and misguided moral persecution. But there are problems, intrinsic to the nature of the novel itself. Anne Brontë was always as much interested in the possibilities of novel construction as she was with the story she was telling. Just as was the case with *Agnes Grey*, her previous novel, the impact is inevitably the result of matters kept from you or perforce read or seen from a particular standpoint manipulated for you by the novelist. Her second novel is a fascinating mixture of those elements which work so well in *Jane Eyre* and *Wuthering Heights* – mysterious characters, atmospheric setting, characters who seek marriage though secretly married already. The trick in *The Tenant of Wildfell Hall* is to make you see Helen Graham as the local gossips see her, and then to see things from her point of view. This is difficult to attempt in television.

Helen, the tenant of Wildfell Hall, arouses suspicion simply because she seems to value her privacy. Add to this the fact she is good looking, young and says little about herself. The additional information that she receives visits from her landlord, Frederick Lawrence, is enough to wreck what reputation she may have left. The narrator of the story so far has been Gilbert Markham, a neighbouring young farmer who has fallen in love with her. He is disturbed at the situation, and there is a violent scene between him and Lawrence. This leaves Helen no alternative but to tell Markham her secret. The narrative voice changes, as we read the story in the form of her diary. So we now have another perspective as we learn of her disastrous marriage to Arthur Huntingdon, a drunken, profligate wretch, who makes her life so miserable that she removes herself and her child from him, seeking asylum by flight to Wildfell Hall, which is owned by her brother, Frederick Lawrence. Arthur Huntingdon is then taken seriously ill, probably the result of his drunken and debauched life. Helen returns to nurse him in what proves to be a terminal illness. His death makes her a wealthy woman, and this proves to be an obstacle to marriage to Markham, but this is overcome. Helen was played by Tara Fitzgerald, and Arthur by Rupert Graves, both of whom came through as rather lightweight for the immense melodramatic burden they were expected to assume. James Purefroy served up an adequate Frederick Lawrence. Gilbert Markham was played by Toby Stephens who scarcely projected that sense of obsession with Helen Graham which goes with the role. He suggested a gentleman farmer who fancied her a bit, but little more. Kenneth Cranham (on to a good line in religious zealots since *Oranges*

Are Not the Only Fruit) shone as the Revd Milward, leader of the moral crusade against Helen. Pam Ferris turned in a sound performance as Mrs Markham, the hero's mother. But the production did not really ignite. For all the talk of the romantic and powerful Brontës, one important element was dreadfully absent – passion. The surface quality was little help here. We get the impression of Wildfell Hall as a vast, decaying, semi-derelict gothic sort of pile, set in a wild landscape in the remote Yorkshire Dales. Somehow, this was all toned down.

This production was certainly seen at the time as part of the '*Pride and Prejudice* factor', merged imperceptibly into a Brontë Effect, and indeed the Pastime chain of retail outlets ran an Austen/Brontë promotion at this period. It was hoped by the management of the Brontë industry centred at Haworth in Yorkshire that it would lead to increased visitors to the Yorkshire shrine as well as a general benefit to the British tourist industry. The usual farrago of psychobabble was deployed to assert the novel's alleged contemporary relevance. The Director of Haworth Parsonage, Jane Sellars, expressed her delight at the televising of *The Tenant of Wildfell Hall*, and the Haworth museum staged an exhibition of costumes from the series during its run November to December 1996. 'I've been a champion of *The Tenant* because I think it is a very powerful but under rated book', Jane Sellars said, 'And it is quite shocking. You find that you can translate the situation into the late 20th century. Helen has been abused. She is a single parent without financial independence who takes the daring step of actually running away to save her child and herself.'[18] She hoped that this television version would lead to a re-evaluation of Anne Brontë, overshadowed for so long by Charlotte and Emily. If the BBC hoped it would be the year's *Pride and Prejudice* they were to be disappointed. However, it was shown in over 20 countries, including Australia, Italy, Belgium, Poland, South Africa, Spain and it earned the Corporation £317 441, a third of the income generated by *Pride and Prejudice*, but not much less than *Martin Chuzzlewit*.[19]

During the Christmas holiday period 1996 BBC-2 transmitted a dramatisation by Kevin Elyot of Wilkie Collins's *The Moonstone*. It was produced by Chris Parr and directed by Robert Bierman, starring Greg Wise, Keeley Hawes, Patricia Hodge, Scott Handy, Peter Vaughan, Paul Brooke and Antony Sher. *The Moonstone*, even more than *The Tenant of Wildfell Hall*, depends for its impact on the way the story is unfolded, as the situations are gradually pieced together from accounts by various characters from differing points of view. It did not prove a simple matter to recast this in a form suitable for serial television drama without losing a very great deal of the novel's peculiar power. It was cast in two hour-long episodes, producing a sense of compression which did no service to its plot complexities. This version reduced the story to a straightforward account of the major events in the novel. Wilkie Collins did not invent the detective novel, but he certainly pioneered the genre. *The Moonstone* is an early classic of the genre. John Herncastle, an English officer, kills three Brahmin guards and steals a precious jewel from the head of a Hindu moon-god during the battle of Seringapatam. In the terms of his will it passes to the hands of Miss Rachel Verender (Keeley Hawes) on her eighteenth birthday. But the Brahmins come to regain it. A mysterious atmosphere is established at the opening of *The Moonstone* with the appearance of three Indian jugglers at the Verinders' house. They are politely but firmly sent on their way by Gabriel Betteredge, the house steward (Peter Vaughan). That night the Moonstone disappears. But it has been stolen by her lover, Franklin Blake, (Greg Wise) in an opium trance. The Indian jugglers are suspected. Blake's rival for Rachel Verender's love, Godfrey Ablewhite, a successful young lawyer (Scott Handy) manages to gain the diamond. But he is murdered in mysterious circumstances.

In the novel, several versions of the narrative intertwine. Who are we to believe? Blake does not realise what he has done. Various innocent people are suspected. The mystery is resolved by the brilliant detective, Sergeant Cuff (Antony Sher). Collins based him on the celebrated police detective, Jonathan Whicher, who solved the infamous Roadhill House murder in Wiltshire. The three-year-old son of Samuel Kent had been found murdered in an outside privy. Whicher concluded the crime had been committed by someone in the household. His theory was based on the fact that whoever killed the child must have had bloodstained clothes, yet no bloodied garment was ever discovered. A night-dress belonging to young Constance Kent went missing, and she later confessed to the crime. Collins makes use of a missing garment and portrays Cuff as Whicher. The novelist mixes several other popular ingredients and works them up into superb entertainment. Victorian newspapers fed the popular appetite for crime, mystery and violence. Foreign news stories were packed with exploits of British soldiers and sailors in far flung parts of the empire – imperialism, at its height in Victorian times, had generated a taste for mysteries with exotic settings, tales of the East, India, and far away places with strange sounding names. William Henry Sleeman's *Ramaseena* (1836), Edward Parry Thornton's *Illustrations of the History and Practices of the Thugs* (1837), Philip Meadows Taylor's *Confessions of a Thug* (1839) and *Tara: A Mahratta Tale* (1863), *Ralph Darnell* (1865) and *Seeta* (1873). Thackeray's *Vanity Fair* is full of echoes of the exotic world of India and abounds with references to brandy-cutchery, brandy-pawnee, tiffin, punkahs, tiger hunts, elephants, mangoes, chutney and curry. Dickens's rich merchant Mr Dombey trades with the East, with its offices near East India House, teeming with suggestions of precious stones, howdahs, hookahs, palanquins and gorgeous princes sitting on carpets with their slippers turned up at the toes. When *The Moonstone* appeared first, in serial episodes, crowds hung around the publishers' offices in Wellington Street and bets were placed on where and how the Moonstone would finally turn up.

When first published, reviews of *The Moonstone* were lukewarm, but Collins wrote to a friend:

> we have only to wait a few weeks, until the book has had time to get talked about. I don't attach much importance to the Reviews – except as advertisements which are inserted for nothing. But the impression that I produce on the general public of readers is the lever that will move anything. . . . It is (in the opinion of more than one good judge) the best book I have written. I believe it myself to have a much stronger element of 'popularity' in it than anything I have written since '*The Woman in White*'. . .

He was right. It has everything we expect in a detective mystery – clues which point in the wrong direction, professional detectives who make mistaken deductions, unlikely suspects, a culprit who seemed the most unlikely, reconstructions of the crime . . . twists and turns as the tale unfolds. Collins wrote: 'Never have I had better reason than this work has given me to feel gratefully to novel readers of all nations. Everywhere my characters made friends, and my story roused interest. . .' *The Moonstone* will always arouse interest and never lose its capacity to excite, and has several times made a good classic novel serial on BBC radio.

In putting the novel together, Collins realised the trick lies in presenting an apparently incoherent and inexplicable mystery cleared up by one who enters the situation from outside, in this case, the professional detective, Sergeant Cuff (Anthony Sher) who in some ways is clearly the prototype for Sherlock Holmes, and he unravels the mystery. And it is right here that the main trouble lies. The difficulty is that the plot details themselves are so neatly put together so as to make sense when revealed, that in itself the plot has little human interest. The fascination generated is the result of the wayward manner in which the details are gradually exposed in the various different accounts and narrations of the same events – an account by Gabriel Betteredge, various family relatives, Franklin Blake, various servants etc. – in just the way, one assumes, as the whole picture would gradually take shape to an investigating detective. Collins's gift as a novelist lay in involving the reader in the unravelling of the clues and unlocking the key to the labyrinth. There is not much else to be had from such novels. This was well perceived by Anthony Trollope, who expressed this opinion:

> Wilkie Collins seems so to construct his novels that he not only ... plans everything on, down to the minutest detail, from the beginning to the end; but then plots it all back again, to see that there is no piece of necessary dove-tailing which does not dove-tail with absolute accuracy. The construction is most minute and wonderful. But I can never lose the taste of the construction... One is constrained by mysteries and hemmed in by difficulties, knowing however, that the mysteries will be made clear, and the difficulties overcome at the end of the third volume...[20]

The acting was proficient. Peter Vaughan, as the house steward, Betteredge, turned in yet another polished characterisation, with presence and gravitas leavened with genuine kindness. Antony Sher, as Cuff, invented some interesting mannerisms, including furtive expressions, grimaces, eccentricities of perambulation, constantly humming 'The Last Rose of Summer' to himself, but did it really add up to a convincing or believable portrait of a great detective? This production, although exquisitely photographed by John Daly, did not generate sufficient period atmosphere and charm to hide the mechanical quality of the plot. Seeing it to its conclusion, with the mysteries resolved, provided much the same satisfaction as completing a crossword.

The television classic novel craze continued into the new year with BBC's six 55-minute episode dramatisation of Sir Walter Scott's *Ivanhoe* in January 1997. This was a BBC/A&E Network co-production. It was written by Deborah Cook, produced by Jeremy Gwilt and directed by Stuart Orme. The production starred Steven Waddington (Wilfred of Ivanhoe), Susan Lynch (Rebecca), Victoria Smurfit (Rowena), Ciaran Hinds (Brian Bois Guilbert), Jimmy Chisolm (Wamba), Trevor Cooper (Gurth), James Cosmo (Cedric the Saxon), David Horowitch (Isaac of

York), Ralph Brown (Prince John), Ronald Pickup (Fitzurse), Rory Edwards (King Richard), Nick Brimble (Front de Boef), David J. Nicholls (Little John), Aden Gillett (Robin of Locksley) and Christopher Lee (Beaumanior). It was advertised by *Radio Times* as 'costume drama of the old school, set in the time of Robin Hood: lavish robes, horses, armour and battle scenes shot in locations all over Britain...'.[21] The BBC had previously serialised this novel in 1970 in ten 25-minute episodes, for the Sunday teatime family audience, with Eric Flynn in the title role. This new version was scheduled on Saturday evenings and, judging by its sexiness and violence (some pretty authentic-looking torture scenes began the series) designed for a more mature audience. Interestingly enough, Christopher Lee, who appeared in this new version, had also appeared (in the German Knight episode) of the BBC Television's *Ivanhoe* series which starred Roger Moore in the more innocent days of 1959. The new version looked rugged and hearty enough, though there was much comment about the hairiness and generally heavy metal-look of the Saxons and their heavy Yorkshire accents. But it pulled in an average audience of 6 million. At times it sounded very modern, with characters cursing 'Bloody hell!', advising each other 'Take care!' and asserting 'A good hot poultice will soon 'ave that sorted!' Some of the rough and tumble during the tournament looked very bloody and bruising.

It is sometimes interesting to detect signs of change in BBC attitude towards the making of classic novel adaptations. Originally the ambition was faithfully to serve the cause of the literary original. This was promulgated in the late 1930s, when the Corporation's radio drama people were actually putting the genre together. But today there are often signs of a desire to somehow, at the same time as dealing with a classic, (by definition, something preserved from the past) to create a product of modern times. It was expressed during the run of *Ivanhoe*, a tale set in the twelfth century, when Richard I was off on the Crusades. Steven Waddington, who played Wilfrid of Ivanhoe, had this to say about his role:

> Personally, I think *Ivanhoe* should possibly be the last hurrah of the period pieces. The public can only take so much, although this is totally different, it's timeless. It's not just about being chivalrous and doing the right thing all the time. Even Ivanhoe has a dilemma – he's in love with two women – and he doesn't just make a decision, it's a long journey before he works out what to do. All those things are very modern.[22]

It is significant that he doesn't say that Ivanhoe's 'dilemma' is time-less. No. It's 'very modern.' As the decade progressed, and more and more classic novels were transformed into costume dramas, we began more frequently to hear that 'so-and-so' had been dramatised 'for the 1990s'. The BBC's education kit to accompany *Middlemarch* actually describes itself on its cover as 'Screening *Middlemarch*: 19th Century Novel to 90s Television'. And indeed, among the latest classic novel dramatisations to appear as this book goes to press, there is a strong feeling that modern dramatic situations and conflicts are being super-imposed upon novels from the last century. This was objectionable enough in BBC-2's 1994 ersatz-Brechtian *Hard Times*, but was even more marked in Tony Marchant's 1999 version of *Great Expectations*.

Convincingly to bring Scott's *Ivanhoe* to the screen a decision has firmly to be made at an early stage as to style – is the aim to produce a version faithful to the romantic historicism of Scott. Or – with the aid of modern scholarship – to go for as authentic a recreation of the past as possible? In other words, are we to have nineteenth century romantic history? Or to go for well researched chronological authen-ticity? Experience would suggest a Walter Scottish style actually works better. Scott (and *Ivanhoe* in particular) – seems to thrive with that historical oil-painting quality, that sense of the carefully posed set piece. We are looking at the work of the man felicitously described by Matthew Arnold as the historiographer royal of feudalism. We are looking at the past through his eyes, the eyes of the man who taught the early nineteenth century how to see their history. There is more of Froissart than Braudel in Scott. Genuine historical realism works against the grain of those timbers with which Scott built his vision of the Middle Ages and the Age of Chivalry. He was writing at the time when Planché was rediscovering (and partly inventing) heraldry, Keats's *Eve of St Agnes*, (published the same year as *Ivanhoe*) Kean's triumphant assumption of the role of Richard III, of chivalric operas such as Rossini's *Tancredi*, Weber's *Euryanthe*, *Oberon*, of massive historical painting – Ingres, David, Delacroix, Haydon – and of the sumptuous pseudo-medieval coronation of George IV (which featured the last ceremonial appearance of the King's Champion),[23] of James Wyatt's Fonthill Abbey and Ashridge Abbey and Jeffry Wayatviller's refurbishments at Windsor Castle and of the rediscovery of Robin Hood, Good Queen Bess and all the apparatus of Merrie England. So plenty of heraldry, ceremonial trumpets and trumpery, banners waived aloft, blazonry, castles, turrets, clanking armour and snorting chargers. Anything less than this effectively devalues what Sir Walter

Scott has to offer. Otherwise we simply remove him from the world he partly created and in which his art lived and thrived. This production seemed to have lacked the nerve to make a decision either way, but erred towards a rather unconvincing historical authenticity. Frankly, it did not work all that well. There was much discomfort in the BBC at its low ratings, and by February 1997 even rumours that it was being internally argued that *Ivanhoe* should not have been made in the first place.[24] Nevertheless, in spite of its cool reception in the UK, it was shown in over 15 countries and earned £506 742[25] – nearly twice as much as *Martin Chuzzlewit*.

In February, BBC-2 began their Saturday evening transmission of the £9 million epic version of Joseph Conrad's *Nostromo*, shot on location in Columbia. This lavish production is bound to go down in television history as an immense curiosity, if nothing else. It is almost certainly more than just that. But at the time its reception was rather grudging, yet its ambitions were considerable. Simply to bring such a complex example of the novelist's art to the small screen, it might well have been thought, would be sufficient a challenge in itself, but on the international scale here attempted it seemed a Pelion-piled-on-Ossa kind of enterprise. *Nostromo* was a co-production by Pixit for BBC Television in association with RAI (Italy), TVE (Spain) and WGBH (Boston), subsidised by Greco as part of the Media Programme for the European Union. It was produced by Fernando Ghia, directed by Alastair Reid and the executive producer was Michael Wearing. It was dramatised by John Hale with music by Ennio Morricone. The director of photography was Franco di Giacomo and the cast, too, was suitably international: Claudio Amendola (Nostromo), Lothaire Bluteau (Decoud), Paul Brooke (Captain Mitchell), Claudio Cardinale (Teresa Viola), Joaquim de Almeida (Sotillo), Albert Finney (Dr Moyneham), Colin Firth (Gould), Arnolde Foa (Giorgio Viola), Ruth Gabriel (Antonia Viola), Fernando Hilbeck (Avillanos), Serena Scott Thomas (Mrs Gould), Salvo Basile (Montero), Xavier Burbano (Ramirez), Ismael E. Carlo (Barrios) and Allan Corduner (Hirsch).

The ambition to make this production was a long time germinating in film executive Fernando Ghia's imagination. With the epic *The Mission* among his credits, Ghia was clearly a man who could act big as well as think big. Robert Bolt told him during the filming of David Lean's *Ryan's Daughter* that there were pretty firm plans for a film version of Conrad's masterpiece, which he was to write and David Lean to direct. This project was obviously abandoned after David Lean died. Ghia then read the novel and was overwhelmed by its power and scope. It is very interesting that as early as that Ghia decided against a cinema film version of *Nostromo* because he thought film length of a cinema release would work against all chance of realising Conrad's intentions. He believed right from the beginning that Lean's ambitions were doomed for that reason. It was the old story of the bottle being too small for the wine. But the subject matter, he always believed, was ideally cinematic. The solution was obvious: 'The material screams out to be a movie', he said, 'but you can't cover it in a feature film. It needs to be at least five hours, and for that, it has to be television.' Ghia put the project to Michael Wearing at the BBC in 1992, and they raised funding from Italy, Spain and the USA, with cast and crew from Europe and Latin America. It was filmed in 1995.

The climate in which *Nostromo* appeared was peculiar. There were rumours that internally the BBC regarded it as a potential turkey, the *Sunday Mirror* led this whispering campaign: 'It's already being branded a flop by the BBC itself' and the *Daily Mail* was asking 'Will *Nostromo* mark the end of the BBC's love of costume drama?' This was before the first episode had even been screened. As Maggie Brown noted in *Guardian*: 'I don't know about you, but I'm looking forward to the first episode of *Nostromo*.... This should be exotic, ambitious stuff, a bleak story of murder, corruption and power set against spectacular shots of the Andes, aided by the fact that Mr Darcy – sorry, Colin Firth – looks great in jodhpurs. This is a project made to challenge...' It was indeed a challenge, not only to the film-makers, but to viewers as well. Its rating figure in UK, 3 million, must seem disappointing, but any attempt to label it a failure must be resisted on the evidence of its impressive success overseas. As well as in USA, it was shown in Africa, Australia, Cyprus, Czech Republic, Denmark, Finland, Greece, Holland, Hong Kong, Hungary, Iceland, Malaysia, New Zealand, Poland, Portugal, Russia, Singapore, Slovenia, South Africa, Sweden, Taiwan, Thailand and Zimbabwe. Its total revenue for the BBC is over £690 898.[26] The problem may well have been with the subject matter.

Conrad's novel makes considerable demands upon its readers and this dramatisation, which certainly showed respect for its literary original, made demands upon television viewers. Conrad has much to say, and says it at some length with some elaboration. The first problem is that of form. Conrad himself was well aware of this as he himself had struggled as a writer throughout his career to find a form suitable for his fiction. He wanted to maintain control over his material as omniscient narrator, yet allow for the possibilities of different points of view towards constructing the realities of his fiction. Additionally, he wanted to allow time for the deployment of irony. He aimed to isolate and dramatise action, to distance himself (and readers) from it. He resorted to the use of an equivalent narrator in his work, Marlowe, who would be telling the story. This enabled him to have Marlowe absent from some things he was trying to incorporate into his narrative, to have the useful perspective of the past or of hearsay on things, and to incorporate the listener/reader into the process of creation. This is a tall enough order in narrative prose fiction – as his readers would testify. But how are such complexities to be translated to the screen? In the case of *Nostromo*, although the work is put together from several different sources and viewpoints – the author's voice as historical narrator, Captain Mitchell's early narrative, Decoud's long letter, the reflections of Dr Monygham, Captain Mitchell's later narrative, Nostromo's own voice – the series of experiences it purports to represent are suspended in a clear chronological sequence. John Hale, in dramatising *Nostromo* for television, concentrated on this thread, this time sequence, and thus rendered the dramatic action fairly coherent. What we lose, to some extent, is the critical edge and irony which different points of view and perspectives might have bestowed on the material.

Nostromo: A Tale of the Seaboard, published in 1904, is set in the fictional South American republic of Costaguana. It is centred on the town and province of Sulaco, the wealthiest region of the area. Originally under the rule of the Spanish Conquistadors, but now being opened up to European and North American interests in the era of European and American capitalist imperialism, with the encouragement of European and American capitalist interests, Sulaco succeeds from Costaguana. The dominant economic force in the area is the San Tome silver mine, and all the leading characters are really defined (or define themselves) by the nature of their relationship to the silver and to the mine. The San Tome silver is what Alfred Hitchcock would have called the Maguffin of Conrad's complex novel, which in so many ways prefigures modern imperialism. Holroyd, the San Francisco financier whose funds support Charles Gould, British owner of the mine, actually seems to prefigure the century of US imperialism:

> We can sit and watch. Of course, some day we shall step in. We are bound to. But there's no hurry. Time itself has got to wait on the greatest country in the whole of God's universe. We shall be giving the word for everything – industry, trade, law, journalism, art,

politics, and religion, from Cape Horn clear over to Smith's Sound, and beyond it, too, if anything worth taking hold of turns up at the North Pole.... We shall run the world's business whether the world likes it or not....[27]

Nostromo, the proud, vain Italian sailor who has been made leader of the port's dockers is concerned with making a glamorous reputation, and intends to use the silver towards realising this ambition. Charles Gould, the young British owner of the San Tome Mine, resolves to make the mines conspicuously successful. For him the success of his mine would be a symbol of progress and the basis for a stable economy:

What is wanted here is law, good faith, order, security.... Anyone can declaim about these things, but I pin my faith to material interests. Only let the material interests once get a firm footing, and they are bound to impose the conditions on which alone they can continue to exist.[28]

For Emilia Gould, his wife, the silver is the agency by which her family is destroyed:

An immense desolation, the dread of her own continued life, descended upon the first lady of Sulaco. With a prophetic vision she saw herself surviving alone the degradation of her young ideal of life, of love, of work – all alone in the Treasure House of the world. The profound, blind, suffering expression of a painful dream settled on her face with its closed eyes. In the indistinct voice of an unlucky sleeper, lying passive in the grip of a merciless nightmare, she stammered out the words 'Material interest'...[29]

For Holroyd, the American capitalist who backs the Gould enterprise, it is a diversion. For Martin Decoud, Costaguano bred but Parisian educated journalist and dilettante, (the adopted child of Western Europe) it represents a means by which to gain the love of Antonia Avellanos. For the spiritually derelict Dr Monygham – who is in love with Mrs Gould – it is his regeneration. For the various political figures the silver is a source of power and a fuel for their ambition. These individuals' destinies are played out in the narrative of the elaborate political upheavals which unfold. Guzman Bento, dictator of Costaguana dies, and there is a power struggle between the legal government of Ribiera and the populist party led by the military chief,

Montero, which naturally centres on the San Tome mine. The silver of the mine has various meanings for these native interests as well. For the corrupt government officials it is the paymaster, it lubricates the system which has served them well enough. To the rebels, it is the prize they win if their revolution is successful. For the other native factions, rather more altruistic in their motive, who are equally opposed to dictatorship and foreign exploitation, the silver is a means of liberating their country from its poverty. To the workers in the mine, it is their daily bread, and the change of ownership will have little impact.

John Hale reduces the various stages and shifts of time and narrative viewpoint to a straightforward chronological account of the action. At the death of Guzman Bento there is a struggle for power which is won by Ribera, who becomes the new dictator. Charles Gould, with Holroyd's backing, supports Ribera's government in the belief the mine will be left alone. Don Jose Avellanos, the old patriot, and General Montero, minister of war, support the new government. We are also introduced to other characters – Dr Monyghan, who had been broken under torture in Bento's regime, Antonia, beautiful daughter of Don Jose, Decoud, her betrothed, Old Viola, who had fought alongside Garibaldi and now lives here with his wife and two daughters, Linda and Giselle, and Nostromo, the Italian dockers' leader. Then there is a further revolution, led by General Montero, who intends to drive Europeans out of South America. The Europeans then unite in a counter revolution to keep Montero from gaining control of the mine. Their success depends on two things. First, hiding the silver mined already to finance themselves, and second, getting through to sympathetic forces up the coast. This venture is entrusted to Nostromo and Decoud. In the darkness their boat is hit by gunfire from a rebel troopship. Decoud breaks under the strain and shoots himself, sinking in the boat weighed down with silver. This is magnificently presented by Conrad:

> A victim of the disillusioned weariness which is the retribution meted out to intellectual audacity, the brilliant Don Martin Decoud, weighted down by the bars of San Tome silver, disappeared without a trace, swallowed up in the immense indifference of things.

Nostromo, realising the extent to which he has been exploited by his allies, decides to hide his load of silver to gain his fortune and reputation when all the troubles are over. But a lighthouse is built on the site where he has concealed his booty. To justify his visits to the site he pretends to be courting Linda Viola, daughter of Giorgio Viola, the lighthousekeeper. However, Nostromo falls in love with Giselle, sister of his betrothed, and they plan to run away together. But on the night he planned to visit her and regain his hoard, Old Viola shoots him, mistaking Nostromo for a former lover of the younger daughter. So the secret of the silver is lost forever.

John Hale effectively reduces this vast canvas to the manageable proportions required for a television drama serial, and there is no mistaking the feeling that we are watching a serious work with intentions greater than simply amusing us. But somehow the engagement, the commitment of Conrad, seems to have been drawn off:

> Conrad saw the world-wide extension of capitalism, the antagonism between imperial and colonial lands, the introduction into the political and economic context of the twentieth century, the intrusion of machines into the jungles, the exploitation of the peasants, the extraction of wealth and its expropriation by foreigners and colonial rulers. It is a world in which progress drinks nectar from the skulls of the slain, a world of directorates and monopolies, of wars and revolutions for the control of wealth and power.[30]

The BBC-2 television version of *Nostromo* was magnificent, but it is a magnificent adventure story. The grisly ironies, the sense of rapacious capitalism and spiritual corrosion – these have gone. That ability to be both immediately realistic and mythical, in which the silver is not only a tangible physical prize men struggle to gain, but also a magical object with the power both to enhance and destroy – like Wagner's *Rheingold* or Tolkien's rings – the poetic power of a vision beyond the immediate surface reality of things, a characteristic of Conrad, is no longer there. *Nostromo* received grudging, mixed reviews in the UK, and in the reviewers' minds (if not viewers') got itself damagingly associated with that year's turkey, *Rhodes*, the £10 million 'flop' shown that autumn: 'Over £10 million spent on a show whose main effect was to boost Jeremy Beadle's ratings by 2.5 million' as one commentator put it.[31] Despite the UK's reluctance to be enthusiastic, *Nostromo* was very successful abroad. It was bought by over 20 countries – including Africa, Australia, Hong Kong, Russia, South Africa, Zimbabwe, Thailand, Greece – and earned the Corporation £690 898.[32]

In March commercial television brought us yet another version of *Jane Eyre*, made by LWT as part of the ITV Drama Premieres in association with Midland Bank (and A&E Television Networks, New York). It was dramatised by Kay Mellor, who came to the task with *Band of Gold* and *A Passionate Woman*, her previous successful television dramas, to her credit. It starred Samantha Morton, the dazzling young discovery, with sterling professional performances as Tracy in *Band of Gold* and Harriet in *Emma*, behind her. Rochester was played by Ciaran Hinds. It was produced by Greg Brenman and directed by Robert Young. Greg Brenman was anxious this production should see things from the female perspective:

> The problem with most adaptations is that they take the male perspective so much they should be called 'Rochester'. It was always our intention to pull the focus back on Jane and make it very much her story, as it is in the book. We also chose a Jane who was the age of the character – Sam Morton was just nineteen when we filmed – often the part is played by a much older actress. What makes the character so interesting is that she is on the cusp of girlhood and womanhood. We did as much as we could to give Jane voice, and I think our film is as close and faithful as you can get.[33]

So far, so good, but then it is revealed that although their researches showed that Jane as a governess would have worn black and costume designer Susannah Buxton decided the colour was too harsh:

> I went for silver grey and a heathery colour, instead. I like clothes to look just that, clothes, not costumes, and that's particularly important with *Jane Eyre*. It's an intense story and it's important that you believe the people and don't see the costumes ahead of the actress.[34]

Unfortunately no amount of good faith good bring this production to life. Despite excellent locations (Naworth Castle in Cumbria for the exterior of Thornfield Hall and Knebworth for the interiors) it lacked atmosphere. Samantha Morton turned in an interesting creation as young Jane but scarcely explored her passion or confusion and Ciaran Hinds carried taciturnity to uncalled for heights of virtuosity. For all its Hollywood ham, Spam and raspberry jam, one longed for a dose of Orson Welles in it somewhere. This LWT *Jane Eyre* was romantic melodrama played with too much decorum for its own good.

In September 1997 the commercial channel broadcast Granada Television's production of *The Ebb Tide*, the remarkable (and under rated) short novel by Robert Louis Stevenson (and Lloyd Osbourne) dramatised in two 50-minute episodes by Simon Donald, produced by Hilary Bevan Jones and directed by Nicholas Renton. *The Ebb Tide* has always been recognized as a curiosity among Stevenson's mature works. It was a complete reworking of an original first draft by Osbourne which Stevenson wrote in Samoa during 1893 – the same period when he composed *Catriona* and immediately prior to his masterpiece, *The Weir of Hermiston*. Stevenson here seems to aspire and, in part, anticipate the spirit of Joseph Conrad in an exotically located tale of the trial and spiritual redemption of three derelict personalities – Captain Chisholm (Robbie Coltrane), Swanson (Steven Mackintosh) and Bunch (Chris Barnes). They are drifters, wastrels, beachcombers, human debris. But they think their fortunes have suddenly changed when they are commissioned to sail a ship with a cargo of vintage champagne to Australia. Even though it is a plague boat and they have been given the job because no one else will undertake it, they feel destiny has struck. They have been called to better things. Chisholm feels that life has finally given him a chance to show what he is made of and is resolved the ship will reach Australia. Swanson and Bunch simply want to consume all the booze. During the voyage they discover the real nature of their voyage. The bottles are empty. It is an insurance scam and they were never expected successfully to complete the voyage. They are just pawns in a much bigger game. This is interpreted as a challenge and they resolve to get the ship through. Chisholm, who hides a dark family secret, lays his hands on enough booze to drink himself into a stupor and a storm represents the torment in his soul. In calmer seas they sight an island and resolve to explore it. Here they meet Ellstrom (Nigel Terry) – a character almost straight out of Conrad – and the story climaxes as he attempts to guard his territory and his priceless pearl collection from them. In a final bloodbath, (not strictly based on the original) matters are resolved. Coltrane's career was then on the crest of a wave, following his smash-hit successful Granada crime series *Cracker*. Hilary Bevan Jones, producer of *The Ebb Tide*, who also worked with Coltrane on *Cracker*, said of the Stevenson story: 'It is a moving story of one man's attempt to find redemption. It is also a dark tale of greed, double-cross and betrayal on the high seas.'[35]

It was produced as part of the ITV Midland Bank Drama Premieres season, and the fact was widely publicised that the drama was filmed on location in the Virgin Islands. The drama was launched in conjunction with a 'Win a Holiday in the Virgin Islands' competition:

...an exclusive trip for two in the beautiful British Virgin Islands. From the seclusion of remote Virgin Gorda, accessible only by sea and in a beautiful protected anchorage, lies The Bitter End Yacht Club. A must for sailing and watersports enthusiasts and popular among the yachting fraternity... The Bitter End Yacht Club has established itself as a relaxing refuge for both the adventurous and the less energetic. Distinguished by its unique architecture, the resort is set on a vast tropical hillside commanding spectacular views.... . Your accommodation will be in one of the property's stylish villas. Dining is British-style with Caribbean accents, and activities, not surprisingly, revolve around the sea...[36]

But ITV subsequently had to announce that the holiday firm concerned – Simply Caribbean – had simply gone into liquidation 'but British Airways Holidays had come to the rescue with the offer of flights to the Virgin Islands for our winner.' This is very interesting evidence of the subtle and sometimes complex connections between the dramatisation of classic texts and the economic and commercial context in which they are produced, packaged and consumed. It is worth briefly commenting on the package, as it has much to tell us as to the manner in which past literary texts are identified as classics with a potential market value which renders them worth resurrecting, and the various processes involved in the financing, production and delivery. There are obvious basic requirements by way of ingredients – an authorship reasonably well known and a dramatic coherent story with good leading roles, an interesting period and offering colourful locations. As overseas sales daily grow in importance, international tastes and expectations must be satisfied. A bit of expert horse trading additionally may lead to various other tie-ins. *The Ebb Tide* in this respect was a revealing product of today's British television industry. Robert Louis Stevenson is a well known, popular classic author. *The Ebb Tide* was new to the market, it offered several good leading roles – with a cast led by Robbie Coltrane on the full tide of his *Cracker* stardom. It would attract sponsorship. And its splendid exotic tropical locations would beg for mutually beneficial collaboration with the tourist industry. Subsequent potential video sales seemed promising. In the event, *The Ebb Tide* was a beautiful production, handsomely filmed by Remi Adefarasin (director of photography) with pleasant and effective music by Bill Connor.

7
Boz Rides Again, and this is where we came in...

In October Channel 4 transmitted Hugh Whitemore's four part (each episode was two hours) dramatisation of Anthony Powell's *Dance to the Music of Time*. This was a *tour de force* and is one of the most seriously underrated classic novel dramatisations of recent years, achieving with deceptive ease (as far as the viewer could see) a feat which, rationally considered, would seem impossible. Consider the literary work in question. It was published in twelve volumes, totalling some 3000 pages. The twelve volume cycle takes its title and sustaining metaphor from the title of Nicolas Poussin's painting *A Dance to the Music of Time* in the Wallace Collection. The work covers a long chronological period from the early part of the twentieth century – it begins just after the First World War, continues through until the end of the 1930s and then reverts to the beginning of the First World War, goes into the Second World War and continues up to the early 1970s – involving the intertwined adventures of a large selection of major characters and numerous smaller groups, who weave in and out of the main actions. But the entire narrative framework is clearly and plainly assembled as a structure. The novels are grouped in threes, representing the four seasons and the four major stages of human life: spring (school, university and sexual awakening): *A Question of Upbringing* (1951), *A Buyer's Market* (1952), *The Acceptance World* (1955); summer (marriage and work): *At Lady Molly's* (1957), *Casanova's Chinese Restaurant* (1960); *The Kindly Ones* (1962); autumn (war years) *The Valley of the Bones* (1964), *The Soldier's Art* (1966), *The Military Philosophers* (1968); winter (postwar, old age and death): *Books Do Furnish a Room* (1971), *Temporary Kings* (1973), *Hearing Secret Harmonies* (1975).

A *Dance to the Music of Time* deals with a vast array of characters. About a dozen of them are dealt with in high definition, but many,

many minor characters are etched in with deftness and brilliance. They are mainly the middle ground of the class system – failed or would-be writers, artists, professionals, publishers, musicians, media-folk and politicos. *A Dance to the Music of Time* is a major work, of profound originality, yet owing much to Proust and at times, something to Evelyn Waugh and P.G. Wodehouse. It is a *roman fleuve*, covering as it does Powell's own life span and paralleling his experience of Eton, Oxford, metropolitan social life, the Second World War and army life, and Britain during the postwar settlement as experienced by the professional classes and artists. In tone and style the work is a strong mixture of comedy and pathos. The comedy arises from the satirical, witty, grotesque and detached view of such a vast canvas. The tragic sense, which grows more sombre, is from the realization of the elemental bargain implicit in life, that life involves death, which grows nearer as time passes and the characters dance their lives away in a vast choreographical pattern. The work has all the social glamour of *Brideshead Revisited*, and the emotional and class tensions of *The Jewel in the Crown*, but it has more. *A Dance to the Music of Time* has a glamorous surface quality and is not averse to social, aesthetic and sexual indulgence, but it is riddled right from the beginning with an awareness of the deeper and darker qualities of life. It encompasses all the high hopes we have when young.

> '...Parents... are sometimes a bit of a disappointment to their children. They don't fulfil the promise of their early years.'[1] and the increasing burden of sadness which accompanies growing older: 'Growing old is like being increasingly penalised for a crime you haven't committed.'[2]

It was one of many achievements to have given so considerable and all-embracing complex of narratives such a sense of shape. The first novel of the cycle, *A Question of Upbringing*, begins with a scene, which calls up for Nick Jenkins, the observer/narrator of the chronicle, the Poussin painting, where people move 'hand in hand in intricate measure: stepping slowly, methodically, sometimes a trifle awkwardly, in evolutions that recognisable shape.' The novel which concludes *A Dance to the Music of Time*, published over 20 years later, *Hearing Secret Harmonies*, closes with a sensitive reference to the same theme. David Thomas wrote about the television series that we could expect to see: '...an astonishing parade of vice and virtue, true love and emotional sadism, ruthless triumph and wretched failure. Important characters meet murderous or perverted ends. Families are bolstered by marriage and decimated by war. This is a yarn thats got rattle to spare.'[3] This complex shifting canvas is observed by Nicholas Jenkins, as first person narrator of the entire saga. And that is one of the major qualities of the work, the voyeur as storyteller. This might have proved a major stumbling block for the writer of the television drama series, but Hugh Whitmore came up with a cracker of an idea – writing the series so that it is the viewer who is the voyeur. As John Spurling commented:

> Not that Jenkins is merely an observer, since he is himself caught up in the whirl. However, his own private life excites him less than everyone else's. It is no accident that one of the climaxes of the sequence is the revelation that its pivotal character, the grotesquely inept but also power-hungry and ruthless Widmerpool, is a sexual voyeur. Jenkins is himself, of course, primarily a voyeur and *The Music of Time* is his account of a life spent puzzling over, laughing and wincing at, but always passionately savouring the sexual antics, power-ploys and survival techniques of others.[4]

There is one overwhelming, immortal character creation in this work, Widmerpool, a role brilliantly assumed by Simon Russell Beale in this production. Despite all the other qualities Powell gives him, there is something of Falstaff about Widmerpool, but also something of what *Just William* and *Billy Bunter* might have been if they had grown up to be Falstaff, with all the corrupting qualities which lie just beneath Falstaff's rolling, jolly exterior. As Martin Seymour-Smith puts it: 'He represents the bureaucratic rot that eats into decency like a corrosive acid, the concealed philistine, the Iago to society's confused Othello – represented by Powell through his characteristic filter of sad and resigned irony.'[5]

To bring this work to the screen and turning the viewer into voyeur was a major success in television drama terms. This works right from the beginning when we accompany Jenkins to the front door of a London house and he rings the bell. We see the door opened by a young lady, naked, except for slippers. And things never look back. Although there are moments when those who really know their Powell will recognize the sequence has been rejigged from time to time so as to accommodate the narrative to television, it should be conceded that this production has employed neither surgery nor butchery to those ends, and that there are many moments when Powell's intentions are

well realized, capturing the tone and style of the original perfectly –
such as Widmerpool's schoolboy running in the mist and Edward Fox
as Uncle Giles ever on the scrounge, Alan Bennett the definitive
Professor Sillery, Sir John Gielgud straight out of Powell's pages as
novelist St John Clarke and Miranda Richardson as Emma Flitton, a
mixture of lust and disgust.

BBC-1 countered this with the five part dramatisation of Henry
Fielding's masterpiece *Tom Jones* by Simon Burke, produced by Suzan
Harrison and directed by Metin Huseyin – who had certainly established his reputation as a dab hand at comedy after directing William
Ivory's dustbin-men comedy drama series *Common as Muck* (*Boys From
the Blackstuff* for the 1990s) for BBC-1 (1995–97). Inevitably, *Tom Jones*
was predictably bruited as a 'romp' and given the full 'Lock up your
daughters! Here comes Tom Jones' treatment on the cover of *Radio
Times*. Reluctant viewers were encouraged to expect something spicy.
They described Fielding's comic-epic rather recklessly as 'an 18th
century rake's progress' where 'the comic depiction of human nature
is free of the usual restraints of period drama.' Tom Jones (former rock-
band-drummer Max Beeseley) we are told is 'in love' with 'genteel'
Sophia (Samantha Morton) but 'in lust' with 'the more down to earth'
Molly Seagrim (Rachel Scorgie). This raises legitimate questions as to
the extent of the dramatisation's fidelity to the spirit and style of
Henry Fielding's novel. Tom is not a rake. A rake is a wholly selfish and
irresponsible man who regards all women as fair game. Fielding goes
to some trouble to show that Tom does have misgivings about his
behaviour, telling us that 'Though he did not always act rightly, yet he
never did otherwise without feeling and suffering for it.' Squire
Allworthy (Benjamin Witrow) says to him, when he learns how Tom
reacted to the news of his recovery during his illness: 'I am convinced,
my child, that you have much goodness, generosity, and honour in
your temper: if you will add prudence and religion to these, you must
be happy.'[6] In the Dedication Fielding says: 'I have endeavoured
strongly to inculcate, that virtue and innocence can scarce ever be
injured but by indiscretion; and ... it is this alone which often betrays
them into the snares which deceit and villainy spread for them.'

He is not writing farce. Fielding thought he was writing comic epic,
and went to great lengths in the introductory chapters to each book
into which he divided *Tom Jones*. He was trying to write a narrative
prose fiction comedy which paralleled the serious or high epic of
Homer. This is why he divided *Tom Jones* into twelve books, as
Homeric epic is divided. He is always present as narrator in *Tom Jones*,

playing the role of the declaiming Bard just as Homer does in reciting *The Iliad*. Fielding believed that epic, just as the drama, is divided into tragedy and comedy. For Fielding comic epic was in direct parallel to serious epic. Instead of gods, goddesses and high-born characters we had characters from every day life. Instead of wars, sieges, battles, we had rough and tumble, fights over cards, and fisticuffs. Instead of the death of heroes and the fall of empires, we have recognition, reconciliation, and marriage. But its function as literature was just as serious.[7] He was confident as the inventor of this kind of novel: 'I am in reality, the founder of a new province of writing, and am at liberty to make what laws I please therein...'[8] His contemporaries did not hesitate to compare his work with the greatest achievements of classical writers – Homer, Virgil, Milton.[9] To play *Tom Jones* entirely as a romp or sexy farce is wholly alien to the spirit of its author: 'I think it may reasonably be required of every writer, that he keeps within the bounds of possibility; and still remembers that what is not possible for man to perform, it is scarcely possible for man to believe he did perform.'[10]

Bearing in mind Fielding's basic assumptions about what he was trying to do makes so much about *Tom Jones* really clear. What could be more appropriate as an epic subject? Tom is a foundling, Squire Allworthy has no idea where he comes from, this is heroic archetype, heroes are frequently born in mysterious circumstances. He brings him up and Tom – like all heroes – is tested in a series of adventures, before his true heroic nature is revealed at the right time. All heroic lives follow this pattern and the hero reveals himself by deed, such as Arthur pulling the sword from the stone, or Siegfried drawing the sword from the tree. Yet, on the face of it, *Tom Jones* has many qualities which would make the task of televising it as drama straightforward if not easy. Fielding worked for years as a satiric playwright before his attacks on Walpole's government led to the muzzling of drama by the 1737 Licensing Act, when he then took up journalism and eventually novel writing. But he carried over into his fiction much of the expertise he had acquired writing for the stage. Much of this is obvious in the novels. The dialogue shows his mastery in putting words in his characters' mouths appropriate to their social station and whether they are country squires, men of the mode or ladies of fashion. He constructs sections of his plots so that threads of action come together as they would at the conclusions of acts in a play, and a long narrative ends with an elaborate denouement. Sequences of action in bedrooms, inn parlours, on the road and so on, are put together more or less as units, as might be found upon the stage, and within these units of action he devises sudden and unexpected appearances – such as Squire Western (Brian Blessed) bursting in at Lady Bellaston's (Lindsay Duncan) house at the moment of Lord Fellamar's (Peter Capaldi) attempt upon Sophia Western (Samantha Morton). The dialogue of this scene would move (as it did) more or less straight off the page and into the dramatisation.[11] And true to the spirit of the dramatic tradition, misunderstandings abound, as Fellamar assumes Western supports his proposals. Tom's discovering Square (Christopher Fulford) behind the hanging rug in Molly's bedroom shows the hand of the dramatist. Yet Fielding constantly prevents *Tom Jones* from lapsing into farce by his presence as narrator, which always keeps the ridiculous at a distance and deploys ironic undercutting, thereby anchoring the reader to the novelist's intentions. This production attempted to go some of the way towards representing Fielding as storyteller, having John Sessions making rather Brechtian appearances and attempt to unfold the storylines, but the temptation of treating this farcically could not be resisted and he was covered with mud by passing coaches, drenched with rain and so on.

Suzan Harrison, the producer, was asked how they could tackle Fielding's novel, which had been the subject of such a successful Tony Richardson film, with Albert Finney in the title role. She answered that this was very much a child of the 1960s: 'Our version for the nineties is very, very different. We are telling the Fielding book much more. Tom is totally led by his youthful libido. It's a simple, romantic story, but fantastically moral.'[12] This production of *Tom Jones* looked right, sounded right, and seemed reasonably faithful to the basic narrative, but it raised several fundamental questions. To what extent did it manifest real understanding of the eighteenth century classic text on which it was based? And the rejoinder to this question – is such fidelity really necessary? The aim of the novelist is fairly clear – to explore the impact of society on a plain and straightforward human being. This much is obvious the moment one starts to ponder the purpose of the character of Blifil in the novel. There is obviously some purpose in the contrast between Tom and Blifil. The novelist shows us that human nature is careless, often thoughtless, impulsive and given to pleasure, yet capable of affection, loyalty and endurance, with the capacity to develop a moral perspective given time and experience. Man is not basically wicked. He shows us Tom staggering from one escapade to another, yet ever striving towards betterment. Blifil, (James D'Arcy) by contrast, has all the veneer and outward show of decorum, good breeding, manners and politesse. Tom is honest. Blifil is treacherous. Here Fielding is writing in a long eighteenth century tradition also manifest in the *De Coverley Papers*, Oliver Goldsmith,[13] Laurence Sterne, especially *A Sentimental Journey*[14] which continues to Washington Irving and even possibly Jean Paul Richter.[15] The echo of these ideas may be discovered in *Pickwick Papers*, and certainly animate the idyll of Christmas at Dingley Dell. Behind the sentimental writing is the strongly held belief that such generosity and goodwill to all men were not exclusively the result of Christian conditioning, but were the natural inclination of humanity uncorrupted by the teachings of the mammonism and vanities of the modern world. This is central to the way Fielding viewed the world and portrayed it in *Tom Jones*. This is why *Tom Jones* is divided into three main parts – the country (the Allworthy and Western estates), the road (with the brilliantly staged action at the inn at Upton) and finally the metropolis, which gives a panoramic sweep of Hanoverian England. Each of the twelve books is prefaced with a chapter in which Fielding appears as master of ceremonies, and explains the whys and wherefores of the novel, giving shrewd insights into character and situation, and justifying the kind of work he offered. Much of this has perforce been sacrificed in making *Tom Jones* 'for the nineties', for the loss of which knockabout and nudity is scarcely much by way of compensation. There was a feeling about this production of secretly being rather pleased with itself, which almost compelled one to ask, what is so special about the 1990s, that literary masterpieces should be so recycled as to be suitably spooned down its spoiled throat? And to what extent can it be argued that such productions continue the classic serial tradition, which traditionally averred its fidelity to the original?

But nevertheless, it had to admitted, the production looked very good, with Mapperton House, home of the Earl of Sandwich, near Beaminster in Dorset, as one of the splendid locations. There was some virtuoso acting, most notably Brian Blessed as a stentorian Squire Western and Samantha Morton certainly delivering the goods as Sophia. The comic characters – in particular Kathy Burke as Honour – were well cast. as All in all, BBC-1's *Tom Jones* was splendid television drama, and worked at its level, but it lacked the bigness of heart and the simple majesty of Fielding's great novel. Any television viewers prompted by the series to read Fielding's novel would be pleasantly surprised. Yet, despite such possibly Leavisite misgivings, it has to be admitted that BBC-1's *Tom Jones* has been among the top earning classic novel dramatisations – realizing £620 300 – almost doubling what *The Tenant of Wildfell Hall*, *Martin Chuzzlewit* and *The Buccaneers* have brought to the BBC, and almost equalling *Nostromo*.[16]

In December 1998 BBC television attempted to duplicate the previous season's success with Wilkie Collins, with the serial dramatisation of *The Woman in White*. It was dramatised in two 90-minute episodes by David Pirie, produced by Gareth Neame and directed by Tim Fywell. It should be ideal for television. The famous opening was supposedly based on fact. Wilkie Collins was walking one evening when he heard a young woman scream and next saw a female figure in flowing white, running from a large house. He went to help her and she told him that she had been held a prisoner there in a hypnotised state for several years. She was soon Collins's mistress and he used her story as the basis for *The Woman in White*. The novel opens at dead of night as a young man (Walter Hartright, a drawing master, played by Andrew Lincoln) walks down a moonlit road. He is suddenly touched on the shoulder by a woman dressed all in white, this is Anne Catherick (Susan Vidler) who is to change his life forever. She bears a striking resemblance to Laura Fairlie (Justine Waddell), the daughter of Hartright's employer (Ian Richardson). Walter has been engaged to teach Fairlie's niece, Laura and her half-sister, Marian Holcombe. Walter falls in love with Laura, and leaves England in desolation when she marries Sir Perceval Glyde of Blackwater Park (James Wilbey). Glyde has a cunning plan. He is after Laura's fortune, and intends to get her to sign a document transferring everything to him, and then to get her confined in a lunatic asylum as Anne Catherick, who has conveniently died – and buried as Lady Glyde. In these dreadful plans he is aided and abetted by his sinister friend, the fat, smooth Count Fosco (Simon Callow). Sir Perceval Glyde will stand to gain her wealth. Walter unravels these machinations with the help of Marian Holcombe and even exposes the fact that Glyde has no right to the title as he was born out of wedlock. To substantiate his claims Glyde attempts to forge documents in the parish register but he is killed in a fire at the church. Anne Catherick was Laura's half-sister. Fosco, in Collins's version of the story, is compelled to provide much of the information which incriminates Glyde, and is himself in turn murdered by members of an Italian secret fraternity which he has also betrayed. Walter and Laura are married.

The BBC has broadcast several outstanding radio versions of this quintessentially Collins performance. Bearing in mind the fool-proof quality of the original, it was surprising this BBC/Carlton production, with WGBH Boston for Mobil Masterpiece Theatre was the disappointment it undoubtedly was. Such a gothic yarn stands or falls by its atmosphere, and although this had its moments – the chase at night with dogs and torches, the sinister dripping fountain, the scene in the grotto and the spooky music by David Ferguson – several key performances were underplayed and there was rather too much sunshine. Sunshine and playful children should be reserved for the end, when this terrible mystery has been resolved. There was room for more melodrama in several of the leading characters. Fairlie is described by Collins as a valetudinarian, a professional invalid, and he could have been far more whinging and self-indulgently sensitive; Ian Richardson did little more than make a retired Oxbridge don of him. Glyde was scarcely darkly villainous enough, coming across as more the golf club bounder than the wicked and destructive demon Collins created. Remember, Collins said of him that he would hesitate at nothing to save himself. Did we believe that of this Glyde? Lumbering James Wilbey with the additional vice of child abuse (not mentioned in Collins novel) as a concession to 1990s media obsessions failed in its attempt to make more of a baddie out of him, as no evidence or suspicion of this was planted in the drama we watched. And Fosco – what a chance blown away! Count Fosco is your actual sinister Italian poisoner, where was that sense of calm malevolence? 'Vast perspectives of success unroll themselves before my eyes. I accomplish my destiny with a calmness which is terrible to myself' he says. Did he make your blood run cold? He should have had at least a foreign accent. After all, he is a member of an Italian secret society, with all that implies. (Though that was not mentioned in this version.) And what ever had happened to his canaries? Over and above all that, this version simply lacked excitement and it lacked fear. We should have jumped out of our seats the minute Anne Catherick placed her chilling hand on Walter's shoulder. There were some good performances in minor roles – Kika Markham as Madame Fosco, John Standing as Gilmore and Corin Redgrave as Dr Kidson, but the powerful and constant performance of Tara Fitzgerald as Marian Holcombe almost makes up for shortcomings elsewhere. It was her ability to bear up and give strength to others which held several parts of this torturing narrative together and led to Glyde's final unmasking. Tara Fitzgerald was the quiet eye at the centre of this mortal storm.

In March 1998 BBC-2 transmitted Sandy Welch's dramatisation of Dickens's *Our Mutual Friend*, which was to win no less than four BAFTA Awards, including Best Drama Serial. It was produced in association with Canadian Broadcasting, by Catherine Wearing and directed by Julian Farino. This was the last novel Dickens lived to complete; *The*

Mystery of Edwin Drood was unfinished at his death in June 1870. Dickens was influenced by his friendship with Wilkie Collins. It is interesting that Sandy Welch came to *Our Mutual Friend* with a reputation established by previous television dramatisations of Barbara Vine, a writer celebrated for complex psychological mystery novels. Collins and Dickens met in 1851 when Collins acted with him in Bulwer Lytton's *Not So Bad as We Seem*. They later collaborated on the melodrama *The Frozen Deep* (in which Dickens starred). Collins joined the staff of his journal *Household Words* and they collaborated on several stories. His novels *The Moonstone* and *The Woman in White* were serialised in Dickens's *All the Year Round*. Collins responded to his tutelage and in turn probably influenced Dickens, turning his inclinations towards complicated melodramatic mystery novels. *The Mystery of Edwin Drood* bears strong evidence, even in its truncated form, of Wilkie Collins's style – lookalikes, rugs, mistaken identities, treachery and murder – and *Our Mutual Friend* similarly has several elements reminiscent of Collins.[17]

The opening of the drama was wonderfully atmospheric, recapturing exactly the stagey qualities which Marcus Stone, the original illustrator, brought to the novel. Gaffer Hexham (David Schofield) and his daughter Lizzie (Keeley Hawes) salvage a corpse from the Thames. At the Veneerings' society dinner it is rumoured that John Harmon, heir to a vast fortune obtained from dustheaps, has been found drowned. Eugene Wrayburn, a disillusioned young lawyer (Paul McGann) and Mortimer Lightwood (Dominic Mafham) leave to go and see the body. Noddy Boffin (Peter Vaughan), loyal clerk to old Harmon, who achieved vast wealth from salvaging dustheaps, will inherit the Harmon fortune. Determined to benefit from his change of fortune, Boffin hires the rascally Silas Wegg (Kenneth Cranham) to read to him, and John Rokesmith (really young Harmon in disguise) as his secretary (Steven Mackintosh). Boffin and his wife (Pam Ferris) invite Bella Wilfer, (Anna Friel) who has been betrothed to John since childhood, to live with them. Young Harmon is able to see Bella in her true colours – she is obsessed with money – and Boffin, by pretending to turn into a miser, is able to cure Bella of her avarice. Wegg and Nicodemus Venus, a taxidermist, (Timothy Spall) conspire to deprive Boffin of his money but fail. This set up is one of the two major elements of the plot. The other element is the rivalry for Lizzie Hexham between Wrayburn and the psychologically obsessive schoolmaster, Bradley Headstone (David Morrissey). Headstone, disguising himself as the riverside scavenger, Riderhood, attempts to kill

Wrayburn, and leaves him for dead but he is saved from the river by Lizzie. Riderhood (David Bradley) realizes that Headstone attempted to incriminate him and they fight. Both are drowned. The novel ends with revealed identities, forgiveness, reconciliation.

This version tended rather to emphasize the murder mystery and curious psychological overtones of the novel and play down the satirical anti-materialistic themes. It was very strong on the Harmon murder, the mystery of the river, and the dark and disturbing psychology at work in such characters as Eugene Wrayburn and Bradley Headstone. Catherine Wearing, the producer, whose two favourite novelists are Dickens and Dostoyevsky, delivered *Our Mutual Friend* with a powerful, unifying sense of style, the result of very close team work. She says: 'It's a collaborative effort. But for me there were three key people in this show – it was me, the writer and the director. We were the heart of why it was the way it was.' She describes herself as:

'....a facilitator. I'm a bringer together of people. I think you have to have a sense of vision of what you're trying to do. For me it came working with Sandy on the scripts. She was so extraordinary. Her way of talking about this book, so much of that, has kind of passed by some magic osmosis from her to me. That came out of the fact that for a year it was just me and her working on the scripts together. Then we found Julian and he got a lot of that instinctively. Then the three of us had a couple of months whereby we did the final draft of the script. That's when we gelled as a trio. I think that the most important thing is that the writer, the director and the producer are all three talking about the same thing. We always had a very, very clear sense of what we were trying to achieve and then everyone we then brought on board, it was purely on the grounds of whether we felt they were going to achieve that and more. I don't pretend that I foresaw everything that ended up on the screen. But enough of it was there initially to get the right people in place and then allow the magic to happen, which is when people start bringing their own expertise and brilliance, and obviously informed the casting as well.... The actual role of the producer is much more subtle than just being the 'boss'. Obviously, you employ a director because you admire their kind of vision and then your job becomes about trying to make everyone work to enhance the director's vision of the piece, and also to make sure that he or she is free to work with the actors while the shooting is going on, and you're sorting out all the practical odds and ends and nightmares. But the producer is the person who basically answers not just the 'who' questions, or the 'how' questions, but the 'what are we making' questions and that's why I'm a producer. Because you commission the script and have ideas. Of course the producer is the person who also has to bring it in on budget, so there's that whole side to it, and also sell the thing – publicity is very much a producer's remit, and selling it abroad and the rest of it...'[18]

What this production achieved was a noticeably heavy, labouring, late-Victorian quality, partly the result of costumes, locations and lighting, but also the result of deliberate, almost ponderous acting and (unusual for television drama) quite long scenes – sometimes running to between five and eight minutes. This effect was certainly assisted by the serialization in four 90-minute episodes, which allowed the pace to settle down comfortably, and each sequence space to establish itself and to breathe at its own rate. As Catherine Wearing says, in some ways this is to revert to an older style of television drama, but here it works: '...it's dead old fashioned. Television used to be like that before the cop shows took over. Then you could only have a scene that's thirty seconds maximum. That's the kind of MTV culture. But television used to have a manner where you could stay with characters and explore things and I think that Dickens more or less dictates what he wants to do with his characters, because of this respect for characters. That's why we have long scenes. What we are aiming at is some kind of emotional reality, using various ways of shooting, using steadicams and moving cameras, not framing everything classically, seeking a kind of energy in film making which will feel very modern and not perioditis, if you know what I mean...'.

What particularly draws her to Dickens is his range and

his extraordinary sense of the imagination involved in life as it is actually lived, rather than we would like it to be...he seems to detect an emotional and imaginative charge in life more than other writers. Sometimes he presents that comically and sometimes he presents that melodramatically and sometimes both at the same time. That is just so extraordinary. Because he saw so sharply, with such immediacy, he had this extraordinary respect for the kind of basic humanity of every single character, however large or small, that he's writing about. I mean every single one of them has a soul that they can lose. That puts him head and shoulders above most writers. I love that, because it just opens up so many possibilities and doors. Because he's such an acute dramatist as well, you never met his characters before you need to and it's always at the perfect dramatic time. I think he is extraordinary.[19]

The mood of this production was evoked from the very dark opening sequence of Hexham and Lizzie scavenging those murky waters of the Thames in the moonlight. The river in *Our Mutual Friend*, the source both of life and death, busy with commercial traffic, a source of livelihood to scavengers, a place where treasures lie hidden and death constantly preys. It is the thread on which the narrative is suspended and connected. Hexham responds to Lizzie's misgivings by pointing out she owes everything to the river. She was born by it. The fire that kept her warm as a baby was made from driftwood from the Thames. Her cradle was made from wood washed ashore by the tide. The river and riverside buildings and dwellings, the sinister almost threatening nature of the Thames, that telling metaphor of life, death, human sewage, were all impressively recreated by production designer Malcolm Thornton and his team by tidal waters near Cardiff. He admits studying David Lean's *Great Expectations* and *Oliver Twist* for their 'visual economy' but also drawing inspiration from Gustave Dore, Victorian photographs and the illustrations to Henry Mayhew's *London Labour* and *London Poor*. The society scenes, so greatly admired during recent decades by literary critics, are greatly reduced, and Sandy Welch uses one or two in each episode, working as a kind of chorus to the rest of the action, pointing up the great divide between the haves and the have-nots. Some may regret the loss of the immortal Podsnap, but, as Chesterton remarked, 'Mr Podsnap is a commercial man having no great connection with the plot'.[20] The lunar landscape of the dustheaps was vividly created in a disused quarry near Merthyr Tydfil. The theme of the life amid the debris of the dead is additionally echoed in Mr Venus and his virtuosity in stuffing the skins and articulating the bones of the dead. His workshop is chillingly recreated here. The paradoxes that rubbish is wealth, that death yields life, hold the complexities of the plot together.

Our Mutual Friend was one of the most thoughtful and original versions of a Dickens novel screened on television. Later that same spring the commercial channel screened Thomas Hardy's *Tess of the d'Urbervilles*. *Tess of the d'Urbervilles* was written, so Hardy claimed, to shield 'those who have yet to be born' from misfortunes like those of Tess, and plans for the novel were begun as early as the autumn of 1888.[21] Just over half the novel was accepted by the newspaper syndicate of Tillotson & Son for publication under the title of 'Too Late Beloved' (or 'Too Late, Beloved'), but when the first sixteen chapters reached proof stage in September 1889, serious objections were raised by the editors at Tillotson and the agreement was finally cancelled at Hardy's request.[22] The story was then declined by the editors of *Murray's Magazine* and also by *Macmillan's Magazine*.[23] By about the end of 1890, the novel was ready for serial publication in *The Graphic* and *Harper's Bazaar*, but it was not until March the following year that Hardy finished the novel. Of the various changes Hardy made to make the novel suitable for serial publication, (this included the loss of the baptism scene)[24] the most notorious is probably that involving Angel's use of a wheelbarrow to carry the three dairymaids in turn over the flooded road – such close physical proximity obviously proving too much for the editors of the day. Ted Whitehead, who adapted the novel for Meridian in 1998, had no such qualms, allowing his Angel to indulge in the closeness Hardy had originally intended for him and before the editors had stepped in. Justine Waddell turns in a superb performance as Tess, whom we see in the process of changing (and of being changed) 'from simple girl to complex woman',[25] and the dramatisation was something of a high-water mark for Hardy enthusiasts.[26]

Tess of the d'Urbervilles tells an age-old story: that of a woman's sufferings in a society whose attitudes towards sex and women have condemned her. As in *Far From the Madding Crowd*, what is at the heart of the novel is a conflict between instinctive behaviour and the social dictates which restrict behaviour – a notion which is brilliantly conveyed by this dramatisation. It is how Hardy presents this simple story which gives the novel its unique fascination; the complexity of characterisation and of theme belying the apparent simplicity of the story itself. That Tess is a victim throughout is underlined by the sub-title Hardy gave the novel: *A Pure Woman* – which makes Hardy's attitude to Tess clear from the outset. And, as in all Hardy's novels, there is the same, fundamental tension between nature and society. A conflict between, for example, the natural love Tess and Angel feel for each other, and the social attitudes which, in Angel's eyes, make Tess a fallen woman. When Angel declares to himself, upon seeing Tess in the fields, 'What a pure and virginal daughter of Nature that milkmaid is!'(p.176) he is summarising the tension precisely: any 'virginal daughter' does not remain long a virgin in Nature, which is an attitude of the social world, not the natural. One of the central issues in the novel was the moral effect of the new impinging upon the old, and this is subtly introduced by the television version in ways which are both unobtrusive yet effective. To Hardy, this issue found a focus in the great de-population of the Dorset villages which went on throughout the tail-end of the nineteenth century: 'the process, humorously designated by statisticians as "the tendency of the rural population towards the large towns", being really the tendency of water to flow uphill when forced by machinery'. (p. 436) Indeed, in *Tess of the d'Urbervilles*, the consequences of the great de-population take a front seat: John Durbeyfield is a poor, struggling farmer, a man dispossessed of his once great family, and of almost any means of sustenance: when the horse, Prince, is killed, the single remaining means of maintaining his family dies with it, and it is this 'spilling of blood', with the death of Prince, which leads Tess to agree to go to the d'Urberville house, which in turn leads to the loss of her virginity, social condemnation and the final, symbolic spilling of Alec's blood when he is stabbed by Tess. This whole notion of raping and the symbolic spilling of blood is handled with extreme dexterity in the dramatisation: we have images of church spires (linking to Angel also, of course), an ancient workman sharpening a scythe by the roadside, Tess's pricking of her lip with a rose-thorn, all of which serve to underscore what leads to Tess's downfall and the final stabbing of Alec by Tess.

But this is a moral issue also, the conflict between the old and the new bring two quite different worlds into juxtaposition. This is presented in the television production with a careful blending of scenes, images, music and diegetic sound which evoke precisely this moral tension. The dramatisation opens with a scene in which the three brothers wander aimlessly into the old world, where a group of maidens are dancing to the sound of rural music, waiting for their beaux to finish work and to join them. Angel wishes to stay and to join in with the country dancing, but the two brothers are concerned that they 'may be seen by somebody' so go on ahead. In a superb televisual moment, Angel eventually leaves the dance in order to catch up with his two brothers. In the background a church bell is tolling, significantly, as it were, calling Angel back to the prejudices of established religion: 'this advanced and well-meaning young man, a sample product of the last five-and-twenty years, was yet the slave to custom and conventionality when surprised back into his early teachings'. (p. 338) And Tess is trapped between these two worlds: Tess, 'who might have been a teacher, but the Fates had decided otherwise' (p. 58), had passed the Sixth Standard at the National School, where she had learned to speak 'correct' English, and has this conflict in her character throughout. On the one hand, 'she spoke dialect at home', while on the other, 'ordinary English abroad and to persons of quality'. (p. 58). Tess, quite literally 'spoke two languages' (p. 58), and this is symbolic of how she is transitionally poised between the two worlds of the old, rural, agricultural community, and the new, social world, which is draining the life out of the old: 'Between the mother, with her fast-perishing lumber of superstitions... and the daughter, with her trained National Teachings... there was a gap of two hundred years as ordinarily understood. When they were together, the Jacobean and the Victorian ages were juxtaposed.' (p. 61) When Tess is herself sent off to make her fortune in this new Victorian age with the family of incomers, the Stokes, who have bought the family name of d'Urberville, the tragedy of the past confronting the present must inevitably follow, and it is a conflict which is perfectly captured by every aspect of this television production, from the whimsical, haunting melodies of composer, Alan Lisk to the studied yet unobtrusive camera-work (director of photography, Richard Greatrex and film editor, Peter Davies). It is a superb rendering of the novel in all respects, never once losing sight of the interests of the original, and the brave use of a narrator (Gerald James) in voice-over to introduce significant moments, serves to guide the production as if through the turning pages of the novel itself.

In April 1998 the commercial channel transmitted Neil McKay's dramatisation of Emily Brontë's *Wuthering Heights*, a LWT/WGBH Boston production, produced by Louise Berridge, and directed by David Skynner. *Wuthering Heights* is a unique masterpiece of English romanticism and should thrive on television. A story of passions elemental in their power to elevate as well as destroy, it seems to emerge naturally from the wild and abandoned Yorkshire landscape in which Emily Brontë conceived it. (Think how this might have been realized by modern television!) Emily Brontë here presents various crises in human relationships – irrepressible violent love, unyielding attachment, ruthless vengeance – passions which seem to exist in a primeval world, beyond human time and space, which are nevertheless recognizably human. As her sister Charlotte wrote of this novel:

In Emily's nature the extremes of vigour and simplicity seemed to meet. Under an unsophisticated culture, inartificial tastes, and an unpretending outside lay a secret power and fire that might have informed the brains and kindled the veins of a hero.... An interpreter ought always to have stood between her and the world....

Dante Gabriel Rossetti commenting on *Wuthering Heights'* 'power' and 'sound style' said the action 'is laid in hell, only it seems places and people have English names there...'. There were times during this television version when one wondered if this was based on the same book, or some other novel which unaccountably bore the same name. It had plenty of fog, drystone walls and blustering weather, but there was something curiously phoney about it. It had a strange Blarney about it, a sanitised Didicoi feel wholly at odds with Emily Brontë's wild vision.

The plot outline is simple, but in *Wuthering Heights* emotion and atmosphere are vastly more important than storyline. Heathcliff is a strange, dark-skinned boy, whom Cathy's father brings back to Wuthering Heights from a trip to Liverpool. He is adopted into the Earnshaw family. Cathy admires his self-sufficiency and endurance but he is systematically victimised by Cathy's brother, Hindley. Cathy and Heathcliff develop an ideal, inseparable partnership. But she mistakenly marries Edgar Linton, the sophisticated worldly young neighbouring landowner of Thrushcross Grange. In her heart, she acknowledges her error:

> If all else perished, and he remained, I should still continue to be; and if all else remained, and he were annihilated, the universe would turn to a mighty stranger. I should not seem a part of it. My love for Linton is like the foliage in the woods; time will change it...as winter changes the trees. My love for Heathcliff resembles the eternal rocks beneath....

The major theme of the novel is the terrible tension between the two worlds – the stormy, wild, emotional and passionate dimension of life represented by Wuthering Heights, and the rational, civilised world of Thrushcross Grange. Heathcliff avenges himself by causing Edgar's sister, Isabella, to fall in love with him, and elope to Wuthering Heights. Cathy and Heathcliff are only reconciled at her death after giving birth to Linton's daughter, Cathy Linton. At the moment of her death, Heathcliff calls upon Cathy's ghost to haunt him forever. Heathcliff pursues his vengeance unto the next generation, contriving the marriage of his son by Isabella with Catherine's daughter by Edgar Linton. His sickly son dies but the young Catherine now controls both Wuthering Heights and Thrushcross Grange. Heathcliff, sated with the ire that has motivated him for so long, sickens and dies, joining his beloved Cathy Earnshaw in a world beyond this one. Little of the violent mythic stuff came across at all in this toothless effort, in which Robert Cavanah, Orla Brady, Tom Georgeson and Polly Hemingway starred.

In July ITV transmitted Philomena McDonagh's four part dramatization of Thomas Hardy's *Far From the Madding Crowd*, produced by Hilary Bevan-Jones and directed by Nicholas Renton.[27] The BBC had only recently shown John Schlesinger's 1968 film (starring Julie Christie and Alan Bates) but the differences were marked, as we shall see. Hilary Bevan-Jones hoped that her production would have 'all the production values but without being glossy. We tried to think "story" rather than "costume drama" because we didn't want to get too distracted by the frocks and scenery.'[28] She was ably backed by her director, who said: 'Obviously you want to make the landscape in which these people live absolutely realistic, but then just lighting a room by fire and candlelight makes it look very different to a contemporary room. But if you watch a really good John Ford western, for example, while you might be aware of the scenery, it's the story that pulls you in.'[29] And Philomena McDonagh certainly does make the story her own, with numerous additions and alterations, presumably to aid the progression of the narrative. For example, in the novel, when Bathsheba's uncle dies, leaving her the farm, we are simply told this has happened. In McDonagh's dramatisation, a number of scenes are added, with doctors, servants, farm workers, sets, the whole paraphernalia – all designed to impart this simple piece of narrative by showing it to us. It may be argued that this is indicative of the difference between the grammar of novelistic storytelling and the grammar of visual storytelling, but is is difficult to see quite where such an approach to dramatisation will end: if a bird is described as singing in the hedgerow, we would presumably have been shown a particular bird singing a particular song in a particular hedgerow – which does seem to defeat Hilary Bevan's claim that the production team 'didn't want to get too distracted by the frocks and scenery.' In the event, and although this production does make good television, it is not a very good dramatisation of the novel. The reason for this is that, as shown, the focus of the production has been shifted away from the novel to accommodate it to the visual. This can be best illustrated by giving some thought to the novel itself.

Far from the Madding Crowd (1874) was the first novel in which Hardy used the setting of 'Wessex', a setting which rapidly asserted itself as a quasi-real place, with its own history, places and personages.[30] The fictional reality of the novel is a simple one, telling a simple story of simple lives in simple rural England, with plenty of opportunities for period costume, Barsetshire accents and ritualised ale-swilling. However, it is also clear that Hardy himself did not conceive of the novel as a piece of historical hokum:[31] the title is an ironic invocation of Gray's 'Elegy Written in a Country Churchyard' (ixx), 1750:

> Far from the madding crowd's ignoble strife
> Their sober wishes never learned to stray;
> Along the cool sequestred vale of life
> They kept the noiseless tenor of their way.

That Hardy's use of Gray's phrasing and sentiment is ironic appears indisputable, but we need to consider the details of the story to see how and where. Bathsheba Everdene refuses an offer of marriage from a small local sheep-farmer, Gabriel Oak, inherits her father's farm and takes over as its owner. In the meantime, Oak's hopes have been dashed by the loss of his flock, and of his farm, and he eventually finds employment on Bathsheba's farm. Bathsheba foolishly sends a valentine card to a middle-aged farmer, Boldwood, and he, believing her to be in love with him, is similarly smitten by her. Bathsheba herself is then swept off her feet by the dashing, sword-swinging and moustachio'd Sergeant Troy, who has deserted Fanny Robin, the mother of his illegitimate child. When Fanny Robin dies in childbirth, and the truth about Troy and Fanny comes to light, he deserts Bathsheba, making it appear that he has drowned. This gives Boldwood hope, and he eventually extracts a promise from Bathsheba that she will marry him after seven years have elapsed. On the night that Boldwood plans to announce to the world his engagement to the captivating Bathsheba, Troy reappears on the scene, ruining Boldwood's hopes forever. Boldwood shoots him, is arrested, and confined as criminally insane. With Troy now dead, Gabriel Oak, who has remained loyal to Bathsheba throughout, announces that he plans to leave the country for California. Bathsheba agrees to marry him, if he will stay, and the novel ends with their marriage, surrounded by the chorus of rural folk who have accompanied them throughout the novel.

Looking back over the outline of the story, it is easy to see Hardy's irony: this is no rural idyll. Hardy's novel, and although it may apparently be set far from the madding crowd's ignoble strife, with its bunch of rustic simpletons and simple rituals, customs and habits, it actually tells a tale which is of a much darker and more dangerous nature also; a tale in which characters are at the mercy of almost uncontrollable passions, instincts and forces, both in themselves, and in nature. This is a story in which an innocent and pregnant woman is left by her seducer to die in the workhouse, a story in which one man is financially ruined, another is murdered, and another confined for life as a madman. Paradoxically, therefore, and while it *is* easy to see Hardy's ironic use of the 'Elegy', there is a very real sense in which Hardy captures something of Gray's philosophical predicament also; simple renunciation of the great, wide world is not enough, for 'from the tomb the voice of nature cries' (Elegy, xxiii) – a sentiment which is echoed in the novel by Troy, to Bathsheba, standing beside Fanny's open coffin: 'This woman is more to me, dead as she is, than ever you were, or are, or can be.... You are nothing to me – nothing... A ceremony before a priest doesn't make a marriage. I am not morally yours.' (pp. 352–3) As ever in Hardy, things are not as simple as they may at first appear. The question is whether the film maker – whose language and grammar is of the descriptive and the visual – can hold the complexity of Hardy's novelistic enterprise together, a complexity which is concerned not just with the presentation of visual *content*, but with the complexity of artistic *form*, also.

In the broadest critical sweep of Hardy's novels, it can be said that their fundamental pattern is that they will contain a character who is a rebel – characters like Bathsheba, Eustacia and Clym in *Return of the Native*, Henchard in the *Mayor of Casterbridge*, Tess, Jude and Sue – and in conflict with the world in which they find themselves. These characters can generally see the value of conformity, but some trait in their personality makes it ultimately impossible for them ever to conform. Their instinctive, natural and human response to others and to situations is at odds with the orderliness of society. This is paralleled by nature itself – the landscape, the weather – which appears indifferent to the plight in which human beings find themselves; sometimes, nature may be not only indifferent, but almost apparently wilfully destructive of all humanity's attempts to scrape a subsistence or to try to create meaning and pattern in the physical world. This fundamental conflict or tension in a Hardy novel – that between society and order on the one hand, and the instinctive unruliness of human behaviour on the other – is certainly evident in *Far from the Madding Crowd*, the novel, but much less so in McDonagh's dramatisation of it. This is best illustrated by looking for a moment at the opening few sequences to the dramatisation, which foreshadow the themes of the production as a whole.

The opening shot is of a sheep auction, with bids taking place loudly, and Oak bidding fifty shillings for a number of lambs. He is then asked by an old man whether he has borrowed to make the purchase. 'Up to here', Oak replies, indicating his forehead. We then cut to a troup of scarlet cavalry officers, focusing in on one (who later turns out to be Troy), with a young woman (who later turns out to be Fanny) trying still to hold lovingly onto his boots as he rides away. The focus of the novel has obviously shifted; while Hardy's novel is thematically focused on the fundamental conflict or tension between society and order on the one hand, and the instinctive unruliness of human behaviour on the other, McDonagh has shifted this to a concentration on money on the one hand (the auction and Oak's borrowing of money) and sex on the other (the cavalry soldiers, Troy, and Fanny Robin). It is interesting to note, for example, that the lamb (which in the novel symbolises the tension between nature on the one hand and the attempt to domesticate it on the other) has become associated only with money in McDonagh's dramatisation. This is part of the *'Pride and Prejudice* effect': taking her cue undoubtedly from Sue Birtwhistle, who, it will be recalled, wanted *Pride and Prejudice* to focus on sex and money. She even goes so far as to create a scene at the end of the dramatisation in which we learn that Oak is to be made a partner in Boldwood's farm. This simply does not happen in the novel, it is sheer invention and not at all in keeping with the nature of the relationship in the novel between Oak and Boldwood. But the power that the money would bring Oak makes him more sexy to Bathsheba – and, more importantly, perhaps, more sexy to this new viewing audience, the one created by the *'Pride and Prejudice* factor'. This is a serious misreading, even misrepresentation of the novel: while *Pride and Prejudice is* arguably about sex and money (or marriage and money at least), *Far from the Madding Crowd* is not. Good television, perhaps. But not very good Hardy.

BBC-1's autumn treat was Andrew Davies's dramatization of Thackeray's masterpiece, *Vanity Fair*. It is interesting that just as the revival of television costume drama and classic serials should be at its height, *Vanity Fair* should be chosen to show off the BBC's capacity in the genre, just as it was chosen to launch the advent of BBC colour television three decades ago. *Radio Times* went overboard in its efforts to establish this as an adaptation 'for the nineties' drawing on the groundswell of enthusiasm for the Spice Girls and featuring it as 'girl power' and assuring readers that although it was 'a polite costume drama of the old school' nevertheless it had an 'anti-heroine' in Becky Sharp – 'a startlingly modern woman who knows exactly what she wants and how to get it, and who is as shocking today as she was 150 years ago.'[32] Although much of this may be put down to hype, there was an element of this from the very earliest stages of the series. There is such a wealth of fine material to choose in Thackeray's wide ranging, dramatic fiction – why not *Pendennis*, or *Henry Esmond*, or *The Newcomes* – all of them rich, colourful, potentially exciting material for the television dramatist? Andrew Davies admitted that he found it difficult to comment on why it was chosen: '....because it is the only Thackeray novel I have read. I particularly like its cynical but compassionate tone, its double-heroine plot construction, the extraordinary, unique, Becky Sharp, the huge sweep of it, and also its parallels with our own glittering and tawdry world. I think it's very funny, too.'[33]

Current BBC budgetary policy combined with market factors affect the commissioning and treatment of television production. Andrew Davies commented:

> These days more and more decisions are taken at the top (i.e. Controller of BBC-1) and interestingly enough, the idea of doing *Vanity Fair* was popular from the start. It's a novel that everyone has heard of (though some people think it's a magazine) and most people have got a vague notion that Becky Sharp is a great character with some naughtiness and notoriety attached to her, like Moll Flanders. It was earmarked for BBC-1 from the start, which means these days that it is supposed to be popular, not just worthy.[34]

Vanity Fair cost nearly a £1 million an episode and initially failed to get the kind of prime time Sunday evening ratings the Corporation had hoped so it was rescheduled to 9.30 p.m. Even so its reception was mixed.[35] But there are important lessons here. Critical reception may have been mixed, the broadsheet papers in particular were reluctant to go overboard and ratings were modest, but international sales have been staggering. By May 1999, scarcely six months after its original British transmission, *Vanity Fair* had earned the Corporation £1 270 645.[36]

Vanity Fair was a co-production with two US subscription channels who are interested in classic novel dramatisations, A&E New York and WGBH Boston, and Andrew Davies believes they attract discriminating audiences and that their executives seek good, sound products: '...they tend to like the originals, and they like faithful adaptations – their influence is benign and helpful. But, I guess they'd find it easier to market *Vanity Fair* than a lesser known novel'.[37]

There seem, then, to have been two fairly strong influences shaping this production of *Vanity Fair*. There was a commercial willingness to fund a fairly well-known Victorian novel, which people had more or less heard of – even if they haven't read – and the fact that Becky seemed a reasonable candidate to launch as a heroine 'for the nineties'. The reputation of *Vanity Fair* is something which cannot be argued with, even though its apparent eclipse of his other novels is unfortunate and unjust, but Becky's resurrection as a prototypical representative of 'girl power' is open to serious question. Her enterprise is not fuelled by any ideological thrust but simply social climbing, admittedly against considerable and unjust odds. Set in Regency times the novel opens with two friends, Becky (Natasha Little) and Amelia (Frances Grey), leaving Miss Pinkerton's Academy. Becky is the orphaned daughter of a French opera girl and a British painter, who survived because she could teach good French. Amelia is the well brought up daughter of a successful London businessman. Becky soon has designs on Amelia's brother, fat, shy, Joseph Sedley (Jeremy Swift), a thriving servant of the British East India Company. A party to Vauxhall Gardens is planned with Amelia's admirer George Osborne (Tom Ward), his fellow officer William Dobbin, who secretly loves Amelia (Philip Glenister). Her machinations are scuppered when Joseph gets drunk, makes a fool of himself and makes his escape back to India. Becky then takes up her post as governess at the household of coarse and scruffy Sir Pitt Crawley (David Bradley). Becky decides to make up to Sir Pitt and Miss Crawley, the family's rich spinster aunt (Miriam Margolyes) who really favours Rawdon (Nathaniel Parker), a rakehell young Guards officer, Sir Pitt's son by a previous marriage. Becky also flirts with Rawdon. She nurses Sir Pitt's wife through her last illness and when newly widowed Sir Pitt proposes to her. Becky has to tell him she has already married Rawdon, who is now cut out of Miss Crawley's will in favour of his elder brother, Pitt (Anton Lesser) an aspiring young politician. Meanwhile, George marries Amelia Sedley and is disowned by his father as Amelia's father has failed in business.

Napoleon's flight from Elba and the gathering storm which leads to Waterloo call them to Brussels. George plans an adulterous affair with Becky but is killed in battle. Rawdon enjoys success at the gambling table and Becky attracts admirers. She bears Rawdon a son whom he adores and Amelia also has a son whom she struggles to bring up in her reduced circumstances. Meanwhile Rawdon and Becky live 'on nothing a year' – he gambles, she flirts. Amelia's fortunes sink and her poverty compels her to hand her child over to her unrelenting father-in-law. Becky is taken up by the notorious Lord Steyne (Gerard Murphy) who showers her with presents and has her presented at court, where the rich Sir Pitt Crawley falls for her. As Becky flaunts her jewels, Rawdon is arrested for debt. He appeals to Becky in vain for help. Unexpectedly released he discovers his wife in a compromising situation with Steyne, and Rawdon thrashes him. Rawdon leaves her forever. (He dies at an outpost of Empire.) Dobbin and Joseph return from India. Dobbin proposes to Amelia who, faithful to the memory of her dead husband, refuses. Amelia, Joseph and Dobbin tour the continent. They find Becky at a run down German spa existing on the favours of various admirers. She renews her wiles on Joseph and this time he succumbs. Becky gets him to take out a substantial insurance and he dies under mysterious circumstances. Andrew Davies did not use this part of tale; there will always be debate as to whether Becky poisons him or not.[38] Becky is now rich. But there is some good in Becky, as her revealing George's duplicity to Amelia finally opens her eyes and she marries Dobbin.

Thackeray's handling of the parallel plot lines tracing the varying fortunes of Amelia and Becky is masterly, as is his detached, yet by no means cynical, view of the characters and action. The most difficult quality to achieve in bringing Thackeray to the screen is this touch. It is accurate and sure. As a satirist he inclines more to the brain surgeon than the butcher. Although all of the same great English school, Thackeray is closer to Jane Austen than to Evelyn Waugh. His delicacy significantly enough was recognized by contemporaries. Robert Bell reviewing *Vanity Fair* in *Fraser's Magazine* in 1848 wrote that he: '...dissects his victims with a smile; and performs the cruellest of operations on their self-love with a pleasantry which looks provokingly very like good nature.' Charlotte Brontë wrote that no author seems to distinguish so exquisitely '... dross from the ore, the real from the counterfeit'.[39] John Forster, reviewing *Vanity Fair* in the year of its publication, wrote that Thackeray only fell short of Fielding 'much of whose peculiar power and more of whose manner he has inherited or studiously acquired' because 'an equal amount of large cordiality has not raised him entirely above the region of the sneering, into that of simple uncontaminated human affection. His satiric pencil is dipped in deeper colours than that of his prototype. Not *Vanity Fair* but Rascality Fair is the scene he lays open to our view....'[40]

Those very qualities his contemporaries praised were absent in this BBC-1 production, which went instead for what was correctly (if infelicitously) described as 'in your face' and for effects which were crude. Rawdon's headbutting of Lord Steyne had more of a Liverpool pub brawl than a slap across the face delivered by a deceived husband.

The scene enacted by Nathaniel Parker and Gerard Murphy does not happen in Thackeray, who quite specifically writes that Rawdon seizes Steyne by the neckcloth until he nearly strangles him then 'struck the Peer twice over the face with his open hand, and flung him bleeding to the ground...'[41] and Rawdon describing the scene to his closest friend says he told Steyne he was a liar and a coward 'and knocked him down and thrashed him'.[42] The translation of this fight scene into the physical language of the 1990s has not improved it. There is additionally something troubling about this Becky. She is one of Thackeray's best drawn characters. A worldly, cunning and self-seeking coquette, Becky is an immortal character in our literature: 'She was small and slight in person; pale, sandy-haired, and with eyes habitually cast down; when they looked up they were very large, odd and attractive...' Early in her life she realises that she exerts the most extraordinarily powerful effect over men. With a single glance of these famous eyes, 'fired all the way across Chiswick Church from the school pew to the reading desk' she causes the Revd Crisp, a curate at Chiswick, fresh from Oxford, instantly and everlastingly to fall in love with her.

> She might appear a child, but she had been an adult all her life ...she had the dismal precocity of poverty. Many a dun had she talked to, and turned away from her father's door; many a tradesman had she coaxed and wheedled into good humour, and into the granting of one meal more. She sat commonly with her father, who was very proud of her wit, and heard the talk of many of his wild companions – often but ill suited for a girl to hear. But she never had been a girl...she had been a woman since she was eight years old...

Becky has much affinity with Blanche Amory in Thackeray's *Pendennis*, as is only to be expected, as both Becky and Blanche are based on Theresa Reviss, the bastard daughter of the novelist's friend, Arthur Buller. Theresa was a monstrous child – arch, precocious, sophisticated and sexually alert way beyond her years. But these wayward qualities are swamped in Natasha Little's assumption of the role, in which Becky becomes a go-getting, materialistic young woman, determined to break through the glass ceiling. In fact BBC-1's Becky Sharp seemed more a product of the Sylvia Young Theatre School than Miss Pinkerton's Academy.[43] *Radio Times* proclaimed her 'J.R. Ewing in a ballgown, Cindy Beale with a brain' and as Thackeray's 'anti-heroine...a liar, a cheat, a seductress, a criminal (possibly a murderer) – and, most heinous of all, she can't stand her own child.'[44]

This production characterised Becky Sharp as 'an accomplished flirt' who ignites an inferno of all-consuming lust. But this only describes her tactics, it takes little account of the basis of her strategy which is her worldly nature, the consequence of her never having been a child, but an adult in a child's body. It is that which enables her systematically to unravel the cryptography of the world as she goes through it. Everyone else in this novel has to live their lives forwards, Becky seems to understand life backwards, like one looking at life retrospectively, with no surprises, nothing unexpected. For her life is just one successful trick after another. It is not that Becky is go-getting, seductive, pushy or whatever – Becky is knowing. That's the thing. The dramatist seems aware of this, for he said:

> I didn't add or change much in this adaptation. I wrote a little prologue scene with Becky running to the pub to get gin for her father and we see her father running a 'drawing class' for fine gentlemen which is a bit like those 'photography clubs' with nude models. Little Becky very much part of that world, sexually aware before the age of ten. And also to indicate the desperate poverty she is trying to escape.[45]

Thackeray is a master of making the reader wonder, really, what does in fact happen. Does Becky go the whole hog with Lord Steyne? Andrew Davies is convinced that she does, although he believes she usually manages to get away with 'implied promises – with George Osborne and Pitt Crawley etc.'[46]

However, BBC-1's *Vanity Fair* had several positive qualities. It was extremely well written for the small screen. Thackeray's vast work was translated into satisfying, interesting, intriguing episodes, each one of which had its own central action (Vauxhall, Brighton, Waterloo, Lord Steyne's masque, the German spa and so on) and a sense of climax. The main narrative threads were handled and sharply focused with the clarity and relevance one would have expected from Andrew Davies. The production design and costumes should have won a BAFTA. Although the Amelia and Becky characters work well as a contrasting pair of heroines, the casting was not immaculate. Becky was rather too imposing. Thackeray goes to some trouble to give us that sense of great power and magnetism exerted by a small woman. There should be no sense of power dressing. Much of Lord Steyne (Gerard Murphy) was right. They had his buck teeth (the implications of rabbit-like libido are important) but not that squat, bow-legged, broad-chested, red-haired quality. Jeremy Swift made a good Jos Sedley, but did not entirely erase memories of BBC-1's last Jos, the immortal James Saxon. The character roles fared better with David Bradley a flesh crawling Sir Pitt Crawley and Miriam Margolyes turning out another beautifully judged performance. Nathaniel Parker as Rawdon was not only a convincing rotter, but also earned one's sympathy. The Waterloo sequence was a bit of a damp squib (but it always is). This is a strange, haunting novel, because behind the deft satire of Victorian society which Thackeray disguised as an account of Regency England there lurks the troubling, shadowy metaphor of Bunyan's vision of the empty, bustling, pointless, materialistic, vacuous, sensual and cruel nature of human society. That echoing, bitter taste is an essential ingredient of Thackeray's novel. BBC-1's 1998 *Vanity Fair* had so much, but this it lacked. It may be impossible to screen, for it comes through gradually in reading the novel and – even more so – pondering when you finally lay it aside. It is this quality which has caused some, mistakenly, to call its author heartless, cynical. There is a quality of pity mixed with sorrow in Thackeray's voice as he says at the end of *Vanity Fair*: 'Ah! Vanitas Vanitatum! Which of us is happy in this world? Which of us has his desire? or, having it, is satisfied? Come children, let us shut up the box and the puppets, for our play is played out.'

In April 1999 BBC-2 transmitted Tony Marchant's dramatisation of *Great Expectations* in two 90-minute episodes. It was produced by David Snodin and directed by Julian Jarrold. The Corporation promised us something different, and it was well publicised that this production had made a determined and self-conscious effort to escape from the shadow of David Lean. For a production to take as its guiding principle the solemn undertaking to be different from a previous version might seem arid and perverse, but that was their manifest aim. 'A darkly different Dickens' is what they promised us, and went on to assure putative viewers that 'the team behind this new version of the Dickens classic haven't flinched from its modern themes.'[47] In translating classical novels into modern television, there are losses as well as gains. Some are understandable, others less so. But *Middlemarch* notwithstanding, after the BBC's previous recent attempts at high Victorians – *Hard Times* (wretched) and *Vanity Fair* (patchy) – expectations were modest. So it was nice to be surprised, if not actually joyous, at least with some pleasure.

First person narrative was not used. We saw the story as events unfolded. What we lost was the fact that Pip's confusions are the result of the distortions through which he perceives the world. It is quite a trick to get viewers similarly confused. We have got to misunderstand the evidence, just as Pip does. Were we credibly led to believe the legacy was Miss Havisham's? Were we really so insensitive as to think that having lost Estella, we could pop Biddy the question? Were we so insensitive that we wanted to chuck Magwitch out the minute he showed up again? Were we really so myopic that we couldn't see Joe's love for Pip was unconditional and had no bounds? It looked good. The director of photography, David Odd, and production designer, Alice Normington, created a fine washed-out quality for the rural Kent exteriors (actually Norfolk), and a bustling sense of London using well selected bits of Edinburgh for the more tenebrous aspects of the metropolis. The bleakness of the marsh country was further driven home by recurring images of circling flights of dreary ducks and melancholy Peter Grimesian music (by Peter Salem). Although Dickens located it earlier in the century, they went firmly for a mid-century look, and several names came to mind – Ford Madox Brown, William Holman Hunt, William Powell Frith among them. These elements were symptomatic of assumptions at the heart of this production. Saying goodbye to the 'teatime classics of yesteryear' – that production line of shallow schedule-fillers – in itself might be no bad thing. Their website made it clear that any version of this masterpiece inevitably emerged in the shadow of David Lean, yet Lean was the product of a very different age 'with very different attitudes'. So the producer, (David Snodin) writer (Tony Marchant) and director (Julian Jarrold) sought to make this version for the close of the twentieth century 'darker and much less sentimental, reflecting the huge changes in values and beliefs which have taken place since 1946...' Well, yes, this may sound desirable and certainly politically correct, but is it sensible?

Those who so frequently come out with this line might be well advised briefly to pause and think, what would life be like devoid of sentiment? Sentiment is one of the comforts of life, which frequently works to good purpose and keeps other less desirable, more competitive and destructive qualities in check. Even Pip admits that much – 'Heaven knows we need never be ashamed of our tears, for they are the rain upon the blinding dust of earth, overlying our hard hearts...' (chapter 19). Art doesn't just reflect life, it is supposed to examine, evaluate, criticise and ridicule it, so we aspire to be better than we are.

The claims that this was a deliberate attempt to eschew previous examples of doing Dickens, and an attempt to produce a darker Dickens more 'suitable' to the 1990s raises some fundamental questions. Are we witnessing a deliberate rejection of one of the genres' basic principles – fidelity to the original literary text? To make a decision to excise comedy and sentiment from *Great Expectations*, and quite fundamentally rejig its narrative, is like a musical director saying as he raises his baton: 'Well Mozart's Symphony number 41 (Jupiter Symphony) is in C Major, which is a rather cheerful, uplifting key. Well we are playing this for the nineties, so we are going to transpose it and play it in D Minor, thus showing a Darker Side to Mozart...' Dickens was quite capable of showing his own darker side when he felt he wanted to, thank you very much. With this production there was a strong feeling of Tony Marchant forcing one of his own plays onto *Great Expectations*, in much the same way as Charles (Theatre of Cruelty) Marowitz was wont to rewrite Shakespeare's *Hamlet* as an anti-Vietnam war drama.

The distortions of this production have strong roots elsewhere. The BBC also told us that Dickens was 'almost as much a journalist as novelist' and consequently we should recognize that his works were not 'all solely dreamed up' but 'based firmly on real people, real events and real places'. These assertions are Grandgrindian, but it meant the vitality of the larger than life was missing. Real life or real places or what – it doesn't matter where these things come from. It is what Dickens creatively does with them that is important, and how he makes them work on our imaginations and our feelings. Remember, fact is stranger than fiction, but fiction is truer. The comic element was almost totally removed. ('Wot, no larks?'). So, no fun with bread and butter at the table, no Trabbs's Boy, no Joe in London, no Wopsle's Hamlet. It was the ladies' show, really. Mrs Joe (Lesley Sharp) was magnificent, generous in her animosity, a simmering bomb ever ready to explode. And for once, we began to understand what a bum hand life had dealt her. Miss Havisham, (Charlotte Rampling) although resembling Dickens's description of her but slightly, was utterly convincing as a once beautiful young woman miraculously preserved, albeit fading fast, in a state of gradual senility. Estella (Justine Waddell) projected in exactly the right proportions qualities of sexual magnetism and emotional paralysis, like one of those fearfully beautiful anautomata from Dr Coppelius's workshop. And as for Molly, Jagger's housekeeper (Laila Morse) – what a pair of wrists! In some ways she was the most perfect translation from page to screen. Dickens describes Molly: '...with large faded eyes, and a quantity of streaming hair. I cannot say whether any diseased affection of the heart caused her lips to be parted as if she were panting and her face to bear a curious expression of sadness and flutter...as if it were all disturbed by fiery air....' The men worked hard. Pip is a rich creation, very self aware for a Dickens hero, anxious to conceal his less attractive qualities, but in telling us his story he lets much slip. This is difficult to bring off in the third person narrative we had here, but this Pip (Ioan Gruffudd) came through as smart and pushy. Joe (though no attempt was made to render him fair-haired or blue-eyed) looked every inch a blacksmith, yet gentle withal (Clive Russell). Magwitch (Bernard Hill) was as rough a diamond as you could find. Jaggers (Ian McDiarmid) was not really bristling and menacing enough, he was insidious rather than portentous. Wemmick (Nick Woodeson) was excellent and we should have had more of his home life and the fortifications so enjoyed by the Aged P.

We lost Joe's wonderfully meaningful incoherence. We lost Tickler; we lost aspects of Orlick (Tom Curran) who looked disconcertingly like something between a 1990s football hooligan and an extra in *Braveheart*; the connections between Compeyson, Magwitch and Miss Havisham and Jagger's motives in saving Estella; and all the fun of the Aged-P's castle. But when they came to it, they lacked the courage to use Dickens's original sad ending. What was all that about being sentimental? Nevertheless this production might well be significant. As the millennium neared its close various interesting influences combined to make Sunday evening schedules a showcase of political correctness and a long overdue recognition of female consumers. One result has been a serious trawl of suitable classic novels for the Sunday evening quality drama primetime slot. Media resurrectionists exhumed that worthy soul, Elizabeth Gleghorn Gaskell. The combined professional talents of producer Sue Birtwistle, dramatist Andrew Davies and director photographer Fred Tammes did all that was humanly possible to bring *Wives and Daughters* to life on the screen. The results were transmitted in the autumn run up to Christmas 1999. In this BBC/WGBH Boston co-production, the characteristic deployment of stock characters in plotting by numbers was as disguised as traditional British costume drama expertise could achieve. Arthur Hugh Clough recorded that there was something of the clergyman's wife about Mrs Gaskell, and Jane Welsh Carlyle was certainly on target when she wrote of Mrs Gaskell in 1849: 'A natural unassuming woman whom they have been doing their best to spoil by making a lioness out of her.'[48] A really superb cast – Justine Waddell, Francesca Annis, Keeley

Hawes, Bill Paterson, Michael Gambon, Anthony Howell and Tom Hollandar starred – exerted themselves beyond the call of duty. It looked ravishing and was served gift wrapped in music by John Keane, which may in the truest sense be described as charming. In shape and texture the music owed much to Schumann and Grieg, (none the worse for that) but was by no means derivative, excellently serving the drama. The same complex of circumstances which brought *Wives and Daughters* to our screens led to ITV's lavish *Oliver Twist* (United Productions/WGBH Boston) being scheduled in the same Sunday evening slot.

This much heralded production of an old favourite was written by Alan Bleasdale. He confessed: 'The three greatest writers the world had ever produced, I think, were Shakespeare, Dickens and Tolstoy. And I dreaded the telephone call that confirmed my commission to write a dramatisation of *Oliver Twist* for television – yet at the same time I was immensely proud to do it. I had a mixture of awe and excitement in doing it.'[49] In the event, this was an unusual and courageous dramatisation. He deliberately tried to recreate the spirit and tone of Dickens's original novel, and to erase impressions generated by the musical *Oliver*! In Bleasdale's version, Fagin (Robert Lindsay) is a failed emigre Czech magician. He is described in the script as 'Failed magician, fence and friend to the under fifteen's.' When the Dodger first takes Oliver to see Fagin, Fagin's gang of boys is sitting down to a splendid supper of sausages, gin and coffee, and the old fence is just reaching the climax of his entertainment – producing hankerchiefs, small balls, watches and as his *piece de resistance* a flurry of doves from all parts of his clothing. Although some may have found this version slow to get up steam, the production never looked back from this moment. In this version the heavily caricatured Jewish qualities so given him by Dickens and traditionally recreated on stage, radio and film[50] enabled this production to pass muster as politically correct because Fagin's Jewish qualities were successfully masked by a general sense of his Central European origins and his skill as a conjuror. But there is much more to it than just paying lip service to PC. Fagin obviously teaches his young charges all his magic tricks as Oliver is mesmerised by the boys' dextrous prestigination. He cannot follow the speed of their hands but sees a blur of spoons, handkerchiefs, playing cards and so on, as they body search the new recruit.

Some viewers found the long exposition of the opening episode a bit much to take, as Bleasdale recasts the opening of the narrative entirely. He described how impressed he was by a section of *Oliver Twist* towards the end of the novel where Dickens gives a striking resume of the plot mechanisms by means of which the entire narrative substance is launched – the details of Oliver's antecedents' relationships before his birth.[51] The dramatist worked these details up and wrote in what is in effect a lengthy prologue before the familiar opening scenes in the workhouse – with which episode one of the serial concluded. The variety of debt acknowledged by this version of *Oliver Twist* – it was produced by Diplomat Films in association with United Productions and WGBH Boston for HTV – might explain much that has been done to Dickens's original, but it has to be admitted, what might appear rather cavalier treatment of a classic novel has considerable compensation dividends. This version of *Oliver Twist* is that comparatively rare thing, a dramatisation for television, written by a writer who has an established reputation as a television playwright. Another obvious example would be Dennis Potter, who dramatised Thomas Hardy's *The Mayor of Casterbridge*. Andrew Davies achieved a reputation as television dramatist for *A Very Peculiar Practice* before he made his mark dramatising classic novels for the small screen.

Alan Bleasdale achieved some impressive effects in *Oliver Twist*. The novel has a plot like a coiled spring, and whirrs away as soon as its catch is released. Bleasdale was anxious about three aspects of *Oliver Twist* which would be 'problematic for a modern television audience' – the level of coincidence, latent anti-Semitism and tendency to sentimentality. He tried to lay the narrative on firm foundations in an extensive 'black story' by way of exposition, which took up most of the first broadcast episode. He was very taken by a section of *Oliver Twist* towards the end of the novel (*Oliver Twist*, Chapter 51 '*Affording an Explanation of More Mysteries Than One, and Comprehending a Proposal of Marriage with No Word of Settlement or Pin-Money*'). 'Because Dickens was writing at such a furious pace and was making it up as he went along, certain things just get thrown away. Genius though he was, he just kept writing and threw those pages over his shoulder. So I've followed along behind him, picking them up' is how Bleasdale describes his method of work. And it works well, although it must have been a bit of shock to those viewers who previously thought they knew the novel. It is not the case that Dickens worked out the plot of *Oliver Twist* before writing it, and then messed it up in the hasty process of scribbling away as the printer's boy waited for copy. Dickens concocted this plot very late in the actual composition of the novel. It is to Bleasdale's considerable credit that so much here actually structurally improved on the novelist's work, provoking though it might be to some textual purists. Bleasdale's hand could clearly be discerned time and again in the way he feeds plot motivation into scenes throughout, toning down the young novelist's tendency to freewheel through the Manichean world he had created to locate the action. Thus he reduces the sense readers experience at the end of the novel, that so much unlikelihood is implausibly pulled together.

In the portrayal of Fagin we can see how political correctness and the need to play to the sensibilities of the international market affect the representation. Every schoolboy knows that David Lean's *Oliver Twist* (1948) was shown in the USA only after some hefty editing had toned down Alex Guinness's portrayal of Fagin, but Alan Bleasdale's Fagin (Robert Lindsay) is a Czechoslovakian conjuror; he does not have a big nose. Robert Lindsay played Fagin on stage in the West End musical *Oiver!* but, as he said, this was a new approach: 'The Fagin in this version is a magician, he's Bohemian, he's from Czechoslovakia and he happens to be Jewish. The fact that he's foreign is beguiling and romantic to the children; he lures them to him with some kind of exotic charisma...'.[52] The exploitation of the character's fascination in his exotic 'otherness' was an interesting idea, and at times Robert Lindsay put one in mind of *Fiddler on the Roof*. But did this compromise Dickens's art? Dickens based Fagin on the real life Jewish criminal Ikey Solomons (1785–1850). Solomons was a master fence for several gangs, who was imprisoned in Newgate in 1831 and eventually transported to Hobart, Australia. He had as much as £20 000 worth of goods sometimes secreted on his premises (concealed in a hiding place under his bed) at Rosemary Lane and another establishment at Lower Queen Street, Islington. It was estimated in 1861 that there were about two hundred gangs of children operating in London, employing some six thousand boys and girls. (Thackeray used the name Ikey Solomons, junior, as his pseudonym when he published his Newgate Novel, *Catherine*, in 1840.)[53] How do we square this with all those trumpeted media ambitions to rid Dickens of sentimentality and the fact that Dickens was trying to portray social realities?

As for the sentimentality, this is ineradicably Dickensian, and distilling it off ruins the authenticity of its taste. This version of *Oliver Twist* countered the sentimental by over compensating on the violent. There were several quite terrible moments. Sikes (Andy Serkis) was homicide waiting to happen. Nancy (Emily Woof) was an utterly convincing and touching victim of the world she found herself in. Her murder realized all the violence which made it one of Dickens's favourite scenes. Monks (Marc Warren) was a towering creation. Mr

Brownlow (Michael Kitchen) was a do-gooder with plenty of good to do in this version – the dramatist upholstered this dimension of the novel to good effect. The female cast was strong – Mrs Mann (Julie Walters), Elizabeth Leeford (Lindsay Duncan) and Mrs Bedwin (Annette Crosbie) turned in performances of seamless excellence. Two young performances were outstanding – Oliver (Sam Smith) and the Dodger (Alex Crowley). This Dodger was a far less jocular and likeable character than Jack Wild made of him in Carrol Reed's film version of Lionel Barth's *Oliver!* The three worlds – workhouse, (filmed at Alston in Cumbria); the Brownlow household (Nether Winchenden House, Buckinghamshire, and around the Chilterns, and the London scenes in King's Bench Walk and Middle Temple); and Fagin's London (filmed in the Czech Republic) – were all solidly presented. The general effect of this production, directed by Renny Rye, was to spread the novel out, seriously altering its pace.

BBC-1 celebrated Christmas, New Year and the new millennium with an all-star production of *David Copperfield*. It was written by John (*Only Fools and Horses*) Sullivan. It was a unique production combining BBC television drama and light entertainment – which was wholly appropriate bearing in the mind the nature of Dickens's genius. The production was not without initial difficulties, and there were reports of late delivery of scripts and considerable rewriting. It was produced by Kate Harwood, who considered the choice of *David Copperfield* as the Corporation's millennium special was appropriate:

> I think one of the great reasons for doing Dickens on television is because he is inclusive. Although he is very southern-half of the United Kingdom, he nevertheless does include all classes and all types of people. He is a very inclusive writer. He writes about rich and poor, high and low. The hard working, the lazy, the fun and the gloom of life. He has such a range of characters and you know, even with the best will in the world, no matter how romantic, Jane Austen, in the end, is about a very narrow band of English society. If you're doing something for transmission at Millennium, and you're trying, via your casting which will be quite popular, to bring in an audience who probably will have heard of your main actors, will probably have heard of Charles Dickens, and at a pinch, of *David Copperfield*, even if the only Dickens they have ever come across is *Oliver!* He is so much better than any other writer for that kind of project. You really do not want people to feel excluded by the BBC in that kind of way.[54]

David Copperfield, she believed, was well suited to this kind of dramatisation on television, because unlike most of his other novels which
are episodic in construction as a result of lengthy serialised compos-
tion, *David Copperfield*, gains a sense of unity as a result of
autobiographical qualities:

> Nothing in the novel makes any sense if it's not about David's
> experience, about David's learning to become a man, about
> David's growing up, about his finding what he lost at the
> beginning. That kind of big, circular sweep is what I think grounds
> everything. This is certainly the thing we're hanging on to most
> firmly, so that all these events, big or small, dramatic, melodra-
> matic, funny – they are all unified in this boy's experiences, and
> then this young man's perception of them, and I think that's what
> makes it make sense to me.[55]

Kate Harwood thinks that there are very strong female qualities in this
book. There's Betsy Trotwood, for example:

> She's fabulous. I think she also has a wonderful journey in this
> book. A wonderful story for her. She's not fixed in aspect at all. She
> learns and grows alongside David. She is so touching at points. Even
> though you think of her as a prickly grotesque. She's not. She's
> actually very tender, and I love the stuff with her and Dora. I love
> the way she understands Dora, even though she feels that David
> made a mistake in marrying her, she is, nevertheless, sweet and
> gentle with her when she is dying. It is very touching. And then
> there is all the stuff about her own marriage. It is a wonderful part.
> I feel there are strong echoes of *Great Expectations* here. She is a
> comic version of Miss Havisham. She's active. Miss Havisham is
> inactive. I mean, she makes things happen on a rather small scale.
> She manipulates but then she sits back and watches the conse-
> quences, whereas Betsy is active. She goes out and makes thing
> happen. She is also full of emotion. Big emotion. Whereas Miss
> Havisham is more retentive and fervent. But they're fuelled by the
> same sort of potential bitterness. That Betsy loses, and in the end
> she finds a family. She so clearly adores David. But I do think there
> are a lot of parallels there.[56]

Dora she sees as a rather modern young woman, and a very important
character who is frequently underrated:

There are plenty of Doras around. She is by no means a character who has disappeared from our lives. When you look at what she says and what she does, she's very funny and there's a slight edge of 'camp' to Dora. She plays. She's very playful. She plays with language a lot. She's always in a little sort of playlet of her own. I think her problem is, in modern terms, that she is very immature and when a crisis comes, it doesn't make her grow. She just retreats into this fantasy world and is very happy within it. But then she has an extraordinary journey. At the end she is very moving. On her deathbed her self knowledge is staggering and terribly moving. In a sense David moves from the child wife to the real wife, with Dora's blessing, almost with her connivance. The triangle between Dora, David and Agnes is extraordinary moving and powerful. That is the focus of the novel.

The production, transmitted in two parts on Christmas Day and Boxing Day, crammed the vastness of Dickens's masterpiece into two episodes. Pondering the leisurely pacing granted *Oliver Twist*, one might be tempted to consider that this BBC-1 *David Copperfield* might have benefited from a bit more space to breath. It was here stripped more or less to its essential narrative. In the process we lost not only Mr Mell and Tommy Traddles and much of Micawber's volubility but also the novel's sense of perspective. *David Copperfield*, has a vastly better constructed plot, but an illusive tone which is very hard to translate to screen. This Christmas *Copperfield* was a joint effort by BBC drama and light entertainment departments and lost the work's sombre dimension. The original title was: *The Personal History, Adventures, Experiences, and Observations of David Copperfield the Younger, of Blunderstone Rookery* (*which he never meant to be published on any account*)). There are some interesting clues here. In the *life-and-adventures-and-opinions* there is a distinct echo of *Tristram Shandy*. Dickens seems to be reverting to his beloved eighteenth-century models, but additionally there is the interesting reference to autobiographical elements which were to be kept secret – as of course they were to most of his readers. The darker parts of the story of course were only known to Dickens himself, Forster and very few others.[57]

The autobiographical tone is established by the celebrated opening words: 'whether I shall turn out to be the hero of my own life, or whether that station will be held by anybody else, these pages will show...' This is indeed the nub of the problem, for as with Dickens's beloved Smollett, the eponymous hero is a bland, often empty central figure, surrounded by raving grotesques and eccentrics. Claran McMenamin did what he could, but the void remained. This production had good moments of brutality and melodrama – young David's thrashing at the hands of Murdstone (the magnificent Trevor Eve) convincingly filmed from a young David's viewpoint, the bottle factory in all its grimness, the hideous Creakle, (Ian McKellen) and the mortal storm which drowns Ham (James Thornton) and Steerforth (Oliver Milburn) – and achieved much of the novel's grotesque comicality. We were blessed with an utterly convincing Mr Dick (Ian McNiece), Aunt Betsy (Maggie Smith) and Dan'l Peggotty (Alun Armstrong). Pauline Quirke was well cast as Peggotty. None of these roles is easy to bring off, but these were vintage performances. Dora (Joanna Page) was silly enough, but scarcely erotic – David is supposed to be besotted with her. While Agnes (Amanda Ryan) was a shade too earnest, Micawber (Bob Hoskins) was a consistently interesting creation, but severely cut back as it was, this Micawber lacked not only his essential Johnsonian prolixity, but also that rhapsodic rhetorical wool-gathering which Dickens might well have caught from his early reading of Sterne. This toning down of Micawber's resourceful eloquence was more to be missed than such other details as the lack of his characteristic eye-glass and bald plate. I think we could to better effect have lost such cameo star turns as Dawn French's Mrs Crupp and Paul Whitehouse's pawnbroker and used the space to fill out Micawber. Nicholas Lyndhurst did some good things with Uriah Heep, but did not wholly erase memories of Martin Jarvis. Mrs Gummidge (Patsy Byrne) was surely too well fed.

Because this production conflated the novel, the tone was altered. *David Copperfield* is deceptive. Beneath the blissful innocence of its finale, and the rooks cawing round the old cathedral at Canterbury, there is a deep, disturbing psychological quality which lingers in the imagination. The scenes of Murdstone's barbarities are haunting, and his insanely reasonable arithmetic problems have a startlingly surreal quality. Equally dreamlike are the sunny innocent moments of retreat, the love and comfort of Peggotty, the stay in the boat at Yarmouth. But the hero has to grow up and face the world. He makes some catastrophic errors of judgement (Steerforth, Dora) and has to endure the pain of maturing, but after the storm he drifts serenely into harbour. With its deployment of the several threads of time, memory, chance and fortune, the past, the present and the future, this is a very revealing novel of middle-period Dickens. He described *David*

Copperfield as 'written memory'. Here he is a successful and established writer, looking back into his past: 'I think the memory of most of us can go further back into such times than many of us suppose...' (Chapter 2) Later he writes: '... The man who reviews his own life, as I do mine... had need to have been a good man indeed, if he would be spared the opportunities wasted...' (Chapter 42). One of the significant qualities of *David Copperfield* is in the perspective of its narrative; that sense of looking back over a past life which seems to have brought personal success, yet with the vision tinged with sorrow. Some of this might well result from the fact that the basic narrative tense of television is present continuous, whereas in narrative prose fiction we have the omnipresent authorial voice dwelling simultaneously in the present and the past. The same problem is posed in dramatising *Great Expectations*, Dickens's only other first person narrative novel. In *David Copperfield*, writing of his mother's funeral, he says: 'All this, I say, is yesterday's event. Events of later date have floated from me to the shore, where all forgotten things will reappear, but this stands like a high rock in the ocean.' Memory in *Copperfield* is not to be tamed. It is a wild and wilful agent which delights and disturbs as it waywardly decides. Like Scrooge, David does not recall the past, but sees it done; it happens again before him. He is in the scene with his former self.

There is a pervading sense of what might have been, a searing awareness of chance in life – the friend not met, the street not turned up, the decision not made – that tormenting if-only, subjunctive past. Many of these qualities were lacking in this new version directed by Simon Curtis. There was some use of narrative voice over (by the admirable Tom Wilkinson) but much of the melancholy, that sense of aspects of life unfulfilled, had gone. BBC-1's *David Copperfield* had a consistently bright surface quality. The sun was always shining, the flowers were out, the trees were leafy, skies were blue, joy was just around the corner as events crowded past one another, as the narrative unfolded. There was ne'er a backward glance. Odd really, for New Year and millennium would have been such a good time to look back, as well as forward.

It might well be, then, that as we crossed the line from one millennium to the next, the classic serial genre was very much alive and well and living in British broadcasting. Just as interesting was the fact that Charles Dickens, original stalwart of the tradition – who provided much lively raw material from the earliest days of broadcasting – after a brief eclipse, seems to be in for something of a revival at a period of immense technical and economic media advancement. His genial face on our banknotes – an image combining the collective potency of creative genius, popular culture, national memory, commerce and the state – would provide the Barthians hours of useful contemplation.

8
The Albatross which was Really a Phoenix

As the century drew to a close the classic serial seemed to be thriving. Few would have predicted this a mere ten years ago when, as it seemed at the time, the BBC had quietly brought the tradition to an end with the last Sunday classic novel dramatisation. But – to mix a metaphor – the albatross rose from the ashes, and soared aloft.

Aesthetics: the form survives

Looking at matters from an aesthetic perspective, it is interesting to see to what extent the actual form and conventions of the classic serial genre have survived over the years. Launched securely on its way in the 1940s the form became so well tried and tested on the BBC Home Service over the years that it easily transferred to BBC Television when that service was resumed soon after the war. The radio classic serials continued on Sunday evenings and the television service offered a Sunday teatime serial, as well as more adult serials on Saturday evenings and occasionally on weekday evenings. When commercial television started in the mid 1950s it seemed little inclined to rival the BCC apparent monopoly of the genre. The enduring strength of the genre was demonstrated by the BBC's last major essay in the genre in monochrome – *The Forsyte Saga* – and the advent of BBC colour transmission was brilliantly heralded with *Vanity Fair* in 1967. Although commercial television demonstrated its effectiveness in historical drama with such series as *Upstairs Downstairs*, BBC television's supremacy in classical serials continued throughout the 1970s and was not seriously threatened until Granada Television's beautiful version of *Hard Times* in 1977. While the BBC struggled to survive in good shape under the constraints of its licence fee, Granada Television went from strength to strength in the 1980s with *Brideshead Revisited*[1] and *The Jewel in the Crown*. The BBC continued its traditional Sunday teatime fare with a rather lacklustre series of classic novel dramatisations and the BBC's classic serial unit was quietly closed at the end of the decade. But the genre survived in vigorous health on BBC Radio Four, almost unaltered and unscathed, untouched by endless revisionism. During this period among many worthy productions there were outstanding versions of *Dombey and Son*, *Tom Jones*, *War and Peace*, *Bleak House* and *Daniel Deronda*. But on BBC television there were perceptible adjustments and revisions as to the manner in which classic novels were selected and translated into television drama. BBC Television's classic serial sprang to life again with *Clarissa* and this was followed by *Middlemarch* and then the stunning success of *Pride and Prejudice*.

There some slight adjustments in the selection of novels and treatment. Understandably there was more interest in doing novels with a greater female interest and, as discussed in the last chapter, Dickens was temporarily dislodged from his premier position, though now he is firmly back in fashion. There was a noticeable tendency readily to abandon the old BBC tradition of faithfully rendering a classic novel in favour of rewriting, or considerably readjusting, novels to suit the perceived and expected feminist or politically correct requirements of today. Thus in *Vanity Fair* (BBC-1, 1998), although certainly acceptable to mid-Victorians, the name Sambo was removed, and some effort was certainly made to present Becky as a Woman of the 1990s. Alan Bleasdale's version of *Oliver Twist* rids Fagin of most of his authentic Dickensian Jewishness. And that is not all. This version of *Oliver Twist*, costing £5 million, as proclaimed its publicity, would for the first time attempt to create a background story for Fagin, to explain why he is such a charming and likeable villain. According to David Liddiment, ITV Director of Programmes, the ringleader of a gang of boys trained as thieves will be portrayed as 'a magical figure with a natural ability to appear and disappear' who has arrived in England from overseas. Following 'clues from the novel' Bleasdale has created 'a character more comprehensible to modern sensibilities'.[2] Tony Marchant very considerably shifted the emotional balance of *Great Expectations*, seeming almost to be trying to infiltrate a contemporary drama of his own into the texture of Dickens's fiction.

These examples suggest some quite fundamental shifting of ground away from the established traditions of the genre in which broadcasting played the role of midwife aiding the delivery of a classic novel into a new life as broadcast drama, almost to the extent that serious questions of legitimacy might reasonably be raised. These examples are also symptomatic of the curious tensions in postmodernism which mixes the desire for authenticity – Shakespeare done, it is claimed, as Shakespeare was performed in his own day; performances of Bach, Vivaldi, Handel and other ancient composers played in 'authentic' style on 'authentic' musical instruments – with an intertextuality which takes all created works as contemporary. What is sacrificed here is the recognition that by an imaginative leap literature and drama may speak across the ages by being read mythologically. Classical works can speak to us in their own language if we can but make the effort to understand. Great literature does not require translation into the patois of the 1990s. If it has in it the ability to speak, it will speak volumes. We must aspire to the classics, not attempt to reduce them to flimflam, but these tendencies show that significant changes may well be developing in the forms and conventions of the classic serial as a genre.

Once the form became established, numerous works of narrative prose fiction from the past were recycled as broadcast artefacts. But now having demonstrably achieved existence in its own right as a form – much like the classical concerto in Mozart's time, or the traditional symphony of the Viennese tradition, or the piano sonata at the turn of the eighteenth and nineteenth centuries – it could be used to bestow classic status on those works it handled. Thus the BBC, like a sovereign bestowing a knighthood with the touch of sword on shoulder, could give the accolade to modern works of fiction, instantly upgrading their literary status, by announcing a work by Evelyn Waugh, Graham Greene, John Fowles or whomsoever, as 'the BBC's new classic serial...which starts on Radio Four on Friday afternoon' and so on. This new genre, the classic serial, brought into being a new kind of translation, that from literary text to serial broadcast drama. The process soon began to work both ways. Novels were translated into broadcast radio or television artefacts, or into films. Well and good. Clearly it was not long before the book trade began to see the media not as rivals, but as partners in the business of literary production. When a work was serialised on radio or television, or made into a film, the original novel would inevitably be contemporaneously marketed, replete with cover picture from the latest production, as the original novel 'now a major television serial' or 'now a major feature film'. Soon occasions arose when films or television drama series were made which in so many ways, especially in their choice of subject or production values, actually resembled 'classic serials' even though they weren't. The market was now established, but there was no original text on which the television drama or film had been based. Nothing daunted, a writer would be commissioned to create a text for the punters to buy in Smiths or Menzies. Thus was the 'novelisation' created. Another new genre.

The process seemed to have gone full circle after the box-office success of *The Piano* in 1993. It was turned into a novel, which sold well in paperback, and then given the accolade by BBC Radio Four. (It has yet to come full circle in the form of a 'major television drama serial' but give them time.) When released, the film was seen as a potent myth, with a message for the 1990s. The leading character is a formidable young Scottish widow, who was struck dumb as the result of some unspeakable trauma. She arrives in New Zealand, with her young daughter and her piano, for an arranged marriage with an insensitive landowner. She seems somehow simply to emerge on to the desolate beach. She has to leave her piano, to which she seems emotionally attached, on the beach. She cannot speak, but expresses herself through playing the instrument furiously. Unsurprisingly, this husband/wife relationship does not flower. She establishes a sexual but inexplicably unconsummated relationship with an almost gone native white man who also scratches a living on the colony. It all comes to nothing. The piano is dropped in the ocean ('not a minute too soon' is a wicked thought which might well have crossed some viewers' minds). Well, what is this Freudian farrago all about? You may well ask.[3] The film was a heady cocktail of Daphne DuMaurier, the Brontë sisters, Sigmund Freud (through Lacan), Andrea Dworkin and Joseph Conrad, heavily laced with elements of the costume drama tradition. Had it been in modern dress it would have been laughed off the screen. But served up in poke bonnets and crinolines, it wowed critics and audiences alike and recharged feminist batteries world wide. It was conceived in the particular circumstances of its post-modernist moment, during the craze for heavily elaborate media reconstructed history, the shrill claim for women's voices to be unstopped for them to speak their case, the rediscovery of Freud through the good offices of Lacan and others, and the feminist recycling of Brontëian romanticism. This film starred Holly Hunter, Sam Neill, Harvey Keitel and Anna Paquin, and was written by Jane Campion, who won an Academy Award for the Best Original Screenplay. It got rave reviews. David Ansen wrote in Newsweek that it was: 'A riveting excursion into 19th century sexuality....' (How this differs from 20th-century sexuality is a question seldom raised by such claims.) Lizzie Francke in *Sight and Sound* said: 'Not since the early days of cinema...could I imagine the medium of film to be so moving.' But as a narrative, whatever terminology seems appropriate, it had become a free standing, literary property with a vigorous and indeed Protean life of its own – it was given the full classic serial treatment on BBC Radio Four. This demonstrates the strength of the ritual – a work which was not conceived as a novel is ritualistically transformed into a classic novel. The matter is worth pondering. There is a significant aesthetic snobbery in our culture, which accords written texts (books=literature) higher status than broadcast media texts (radio drama, films and television drama). We have all heard it. 'Did you see *Middlemarch* on the telly last night?' – 'No. But I have read the book...' Well, a work such as *The Piano* poses an interesting problem. Here you have a cinema release which looks like a classic novel adaptation, but is not actually based on a novel – classic or otherwise. Naturally, to maintain one's cultural well-being, one would like to read the book. But there isn't one. What is the worthy punter supposed to do? Fortunately help is at hand. Though arguably not in the same class as water into wine, a modest miracle turned *The Piano* into novel form in time for the Oscars ceremony in March 1994. Kate Pullinger, author of *Where Does Kissing End*, was able to oblige, and *The Piano* was published the following month.[4]

Another interesting example is the retelling of the mutiny on HMS *Bounty*. This was the basis of bestsellers by Charles Nordoff and James Hall, two former American airmen who served in the First World War. They subsequently went to live in Tahiti and intended to write about Polynesian life. After some success with several travel books and adventure books for boys, they produced a number of bestsellers between 1929 and 1945 – several of which were filmed. Between 1932 and 1934 they published their trilogy of novels about William Bligh, Fletcher Christian and the mutiny on HMS *Bounty*.[5] Their achievement earned additional credit as a result of the Academy Award winning film *Mutiny on the Bounty* (1935), which memorably starred Charles Laughton and Clark Gable. Nevertheless, it could be argued that even more prestige was bestowed upon Nordhoff's and Hall's work by the production of *Mutiny on the Bounty* as a BBC Radio Four classic serial. This starred Oliver Reed as William Bligh, and when the actor died in 1999 this performance was listed as among his finest roles by obituarists.

The marketing and consumption of the classic serial has considerably affected the aesthetic nature of the classic serial. Not only has it become tied in with the marketing of books, but with the video cassette revolution, classic serials are now available as artefacts for hire or purchase and may be consumed at home. They are also often aimed at the educational market and may be accompanied by various study packs for classroom use. Thus the form has developed in ways which could not have been anticipated by the genre's originators and early pioneers.

Rituals and the social order

The classic serial as a genre can tell us a great deal about how a culture speaks to itself and the evolving social order. The classic serial was able to evolve in the way it did at the close of the 1930s very largely as a result of the BBC's taking soundings as to the kind of broadcast drama its consumers wanted, and also because the very nature of the Reithian monopoly and its imperatives enabled the producers to assume the role of cultural evangelists and give audiences not only what they wanted but always to offer them something a little further than the accepted and expected popular taste. These broadcasts certainly introduced many listeners to works of literature they might not have been tempted to try on their own. When the classic serial began it would be fair to say that drama producers initially went for well established, mainly English authors, but from the very earliest days frontiers were pushed forward and boundaries extended. There was plenty of Trollope, Jane Austen and Dickens, but also ventures into such American and European authors as Dumas (*Count of Monte Cristo, Viconte de Bragellone*), J.P. Marquand (*So Little Time*), Tolstoy (*Anna Karenina*), Stendhal (*Charterhouse of Parma* and *Scarlet and Black*), Jules Verne (*Around the World in Eighty Days; Twenty Thousand Leagues under the Sea*), Flaubert (*Madame Bovary*), Dostoevsky (*Brothers Karamazov*) and Balzac's *The Rise and Fall of Cesar Brigotteau*. The BBC classic serial led as well as followed public taste. But in the main the taste in fiction was very much the taste of the educated middle-class middle-aged English male and male values tended to dominate. Hence the predilection for Galsworthy, Dickens and Trollope. Culture is not static, it is constantly reconstituting itself. Market factors very much impact upon the choice of subject and the manner of its treatment, which provides interesting evidence of the ways in which our culture communicates to itself. Recent changes in the organisation of the television industry encourage the bigger companies at the expense of the independent production companies, which again will serve to buttress and support the British, traditional, authoritative style in which these classic novels are dramatized and produced for television.

The high quality aura is an important factor in their marketability. These productions seem to satisfy particular demands in American viewers. Susan King, television critic of the *Los Angeles Times*, in welcoming 'British masterpiece' *Jane Eyre*, spoke of the way British television had enchanted viewers 'with its sparkling adaptations of the Austen classics' and assured readers of its authenticity, having been 'filmed in Hertfordshire and Oxfordshire, England'.[6] Yet, at the same time as hoping openly to trade on the cultural and literary associations of such drama series, television executives in the USA are attempting to realize a niche in more popular ratings, which identifies a role for British classic serials as part of a much broader scheduling strategy. When *Pride and Prejudice* was screened in America by A&E it was the most successful show they had screened in their 12-year history. Sarah Frank, the President of New York based BBC Worldwide Americas, which co-produced *Pride and Prejudice*, commented that: 'We're trying to be mass marketers of a niche product.'

An American media journalist wrote: 'Despite the BBC's erudite image, Frank's niche is pretty broad. For every Jane Austen production, there's an *Absolutely Fabulous*, the BBC comedy series about two vodka-swilling, chain-smoking Ivana-bes that Frank ran on Comedy Central. The show quickly quadrupled the channel's ratings, and spawned US clones....'[7]

Television has been part of our culture for sufficient time to have elapsed for a classical canon of past productions to begin assembling itself. Video cassette technology now enables these past products to be reproduced for the market and, like printed books in previous generations, videos of television programmes can be purchased in retail outlets for domestic consumption. Among the most consistently selling are videos of successful past televised classic novels. Several achieved classic status as gifts. And it is significant that the traditional British classic novel continues to be seen in the US as a BBC product. Paul Bauman, meditating on his Christmas indulgences, was pleased to say that Santa got it right, as there among his presents under the tree, impressively alongside 'the keys to my new Maserati' were 'all six videocassettes of the now antique BBC miniseries '*Brideshead Revisited*....'[8] Thus the television production and marketing of classic novels is not only ongoing, but has become a highly prized and eminently marketable commodity. Certain economic, commercial and technical imperatives have revised and sharpened the classic serial as a genre, and as we have seen it is experiencing a significant revival. Mary Collins, Head of Press and Public Relations

(International) and BBC Broadcasting House commenting on sales to the USA, said:

> Period dramas like *Pride and Prejudice* and *Tom Jones*, children's programmes like *Little Lord Fauntleroy* and *The Borrowers* ... do very well over there... We have a thing called the BBC Showcase once a year which involves buyers from all over the world coming to Brighton for four days to watch BBC programming. We are Europe's biggest exporter of television programmes.[9]

The current state of play, at the time of writing, is that despite various predictions about new opportunities for independent production companies, the major companies continue to dominate the production of classic novel serials. The BBC, which invented the genre, has without doubt created a leading role in the market with its productions of *Middlemarch* 1994, *Pride and Prejudice* 1995, *Our Mutual Friend* in spring 1998 followed in the autumn by *Vanity Fair* 1998 and *Great Expectations* in spring 1999, and with *Oliver Twist* and *David Copperfield* in production. Despite the considerable element of co-production cash involved in such productions, (mainly from the USA and Australia) the major commercial companies and the Corporation successfully managed to maintain artistic control. This control shows in the tone, style and fidelity of the products. Even the comparative failure in the UK of recent major BBC drama series, such as *Ivanhoe*, *Rhodes* and *Nostromo*, is deceptive. In fact, *Rhodes* and *Nostromo* were among the most successful BBC programmes in terms of total sales revenue 1996–97. Their poor ratings and weak critical support in the UK belie their very healthy overseas sales.[10] Thus, the BBC continues to maintain a leading role in the classic novel market. In recent years, in a new development, various of the British commercial television companies have entered this market to produce classic serials – *Emma*, *Moll Flanders*, *Charlotte Brontë*, *Wuthering Heights*, *Tess of the d'Urbevilles*, *Far From the Madding Crowd*.

On the face of it, the position should be otherwise. The major channels in Britain are required to purchase at least 25 per cent of their programming from the independent companies but this figure is often exceeded. According to the evidence of the ITV Network Centre approximately 27 per cent of network television hours, together with 36 per cent of the £515 000 000 budget for last year, was accounted for by the independent producers' programmes. In spite of the fact that 11.3 per cent (125 hours) of the network was awarded to Thames, the former Channel 3 operator which was formed into an independent production company after failing to gain its franchise under the new bidding scheme. It is estimated during 1994–95 the independents produced 29 per cent of the hours of programming, and earn 37 per cent of the £540 000 000 spent on programme making. Further optimism might be generated by pointing out that many of the most celebrated programmes broadcast have in fact been made by companies independent of the BBC and the major television companies – *Sharpe's Rifles, Hollywood Women, Drop the Dead Donkey*. The independent companies are assured direct access to the ITV Network Centre, thus ensuring that they are not pushed aside by the big boys. Several of the new companies, such as Meridian and Carlton, are publisher/broadcasting companies, with no programme libraries to draw upon, and a limited programme production policy. This should provide independent companies with slots to fill. Satellite and cable developments would additionally seem to herald further opportunities for independent enterprise. But none of the factors seem to have encouraged independent productions. The major programme making initiatives, and this applies to drama series possibly more than to other kinds of television production, remain with the larger companies. The freeing and opening up of markets in this way would seem to be an incentive to the independent production companies to move in on territory which up to now has been dominated by the big players.

Why, then, do the productions of the major 'classic' novel series remain in the hands of the BBC and just one or two of the major television companies? The answer is simply economics. A drama production with the required production values, which the markets traditionally take for granted as far as classic novels series are concerned, costs about £800 000 for every hour of screen time. The nub of the problem is cash flow. The industry is seriously short of the immediate wherewithal which provides large advances to finance programmes. The companies are unable to build up the large reserves to fund future productions. There is considerable and frequent outlay required during production, which means the production company finances the drama production as it is being made and only recoups when the production is finally delivered. Many weeks and months will inevitably elapse between the commissioning of a programme and its screening. Costume dramas, historical epics, classic novel adaptations – call them what you will – continue very much to be the property of the BBC or the larger commercial companies, who can often stump up the cash as the result of co-production deals with

American or Australian television companies. This will inevitably influence the choice of material and even further, the manner of its treatment. Having pioneered the 'British' way of 'doing the classics' the BBC may accidentally have created a prototype. This is seen as the way to do the classics, or to handle history (or even indicate what 'history' actually is).

The BBC has achieved such a *coup d'état* in our nation's cultural production, that this assertion of the 'authentic' is seldom, if ever, challenged. The BBC was able publicly to claim on air[11] that their Christmas television series of Dickens readings given in costume by Simon Callow was an 'authentic recreation' of Charles Dickens's public readings. This is highly questionable. True, Callow looked the part, bearded and in the kind of clothes Dickens wore for the readings; the corrected texts, edited by Dickens for the readings, were used; the famous desk had been recreated. But these were all trimings. The whole thing, replete with audience rigged out in Victorian oddments, resembled something between elaborate family charades and an edition of the *Good Old Days*. But the performances were not convincingly authentic. The voices were insufficiently differentiated and the delivery lacked commitment, and that demonic spirit which is attested to by those who heard Dickens perform. The Sikes and Nancy murder would have caused no one to faint and his rendition of *Pickwick* scarce raised a laugh. Yet the evidence of contemporary audiences is that Dickens produced laughter, tears, shreiks, screams and hysterics. Clearly, there are degrees of authenticity. But if this is the kind of thing which media conventions have conditioned audiences to accept, then this is what they will have to be given. The style has been created, marketed and approved. It will then have to be the way these things are done. The elaboration of media authenticity is impressive. ITV's drama series *Bramwell* is a wonderful example. It tells a modern story – the career of a modern emancipated young female medic, set in a rich late Victorian period context. A very great deal of trouble has been gone to in order to 'recreate' the look, feel and sense of the past. The effect is as if the retail stock of Pastimes had come to life.

Each episode begins with Dr Eleanor Bramwell leaving her GP father's house and passing through the streets of Victorian London *en route* to the Thrift Hospital, where she works. We see her perambulating legs and through her eyes see the sights she would see – and it is all there, a complete gallery of figures from Mayhew's London – well dressed young ladies flirting with an army officer in red coat, a handcart trundling old clothes, bow-fronted shops on the steps of which stand proud be-aproned members of the Victorian shopocracy, a toff giving money to a beggar girl, a man in bowler hat takes a photograph with a huge tripod camera and a flashlight, workmen at a flaming brazier, some scuffling drunks, a dustman with leather cap *à la* Mr Doolittle, a barrel-organ grinder, (where would such period dramas be without their resident barrel-organ grinder?) beggars, a prostitute and client, urchins appropriately dashing in and out of alleyways, a wheelwright proudly spinning a new-made product – the streets are filled with swirling smoke and there is much grubby washing drying across the streets.... But it is not simply a question of an intensified interest in our past, it is the way in which aspects and elements of the past are of use to the present. This affects what kind of subject matter is taken up, and the manner in which it is accommodated for today's market needs. As we have seen, there is a particular interest in material which deals with women and female experience. As Kate Lock commented as this great tide started to come in:

> It's been hailed as a clash of the corsets. Headlines such as 'ITV charged With Bodice Snatching' greeted new season line ups that see costume dramas prominent on both sides.... Suddenly, it seems, drama commissioners are after anything in a period frock....[12]

This was in 1996 as the 'Factor' began to take hold, but the triumph of *Pride and Prejudice* is to be seen as the crescendo of a process which goes back several years. At the opening of the decade, Samuel Richardson's novel *Clarissa* proved a rich seam which yielded much material of direct interest to its moment. Serialised on BBC-2 it spoke across the centuries to audiences today, illuminating themes of materialism, social ambition and the treatment of women in a patriarchal society. Although the drama's publicity went to some lengths to emphasize the elaborate exactness of its authentic costumes and locations, shed of its period garb *Clarissa* told an all too familair story of subjugation and exploitation. Granada's *Moll Flanders* put before us a young lady of the 1990s doing her best to survive in society by exploiting what advantages nature had given her, and she addresses the audience directly to state this very contemporary position, earning ratings of 13 million in the process.[13] *Tess of the d'Urbervilles, The Tenant of Wildfell Hall, Far From the Madding Crowd, Jane Eyre* – all dramatised for television in the wake of the '*Pride and Prejudice* effect' – were given a 1990s' spin in emphasizing as never before the problems and inhibitions facing the heroine's realization of personal potential in the face of society's restrictions. The leading roles were given to actors with gutsy presence such as Saskia Wickham, Samantha Morton, Tara Fitzgerald and Alex Kingston.

With what amounts to the creation of a canon of classics, such a commanding position in the marketing of accompanying study-aids, publications and videos, the BBC is now in a monopoly position. Most of the major new classic novel dramatisations are accompanied not only by a considerable amount of influential hype, but also with additional merchandize. This includes educational packs, study kits which contain not only material designed for classroom use – 'behind the scenes' material (audio cassettes, video tapes and so on) about how the production was made – but also booklets and printed material, interviews with actors, production staff and writers. Additionally the BBC offer considerable information by means of websites. These are interesting developments which may well repay further research. What may be happening is that the baton of literary opinion leadership is being quietly passed from academic to media hands. This is worth comment. In other comparable areas – medicine, the law, engineering – professional theory and practice would be a responsibility exercised by leading qualified and experienced members of the profession. Traditionally the identification, evaluation, custodianship and teaching of our literary heritage was in academic hands. It has to be admitted that this has not always been for the best. Dr F.R. Leavis argued in *The Great Tradition* (1948) that all roads led to D.H. Lawrence, and implied that the work of Fielding, Jane Austen, George Eliot, Henry James and Joseph Conrad had been in the nature of the ancient prophets preparing the way for D.H. Lawrence; life is too short to spend any time reading Fielding and J.B. Priestley, and Dickens – whose *Hard Times* alone was spared the flames – was shoved into the grudging obscurity of an Appendix. Dr Leavis preached that (apart from *Hard Times*), Dickens's novels lacked 'total significance of a profoundly serious kind' and the distinctive creative genius which controlled that 'unifying and organising significance' which the truly great novelists always manifested. He admitted that Dickens's works continued to be read, but believed his genius 'was that of a great entertainer' who lacked the profound responsibility he expected of a creative artist: 'The adult mind doesn't as a rule find in Dickens a challenge to an unusual and sustained seriousness.' This estimation of Dickens affected his reputation for several generations until retracted and revised.[14] But it may currently be replaced by a more far-reaching influence exercised by media professionals whose authority might be debatable. While it is incontrovertibly true that the BBC achieved a *coup d'état* over the production and distribution of our culture more than half-a-century ago, their imperial sway has been considerably strengthened by these developments in merchandising and information technology.[15]

Deals involve so much money and so many rights that caution rules. As Lisa Buckingham commented in the *Guardian*, the sugar daddy turns out to be either the BBC or one of the major British commercial television companies. Even though an independent producer takes a programme idea to one of these big boys, and the idea proves to be attractive to them, terms are then negotiated. The company agrees the production fee, which covers the cost of making the programme, plus a bit of profit. The deal will also include programme rights. In return for putting up the £X million for this project, they will demand rights for its first screening and for any repeats. They will earn two per cent above the rate at which the banks lend to each other for this generosity. They will also stick out for international rights, for marketing the programme as a video, or as a book and any other merchandise which may accompany it. If the programme is to be made by a commercial television company, they will also thrive on the advertising revenue gained from selling the commercial space around the programme. This has traditionally made serial versions of the classics a very good proposition.[16] Malcolm Craddock, of Picture Palace, which made *Sharpe* (starring the bankable Sean Bean) for the British commercial television channels, commented: 'There is not an independent producer who doesn't think the situation couldn't be improved. Bank finance of some sort is always available, but the reality is that margins are very slim and bank finance has to be paid for. Interest charges are another slug out of the production margin.'

A curious state of affairs was revealed in the spring of 1999 as reports of the decline in morale in the television industry were circulated when the belief spread that production standards were in sharp decline. There were serious worries about faked documentaries, bogus guests on chat shows, distortion of the truth in news and documentaries programming in order to create excitement or controversy to boost 'entertainment' value. A BFI report, based on interviews with 500 executives, researchers, producers and camera crews, published on 24 May revealed that there was widespread belief that television programming was 'dumbing down', becoming formulaic and going for the lowest common denominator. Quality of output was sacrificed to making docu-soaps, game and chat shows. Another report, *Building a*

Global Audience, funded by the Department for Culture, Media and Sport, published in April 1999, revealed that international television distributors were actually reluctant to buy British television programmes. Received wisdom in the industry had it that John Birt has put the BBC on a sound business footing, but with the changeover at the top, his successor must be one who has regard to high standards in what the Corporation actually makes – programmes. Interestingly enough, this desirable high quality was found only in classic serials.[17] If classic novels become more and more regarded as desirable production commodities, it is going to be very interesting to observe the various factors at play which may influence the choice of novel, and the manner of production. Given these economic and market factors, it can be seen that certain authors and texts are favoured for production over others. And that the historic past, the social context in which these stories unfold, is reconstructed in ways acceptable to the market. Consumers, both in Britain and abroad, inevitably build up an apprehension of English literature and the British historical past from the evidence continually recycled in these products.

It is a fact that for generations, classic serial production in Britain was dominated by Dickens. Consequently, a particularly Dickensian construction of Victorian England might well have been the result. This is the price continually paid for the fallacy universally acknowledged that Dickens and moving pictures were made for each other, and this is why there were so many films and television adaptations of Dickens's novels. For a time it seemed as if Boz was eclipsed by the 'Pride and Prejudice Factor', or the Battle of the Bodices (the sudden craze for the Brontës and Wilkie Collins), but with the stunning success of BBC-2's BAFTA winning *Our Mutual Friend*, which was followed soon afterwards by ITV's *Oliver Twist* and the BBC's millennium production of *David Copperfield* it looked as if Dickens had suddenly regained his traditional eminence.

The ideological dimension

How will this revival of the classic serial and developments in the manner of productions affect the way we view the world? In some respects, the revival of the classic serial as a high quality media product for the international market should be seen as part of the contemporary fascination for the past, which has many parts and numerous aspects. Our construction of the past, of the history which shaped us and made us what we are, might well tell us something about how we view ourselves. Television plays a considerable role in such cultural processes. It is worth looking at some of the ways in which television recycles or recreates the past, as it is within this context that classic serials are now seen and consumed.

The three particularly strong elements in the television experience of history might be called remembrance, memory and myth. Remembrance is the official, 'public service', Reithian manner in which broadcasting is used – drawing on a vast battery of resources including archive film, elaborate reconstructions, sound effects, music, authoritative voice-over narrative – to tell the nation its own history. Often the form is cast as a well publicised series, with accompanying book and other merchandise, such as BBC 2's series on the First World War.[18] Other examples would be: *Victory at Sea* (1952),[19] *The Great War* (1964),[20] *The Lost Peace* (1966),[21] *The World at War* (1975),[22] *Alistair Cooke's America* (1972),[23] *The Ascent of Man* (1974),[24] *Churchill's People* (1975),[25] *Civilisation* (1969),[26] *Seapower* (1981),[27] *Ireland: A Television History* (1981)[28] and *The Troubles* (1981).[29] The BBC continues to make these prestige historical series – *The People's Century*, *Hitler: A Warning From History*, *War Walks* have all proved to be more recent successful examples. Commercial video recording makes such material available as a commodity for domestic consumption as well as in schools, colleges, universities and other institutions such as public libraries, and media artefacts then begin to assume the legitimacy of orthodox academic histories. The historical veracity of classic serials is buttressed and supported by the accompanying television documentaries for various classic serials of the 'behind the scenes at the making of such-and-such' variety. This was very noticeable in the case of BBC-2's *Our Mutual Friend*, which was accompanied by *The Last Chapter*, a programme which attempted firmly to represent Dickens's last novel, not so much as a timeless masterpiece, as to root *Our Mutual Friend* firmly in some alleged historical moment.

The broadcasting media have achieved credibility and authenticity over past generations in having regularly relayed news and current affairs. Television may also be seen in its role of official chronicler in the manner in which particularly selected past events are given major television treatment. This calendarisation of history may be regular – such as Remembrance Sunday, the Queen's Birthday, the State Opening of Parliament – or particular events recalled as part of a national anniversary – such as D-Day, the Great War, VE Day. We also see television at work in this role in its coverage of the funerals of the greats such as Winston Churchill, Bernard Montgomery and the most striking example in recent years, the public grief and non-state funeral of Diana, Princess of Wales. The media model for this was certainly pioneered by Richard Dimbleby. In Richard Dimbleby's commentaries, as well as in the command of language used to convey the immediate sense of occasion, there was always the power to imply that what was being seen was an ancient but oft-repeated ritual, or ceremony frozen in its place in our sense of history. Rituals and ceremonies are in essence dramatic re-enactments of significant moments in the nation's past. In the way that the nation's past is constructed in our culture, they are melting moments in frozen time. Richard Dimbleby was a master builder of this edifice. If putting together a CD or video of 'Richard Dimbleby's Greatest Hits' there are two performances which would simply have to be represented – his commentary on the lying-in-state of King George VI, and his voice-over of the Coronation of Queen Elizabeth II. Both these were major television events and have their place in our collective cultural memory. It is not only in the hushed genuflecting tone of that unmistakable voice, but in the vocabulary, syntax and images of the language, that the Dimbleby enchantment must ultimately be sought:

It is dark in New Palace Yard at Westminster tonight. As I look down from this old, leaded window, I can see the ancient courtyard dappled with little pools of light where the lamps of London try to pierce the biting, wintry gloom and fail. And moving through the darkness of the night is an even darker stream of human beings, coming, almost noiselessly, from under a long, white canopy that crosses the pavement and ends at the great doors of Westminster Hall...

They are passing, in their thousands, through the hall of history while history is being made. No one knows from where they come or where they go, but they are the people, and to watch them pass is to see the nation pass...

It is very simple, this lying-in-state of a dead king, and of incomparable beauty. High above all light and shadow and rich in carving is the massive roof of chestnut, that Richard II put over the great Hall. From that roof the light slants down in clear, straight beams... There lies the coffin of the King.

The oak of Sandringham, hidden beneath the rich golden folds of the Standard; the slow flicker of the candles touches gently the gems of the imperial Crown, even that ruby that King Henry wore at Agincourt... How real the tears of those who pass and see it...

Who can know what they are thinking? Does that blind man whom they lead so carefully down the thick carpet sense around him the presence of history? Does he know that Kings and Queens have fasted here and stood their trial and gone to their death? And that little woman, with the airman by her side – does she feel the ghosts that must be here in the shadows of the Hall? The men and the women of those tumultuous days of long ago, of Chaucer, Essex, Anne Boleyn, Charles and Cromwell, Warren Hastings and those early Georges?

I thought when I watched the Bearers take the coffin into this Hall yesterday that I had never seen a sight so touching. The clasped arms of the Grenadiers, the reverent care with which lifted and carried their King. But I was wrong. But in the silent tableau of this Lying-in-State there is a beauty that no movement can ever bring. He would be forgiven who believed that these Yeomen of the Bodyguard, facing outwards from the corners of the catafalque, were carven statues of the Yeomen of the Tudor Henry's day. Could any living man ... be frozen into this immobility? The faces of the two Gentlemen at Arms are hidden by the long, white helmet plumes that have fallen about them like a curtain as they bowed their heads. Are they real, those faces, or do the plumes conceal images of stone?...[30]

Dimbleby's supreme achievement in this respect is undoubtedly the commentary on Queen Elizabeth II's coronation. This definitively placed in the public consciousness the concept of an ancient ceremony going right back to the roots of the nation's past and miraculously preserved and re-enacted before our eyes. Or, as Richard Dimbleby later described his feelings of that day:

I felt profoundly that I was seeing history in the making, and indeed the whole pageant on the floor of the Abbey moved with a slow irresistible rhythm that seemed to lift it out of time altogether. I thought at one moment... that I might be watching something that had happened a thousand years before.[31]

Richard Dimbleby lent his considerable media authority to the way sundry public ancient, traditional rituals and national events were broadcast – especially royal and state events such as coronations, weddings, funerals, the state opening of parliament, trooping the colour. This way of doing things, very largely the personal and idiosyncratic invention of Richard Dimbleby, has unquestioningly become the traditional way these things should be done, and Tom Fleming, David Dimbleby and others consciously or unconsciously speak in the tones and with the cadence of this great original.

Television as media memory may be seen either as a means of focusing attention on the life and career of a person deemed important in history, who appears before the cameras and rehearses past events in which they were personally involved, such as the extremely controversial series *Lord Mountbatten Remembers* (BBC 1980), or at the more general level of human experience in which television enables ordinary every-day folk to talk about their experiences – such as the extremely powerful and moving series about working life in twentieth-century industry, *All Our Working Lives*.[32] The great pioneering effort in this tradition was *All Our Yesterdays*.[33] Myth, which embraces literature and drama in all its aspects dwarfs both remembrance and memory in its scope and indeed its probable impact. Television's appetite for stories is vast and endless. Not only are there so many hours of schedules to fill, and not only are programmers fully aware of human appetite for stories, ('Tell me a story!' is one of the first complete sentences we learn to employ on our parents) but there are constantly fresh generations who need to be introduced to the way television tells stories and to the vast repertory of stories which they will need to be told. In this role television realizes itself in several striking ways.

Obviously, television rehearses selected classics of the nation's literature. The selection is instructive. Classical drama, apart from the obligatory respect for Shakespeare, (and even he is neglected – when did you last see a Shakespeare play on television?) British classical (or even popular) stage drama is not deemed of much use to television. To be sure, Sheridan, Shaw, Priestley, Wilde may crop up here and there in the schedules (especially at Christmas) but these productions are seldom part of television's routine offerings. When we come to novels there is an interesting selective process at play. Dickens, of course, is standard fare. Jane Austen, the Brontës... but what else? Hardy crops up from time to time and seems in a revival – *Jude the Obscure* was filmed in 1996 and *The Melancholy Hussar* (as 'The Scarlet Tunic') in 1997. Recently both *Tess of the d'Urbervilles* and *Far From the Madding Crowd* have been given the classic serial treatment on commercial television, with *The Woodlanders* currently in the pipeline. Little from the eighteenth century – *Clarissa* caused a sensation – we had truly never seen anything like it, that is surely the point and the BBC serialised

Tom Jones on Sunday evenings in autumn 1997 – George Eliot, the odd Thackeray, a burst of Trollope.... Compared to the vast array of English novelists – Goldsmith, Sterne, Smollett, Fielding, Gaskell, Gissing, Meredith, James, Conrad, Lawrence, Forster, Wells, Huxley, Bennett, Woolf, Walpole, Galsworthy – the amount of classical fiction which actually gets the treatment is significant not only because it is so limited, but the very selection is interesting. Also part of television's output of myth are the historical dramas which aspire to the production values of 'classic adaptations' but are in fact written for television by contemporary writers – *The Six Wives of Henry VIII* (BBC, 1968), *Elizabeth R* (BBC, 1971), *Henry VII* (BBC, 1974), *Edward and Mrs Simpson* (Thames, 1978) and absorbing a very considerable proportion of the BBC's drama budget for the year, *Rhodes* (1996). Significantly several of these, apparently finding themselves in need of something which might pass as a literary/textual authoritative anchorage, are accompanied by published volumes amusingly called 'novelisations'. The mixed metaphor is interesting to note – original television programmes anxiously assert literary associations and attempt to turn themselves into books. (In the case of *Rhodes*, the book was more consistently interesting than the drama series). And when television programmes appear as commercial videos they are packaged so as to resemble volumes and open to consumers like books. Thus, on sale in W.H. Smiths and Waterstones, these vulgar products of the mass media are allowed to mix among Booker Prize winners and literary polite society.

There have been attempts to dramatize historical events from the ordinary viewpoint, in such series as *Family at War* (Granada, 1973) and *Sam* (Granada, 1973–75). One of the most lavish and admired of these historical productions was BBC-1's six-episode £6 million dramatisation of Stella Tillyard's acclaimed 1994 biography of the eighteenth-century Lennox sisters, *Aristocrats*. This was an Irish Screen Production for BBC-1 and WGBH Boston, superbly costumed and filmed in impressive eighteenth-century locations, it almost stultified itself with its own production values. While it was running during June and July 1997 its historical authenticity was regularly under-written by exhortations to read 'How the true story of the Lennox sisters was brought to the screen' in the pages of the then current BBC *Home and Antiques* magazine.[34] Then there are the highfalutin attempts to use television drama as a vehicle for the serious retelling of modern history by such dramatists as Ian Curteis, whose *Suez 1956*, and *Nye Bevan* (BBC, 1981), *Churchill and the Generals* (BBC, 1979) were models of historical drama for television. Although beyond the bounds of the present discussion, it must be pointed out that significant ideological tensions arose between Ian Curteis and the BBC during the initial stages of the Corporation's attempt to produce his television drama *The Falklands Play* which was withdrawn from production amidst considerable acrimony.[35]

There is a populist dimension to these endeavours to reconstruct the past which finds expression in the craze for television adaptations of R.F. Delderfield[36] and those authors who in some measure seem to follow in his tradition, such as Catherine Cookson, Barbara Taylor Bradford and Winston Graham[37] and the epoch-making series written for television by John Hawkesworth *Upstairs Downstairs* (Thames, 1970–75) and *The Duchess of Duke Street* (BBC, 1976–77) and *Berkeley Square* (BBC-1, 1998).

Even then this ocean of history is by no means trawled – there is a comic level of historical perspective supplied in such series as *Blackadder* (BBC, 1983–90), *Brass* (Granada, 1983–84), *Dad's Army* (BBC, 1968–77), *It Ain't Half Hot Mum* (BBC, 1973–81) and *'Allo 'Allo* (BBC, 1984–90) and to show this furrow is by no means ploughed, commercial television in August 1994 launched yet a further example of constructed nostalgia in *Which Way to the War?* The derivations of the leading items in this genre are often illuminating. *Dad's Army* owes much to the comic volunteer army run by Captain Waggett in *Whiskey Galore* as well as *Fred Karno's Army*. *'Allo 'Allo* is a rich bouillabaisse of ingredients fished from thousands of 1940s' British and American war films peopled with comic Frenchmen, sexy resistance girls, bullying krauts in conflict with plucky members of the British public school educated officer class. The genre had a considerable longevity and survived in excellent condition as late as *The Longest Day*, which was released in 1961. *Which Way to the War?* draws heavily on such originals as *Ice Cold in Alex*, *Sahara* and *Hotel Sahara*.

The selection and treatment of subject matter from this reservoir of the past is considerably affected by contemporary cultural considerations. Subject matter has to be suited to contemporary taste, and presented in a style and manner which makes it palatable to modern audiences, both at home and abroad. It is not simply a matter of archaeology. The past is not only dug up, it has to be restored to life in a form which is acceptable to modern consumer taste. The classic serial needs to be seen and evaluated in this ideological context. Thus at the close of the twentieth century it seemed likely that the classic serial as a genre was very much alive, growing and developing. As this history has demonstrated, the genre is by no means the proprietory right of the BBC – the commercial television companies have amply demonstrated mastery of the genre. It is encouraging to note in conclusion that as a living thing the genre certainly appears vital, and with a life of its own.

Notes

Introduction

1. Marcus Aurelius: *Mediations*, Book IV, sec. 36.
2. See Peter L. Berger, *Invitation to Sociology: a Humanistic Perspective* (1963), Harmondsworth, Penguin, 1966, pp. 83–8.
3. See Robert Giddings: 'Super Product' in *New Society*, 13 July 1978, pp. 83–4.

1 Definitions, Early History: the Classic Drama Serial

1. E.M. Forster, 'Does Culture Matter?', in *Two Cheers for Democracy* (1951), 1976, p. 108.
2. John Reith, speech to the Adult Education Conference, October 1928, quoted in Asa Briggs: *The History of Broadcasting in the United Kingdom: The Golden Age of Wireless 1927–1939*, Oxford, Oxford University Press 1995, p. 7.
3. Henry Val Gielgud, 1900–81, the elder brother of Sir John Gielgud, he was Director of Productions at the BBC from 1929 to 1963 and worked in television drama between 1949 and 1951. Gielgud published fascinating volumes of autobiography – *Years of the Locust* (1947), *One Year of Grace* (1950) and *Years in a Mirror* (1965).
4. See John Drakakis (ed.): *British Radio Drama*, Cambridge, Cambridge University Press 1981, p. 3.
5. Quoted in Asa Briggs: *The History of Broadcasting in the United Kingdom*, Oxford, Oxford University Press 1961, Vol. 1, p. 282.
6. See Robert Giddings, Keith Selby and Chris Wensley: *Screening the Novel*, Macmillan 1989, pp. 43ff.
7. Anthony Smith: *The Shadow in the Cave*, 1982, p. 14.
8. Paddy Scannell and David Cardiff: *A Social History of British Broadcasting*, Volume One: 1922–1939: *Serving the Nation*, Oxford, Blackwell 1991, p. 135.
9. Ian Rodger: *Radio Drama Methuen*, Macmillan 1982, p. 14.
10. See Lance Sieveking: *The Stuff of Radio*, Cassell 1934.
11. Sieveking invented the squared plan of the football field which featured in the *Radio Times* and helped generations of fans, giving rise to the cry: 'And back to square one!'
12. Briggs op. cit., p. 55.
13. He adapted Pirandello's *The Man With a Flower in His Mouth* for J.L. Baird's experimental television broadcasts in May 1930. See Briggs op. cit., pp. 509–10.
14. Louis Napoleon Parker 1852–1944, former music master at Sherborne, invented the pageant and became in effect the nation's pageant-master. Among the most famous civic pageants were those at Bath, Dover,

211

Sherborne, Warwick and York. He staged patriotic pageants during the first World War and devised *The Pageant of Drury Lane* in 1918. Another obvious key work of this vogue for the spectacular historical show is Noel Coward's *Cavalcade* (1931). Charles Chiltern adapted the pageant style for such characteristic radio stories-with-music historical sagas as *Riders of the Range* (which ran from 1939 to 1953), *The Blue and the Grey* (1961) the story of the US Civil War, *Blood on the Prairie* (1963) which told the story of the Souix Indian wars. The influence clearly continued in *Oh, What a Lovely War!* which Chiltern wrote for Joan Littlewood in 1963.

15. See Scannell and Cardiff op. cit., p. 146.
16. See Briggs op. cit., p. 149.
17. Val Gielgud: *British Radio Drama* 1922–1956, 1957, p. 36.
18. *Radio Times*, 20 February 1931, p. 414.
19. See Scannell and Cardiff op. cit., p. 370ff.
20. See Jon Stallworthy: *Louis MacNeice*, Faber and Faber 1995, p. 334.
21. D.C. Bridson: *Prospero and Ariel* 1971, p. 57.
22. Val Gielgud: *British Radio Drama* op. cit., pp. 60–1.
23. Broadcast on the Chelmsford station on 29 July 1924. We are indebted to James Codd of the BBC Written Archives Centre at Caversham for this information, and for details of many of these early broadcasts of classic novels.
24. The proposal scene from *Pride and Prejudice* was broadcast on 15 January 1924; Lady Catherine's visit from *Pride and Prejudice* transmitted on 16 January 1925 and various scenes from Jane Austen on the theme of love and friendship were adapted and produced by M.H. Allen on 17 August 1936. A version of Kingsley's *Westward Ho!* was transmitted on 19 November 1925. *Jane Eyre* was broadcast in 1931 and 1933; *Wuthering Heights* was broadcast in 1934.
25. Asa Briggs: *The Golden Age of Wireless* op. cit., p. 152.
26. *Radio Times* 31 March 1939, p. 6.
27. Ibid., p. 7.
28. Ibid.
29. Tom Hickman: *What Did You Do in the War, Auntie? The BBC at War 1939–45*, BBC 1995, pp. 77–8.
30. *David Copperfield* Omnibus/Sagittarius, American TV film 1970. It was written by Jack Pulman, produced by Frederick H. Brogger and directed by Delbert Mann. It starred Robin Phillips as David, Edith Evans as Betsy, Michael Redgrave as Peggotty, Susan Hampshire as Agnes and Corin Redgrave as Steerforth. Richardson's performance as Micawber is superb.
31. F. Dubrez Fawcett: *Dickens the Dramatist: On Stage, Screen and Radio*, W.H. Allen 1952, pp. 215–17.
32. John Swift: *Adventure in Vision* Lehmann 1950, p. 46–7.
33. It began in 9 April 1954 and ran until 28 June 1957.
34. Letter dated 30 May 1947, quoted in Asa Briggs: *Sound and Vision, The History of Broadcasting in the United Kingdom*, Oxford, Oxford University Press 1979, Volume IV, p. 214.
35. It was based on Clemence Dane's stage version, produced by George More O'Ferrall, with music by Richard Addinsell and was transmitted live on 21 December 1946.

36. Jan Bussell: *The Art of Television,* Faber and Faber 1952, p. 103.
37. *Radio Times*, 4 March 1949.
38. 'How We've Covered Dickens', in *Radio Times* 5 November 1994.
39. Interview with the authors, April 1998. Peter Vaughan – whose career in Dickens spans the controversial *Oliver Twist* of 1962 and *Our Mutual Friend* 1998 – added that in shooting television today, on film: '... we're really working as we would on location in the cinema, which means that you can have much more manoeuvrability and be much more malleable in your choice of shots and in your lighting. I think the quality of the work has proved that over the years.'
40. Interview with the authors, April 1998.
41. As well as improvements in Welsh and Scottish television services and more educational programmes for adults. See Asa Briggs: *The History of Broadcasting in the United Kingdom, Volume V, Competition 1955–1974,* Oxford, Oxford University Press 1995, p. 294.
42. Report of a Meeting with Drama Producers, 9 November 1960, quoted in Briggs op. cit., pp. 286–7.
43. Newman's contribution to the development of television drama in Britain in the 1960s is discussed in Irene Shubik: *Play for Today: The Evolution of Television Drama* Davis & Poynter 1975.
44. See Tise Vahimagi: *British Television: an Illustrated Guide,* Oxford, Oxford University Press/BFI 1994, pp. 134–45.
45. Kenneth Passingham: *The Guinness Book of TV Facts and Feats,* Guinness Superlatives Ltd. 1984, pp. 227–8.
46. *Tom Grattan's War* was written and produced by David C. Rae and transmitted as 24 30-minute episodes.
47. *The Fall of Eagles,* 13 75-minute episodes, superbly cashed in on the craze for costume drama reinvigorated by the advent of colour television and BBC-2. The series was written by Robert Muller and starred Maurice Denham as Kaiser Wilhelm I, Curt Jurgens as Bismarck, Barry Foster as Kaiser Wilhelm II, Marius Goring as Hindenburg and Laurence Naismith as the Emperor Franz Josef.
48. The series starred Ronald Pickup as Randolph, Lee Remick as Jenny and also starred Christopher Cazenove.
49. See Mollie Hardwick: *The World of 'Upstairs, Downstairs': an Illustrated Social History from the Turn of the Century to the Great Depression,* Newton Abbot: David and Charles 1976.
50. Lord David Cecil: *The Cecils of Hatfield House,* Constable 1973, p. 267.
51. Samuel Hynes: *A War Imagined: the First World War and English Culture,* Atheneun 1991, p. xiii.
52. Leslie Halliwell with Philip Purser: *Halliwell's Television Companion,* Paladin 1987, p. 287.
53. Quoted in *Radio Times* 28 December 1967, p. 59.

2 The 1970s: Signs of Change

1. Comment quoted in Asa Briggs: *The History of Broadcasting in the United Kingdom, Volume 5 Competition 1955–1974,* Oxford, Oxford University

Press 1995, p. 937.

2. Curiously enough, the Japanese Thomas Hardy Society was founded a decade earlier, in 1957, to foster interest in Hardy's novels and visiting sites of interest in Dorset. At the Society's formal meetings the Japanese members dutifully drink up cups of furmity, Henchard's favourite drink, made of wheat stewed in milk, raisins, sugar, spices mixed with rum.

3. Alan Bates as Michael Henchard, Janet Maw as Elizabeth-Jane, Jack Galloway as Donald Farfrae and Anna Massey as Lucetta, the music composed and conducted by Carl Davis, produced by Jonathan Powell, directed by David Giles, dramatised by Dennis Potter.

4. See, John R. Cook, *Dennis Potter: A Life on Screen*, Manchester University Press, Manchester, 1995, p. 101.

5. Christopher Ricks, 'Translating Hardy for TV', *Sunday Times*, 5 February 1978.

6. W. Stephen Gilbert, *The Life and Work of Dennis Potter*, Sceptre, London, 1995, pp. 229–30. The writing completed, Potter called it 'a general drama of pain... there were times, working on the dramatisation, when I did indeed feel a certain lowering of the spirits.'

7. See Cook, op. cit. p. 101 who argues that this was a connection exploited by Potter when he later cast the leading actor of *The Mayor Casterbridge*, Alan Bates, in *Secret Friends*, the film version of his novel, *Ticket to Ride*. This concerns a man who begins to confuse his wife with a prostitute.

8. *War and Peace*, written by Sergei Bondarchuk, was released in the USSR in 1967. It lasted over eight-and-a-half hours. Its tone is reverent, dignified and the film contains some of the most spectacular and convincing battle scenes ever filmed. Bondarchuk directed and starred as Pierre. This too was a long-term project, taking five years to make and costing an estimated $60 000 000. It has twice been shown on BBC television. The BBC-2 version was inevitably influenced by Bondarchuk's film.

9. See Ariel 29 September 1972, p. 3.

10. See Leonard Miall: 'Working With European Broadcasters' *EBU Review*, June 1972.

11. Clive James: 'Tolstoy Makes Television History' *The Observer* 22 October 1972.

12. Harold Child: 'Jane Austen' in A.W. Ward and A.R. Waller, eds: *The Cambridge History of English Literature, Volume XII, The Nineteenth Century*, Cambridge, Cambridge University Press 1932, p. 239.

13. Jane Aiken Hodge: *Passion and Principle: The Loves and Lives of Regency Women*, John Murray 1996, p. 16.

14. Peter Parker (ed.) *The Reader's Companion to the Twentieth-Century Novel*, Fourth Estate, 1994, p. 197.

15. Hilary Kingsley and Geoff Tibball: *Box of Delights* 1989, p. 150.

16. Raymond Williams: 'Isaac's Urges' in *The Listener* 31 January 1974, in Alan O'Connor, ed.: *Raymond Williams on Television*, Routledge 1989, p. 2.

17. Roman biography developed from funeral oratory and tomb inscriptions.

18. Alistair Cooke: *Masterpieces: A Decade of Classics on British Television*, Bodley Head 1982, p. 19.

19. Clive James, in *The Observer* 21 November 1976.

20. This is a curious state of affairs. This novel had been given pride of place in

the Dickens canon by the influential Dr F.R. Leavis, *The Great Tradition* (1949) whose word was readily spread by his numerous disciples in the teaching profession. Its neglect by the media, in whose ranks many Cambridge graduates may be found, is therefore odd.

21. His early plays dealt with sporting subjects – hill walking (*Mosedale Horseshoe*), bowls (*The Panel*) and cycling (*The Birthday Run*). He caught the diusillusionment with Harold Wilson's Labour Party perfectly in *The Nearly Man* (Granada, 1974). Other televison plays followed, including classic adaptations; he won the BAFTA Writers Award in 1986 for *Bleak House* (BBC-2, 1985).

22. Cf. Clive James, *The Observer*, 6 November 1977. 'Dickens did not talk down. He was genuine in everything, even his sentimentality, which was really just a powerful assertion that people could be noble beyond their circumstances ... *Hard Times* (Granada) continues to be remarkably successful in transmitting the largesse of his spirit.

  Dickens knows, and lets you know he knows, that he is writing melodrama: one of the functions his style performs is to win your consent while he simplifies. It follows that a dramatisation must find a style to match, and here it has happened.'

23. See F. Dubrez Fawcett: *Dickens the Dramatist: On Stage, Screen and Radio*, W.H. Allen 1952, p̂. 29.

24. A long running soap opera about a GP's family. *Mrs Dale's Diary* began on the Light Programme in January 1948 and ended on Radio 2 in April 1969, by which time it was called *The Dales*. The Queen Mother's comment amply sums it up: 'It is the only way of knowing what goes on in a middle class family.'

25. Interview with authors, June 1998.

26. *Pickwick Papers*, *Bleak House* and *Little Dorrit* were not released. The others are available.

27. A BBC co-production with Time-Life and Playtel.

28. Philip Purser, quoted in Leslie Halliwell: *Halliwell's Television Companion*, Paladin 1986, p. 816.

3 The Blockbusters

1. Clive James, *The Observer* 16 March 1980.

2. Jane Harbord and Jeff Wright: *Forty Years of British Television*, Boxtree 1995, p. 86.

3. This might explain another curious obsession currently in vogue: the craze for authentic performances of ancient music, or putting on Shakespeare's plays in the 'genuine' and 'original' Globe Theatre.

4. Cf Robert Colls and Philip Dodd, eds: *Englishness: Politics and Culture 1880–1920*, Croom Helm 1987.

5. *Sorry!* ran until 1988 and in some ways continued a tradition which had featured BBC-1's 1971–73 sitcom *Now Look Here!*, in which Corbett had also starred, and the Terry Scott vehicle, BBC-1's 1973 sitcom *Son of the Bride*. All of these series centred on adult males who had never really cut themselves free of their mothers.

6. It has long been a rule of thumb among media pundits that a second-rate novel stands a greater chance of making a first-rate dramatisation.

7. Evelyn Waugh: *Brideshead Revisited*, Chapter 1, Harmondsworth: Penguin 1981, pp. 31–2.

8. Ibid., pp. 29–30.

9. Jane Austen, letter to Anna Austen, 9 September 1814.

10. Alistaire Cooke: *Masterpieces: a Decade of Classics on British Television.* Bodley Head 1982, p. 55.

11. Details taken from Pat Chapman, ed.: *The 1998 Good Curry Guide*, Hodder and Stoughton 1998, pp. 200–21.

12. See George Brandt: 'The Jewel in the Crown' in George Brandt, ed.: *British Television Drama in the 1980s*, Cambridge, Cambridge University Press 1993, pp. 206–11.

13. See John Bayley: 'The Matter of India', in *London Review of Books* 19 March 1987 p. 195 and cf Andrew Robinson 'The Jewel in the Crown' in *Sight and Sound*, 53, 3 Summer 1984, pp. 1988–9.

14. See, for example, Julian Barnes in *The Observer* 11 January 1984 and Sean Day-Lewis in the *Daily Telegraph* 15 February 1984.

15. 'Outside the Whale' in Granta, April 1984.

16. See George Brandt, ed.: *British Television Drama in the 1980s*, Cambridge, Cambridge University Press 1993, p. 200.

17. *The Monocled Mutineer*, a drama in two 75-minute episodes, by Alan Bleasdale, based on the book by William Allison and John Fairley, dealt with the career of Percy Toplis, a minor criminal who as a private in the army led a mutiny at Etaples in France just before Third Battle of Ypres in 1917. He then returned to England and was later killed while resisting arrest. The production caused much controversy over its authenticity, originally publicised as a true story. The BBC later backed down and admitted that parts of the story were fictionalised. The Conservative government and its supporters in the press attacked it as left-wing propaganda. The production starred Paul McGann, Cherie Lunghi, Matthew Marsh and Timothy West and was produced by Richard Broke. *Tumbledown* was based on the true story of 'X' who was an officer in the Scots Guards and was wounded in the Falklands war and was critical of his reception on returning home. Ian Curteis had already written successful plays transmitted by the BBC about the Suez War and Winston Churchill. The BBC had commissioned his *Falklands Play* but difficulties with casting Mrs Thatcher and other problems caused the Corporation to drop the production. Curteis leaked the story to the Freedom Association and it was then debated by the *Evening Standard* and the rest of Fleet Street, to the embarrassment of the Corporation. See Chris Horrie and Steve Clarke: *Fuzzy Monsters: Fear and Loathing at the BBC*, Heinemann 1994 p. 129. and Michael Leapman: *The Last Days of the Beeb*, Allen and Unwin 1986, pp. 185–90.

18. *Brass*, Granada 1983–84, written by John Stevenson and Julian Roach, who were veterans of *Coronation Street*. The series was produced by Bill Podmore and directed by Gareth Jones, it starred Timothy West, Caroline Blakeston, Barbara Ewing, Geoffrey Hinsliff, David Ashton and James Saxton.

19. BBC Annual Report and Handbook 1987, p. 173.

20. Interview with the authors, April 1998.

21. Interview with the authors, April 1998.

22. And based on very interesting evidence cf John Sutherland *Is Heathcliff a Murderer?*, Oxford, Oxford University Press 1996, p. 66.
23. Olivia Manning, *The Balkan Trilogy*: *The Great Fortune* (1960); *The Spoilt City* (1962) and *Friends and Heroes* (1965). *The Levant Trilogy*: *The Danger Tree* (1977); *The Battle Lost and Won* (1978) and *The Sum of Things* (1980).
24. R.D. Smith was later a distinguished BBC radio drama producer on the Third Programme, who included several classic novel dramatisations to his credits, including Milton's *Samson Agonistes* (1960), which ran for one-and-three-quarter hours.

4 The 1990s: Renaissance of the Classic Serial

1. See Michael Leapman: *The Last Days of the Beeb*, Allen and Unwin 1986, p. 13, to which we are considerably indebted for this section.
2. See Leapman op. cit., p. 191.
3. See Robert Hewison: *Culture and Consensus: England, Art and Politics Since 1945*, Methuen 1995, pp. 216–19 and Chris Horrie and Steve Clarke: *Fuzzy Monsters: Fear and Loathing at the BBC*, Heinemann, 1994, pp. 11–13 and 47–9.
4. *BBC Annual Report and Handbook* 1987, pp. 64–5.
5. *BBC Annual Report and Accounts 1996–97*, pp. 50–1, p. 79.
6. Bill Borrows: 'Fat Profits' in *The Guide*, *Guardian* 29 August 1998, p. 12.
7. See Robin Nelson: *TV Drama in Transition: Forms, Values and Cultural Change*, Macmillan 1997, p. 30.
8. Joseph Highmore (1692–1780), portrait painter, friend of Samuel Richardson, he studied at the Kneller Academy and painted twelve illustrations for Richardson's novel *Pamela*. Francis Hayman (1708–76), began as a scene painter at Covent Garden Opera House, and decorated boxes and pavilions at Vauxhall Gardens. He was celebrated for his Conversation Pieces. William Hogarth (1697–1764), began as engraver and painter of Conversation Pieces, now acknowledged the greatest English master of satiric narrative paintings – *A Harlot's Progress*, *Marriage à la Mode* and *A Rake's Progress*.
9. Sir A. Ward and A.R. Waller, eds: *The Cambridge History of English Literature, Volume X: The Age of Johnson*, 1932, p. 1.
10. Interview with the authors, May 1998.
11. David Nokes: 'It Isn't in the Book' in *Times Literary Supplement* 26 April 1996.
12. Richard Last: 'The Perils of Being Pure' in the *Daily Telegraph* 8 August 1991.
13. Peter Waymark: 'Suddenly It's the Dawning of the Railway Age' in *The Times* 8 January 1994.
14. Lynne Truss: 'Middlemarch is Definitely Worth a Detour' in *The Times* 13 January 1994.
15. These details are from interviews by the authors with Ros Borland, Commercial Manager, Drama, BBC Television, Amanda Knott, Assistant Commercial Manager, Drama, BBC Television and Martin Rakusen, Commercial Executive, BBC Rights Agency.
16. See Jenny Rice and Carol Saunders: 'Consuming *Middlemarch*: The

Construction and Consumption of Nostalgia in Stamford' in Deborah Cartmell, I.Q. Hunter, Heidi Kaye and Imelda Whelehan, eds: *Pulping Fictions: Consuming Culture Across the Literature/Media Divide*, Pluto 1996, pp. 85–98.

17. Libby Purves: 'Remaining Faithful to the Bitter-sweet End' in *The Times* 8 January 1994.
18. Andrew Davies, interview with the authors, May 1998.
19. Ibid.
20. Andrew Davies, quoted in Cary Bazalgette and Christine James, eds: *Screening 'Middlemarch': 19th Century Novel to 90s Television*, BBC Education Developments 1994, p. 29.
21. See E.J. Hobsbawm and George Rude: *Captain Swing*, Lawrence and Wishart 1969, p. 97, Elizabeth Longford: *Wellington: Pillar of State*, Weidenfeld and Nicolson 1972, pp. 226–8 and Jasper Ridley: *Lord Palmerston*, Hutchinson 1970, p. 148.
22. John Morley: *The Life of Richard Cobden* Chapman & Hall 1881, pp. 90–1.
23. See R. Athill: 'Dickens and the Railway' in *English Number 13* 1961.
24. See Ernie Trory: *Truth Against the World: The Life and Times of Thomas Hughes, Author of 'Tom Brown's Schooldays'*, Hove, East Sussex: Crabtree Press 1993, p. 117.
25. William Makepeace Thackeray 'De Juventute' 1860, in *Roundabout Papers*. See David Newsome: *The Victorian World Picture*, John Murray 1997, pp. 27–32.
26. Cary Bazalgette and Christine James: *Screening 'Middlemarch': 19th Century Novel to 90s Television*, BBC Educational Developments 1994, p. 26.
27. The first episode was 85 minutes long, the remaining five were of 55 minutes.
28. Interview in *Who Framed Charles Dickens?*, BBC-2 7 November 1994.
29. Richard Johnson: 'Curtain Up on a Classic' in *Radio Times* 5 November 1994, p. 27.
30. Ibid., p. 29.
31. David Lodge: 'Visions of Victoriana' in *Observer Review* 4 September 1994.
32. David Lodge: 'Three Weddings and a Big Row' in *The Independent* 13 December 1994.
33. Ibid.
34. Letter, quoted by Charles Dickens the younger, Introduction, *Great Expectations and Hard Times*, Macmillan, 1930, p. xv.
35. It had last been on television in 1971 when it was dramatised by Julian Mitchell, produced and directed by Howard Baker, starring Bryan Marshall and Ann Firbank.
36. Quoted in Andrew Culf: 'TV and Film Vie Genteelly for Jane Austen Blockbuster' in *Guardian* 13 October 1995.
37. In the event 35mm shooting was abandoned and it was actually filmed on Super 16.
38. Ibid.
39. Jane Austen: *Persuasion*, Chapter 11.
40. Nick Radlo: 'Powers of Persuasion' in *The Journal of the Royal Television Society*, November/December 1995, p. 17.

5 The '*Pride and Prejudice* Factor'

1. Colin Firth played Fitzwilliam Darcy and Jennifer Ehle was Elizabeth Bennet. Jane was played by Susannah Harker, Kitty by Polly Maberly, Mary by Lucy Briars and Lydia by Julia Sawahla. Benjamin Whitrow was Mr Bennet and Alison Steadman played Mrs Bennet.
2. Sue Birtwistle and Susie Conklin: *The Making of 'Pride and Prejudice'*, Penguin Books, BBC Books 1995, p. v.
3. Simon Langton, interview with the authors, June 1998.
4. Sexual intercourse with girls under twelve was criminalised by Edward I's first Statute of Westminster 3 Ed.I c. 13 (1275). It was a Felony, without benefit of Clergy, with girls under ten by a Statute of 1586.
5. Cf Rosamond Vincy in *Middlemarch*.
6. Samuel Johnson: *The Rambler*, number 170, 2 November 1751. *The Gentleman's Magazine* 1768, Vol. 58, p. 49.
7. A.D.Harvey: *Sex in Georgian England*, Duckworth 1994, pp. 22–3.
8. Rosemary Hawthorne: *Knickers: An Intimate Appraisal*, Souvenir Press 1991, pp. 11–13.
9. *The Gentleman's Magazine* 1788 Vol. 58, p. 491.
10. George Hanger: *The Life, Adventures and Opinions of Colonel George Hanger*, William Combe 1801, pp. 17–18
11. William Hickey: *Memoirs of a Georgian Rake*, edited by Roger Hudson, Folio Society 1995, p. 12.
12. Sarah Ellis: in a book published 1842, cited in Reay Tannahill, *Sex in History*, Scarborough House 1992, p. 349.
13. Jane Austen: *Pride and Prejudice*, Vol. III, chapter 4.
14. Ibid.
15. Book of Common Prayer, The Form of Solemnisation of Matrimony.
16. See Maggie Lane: *Jane Austen's World*, Carlton 1996, pp. 54–5.
17. Simon Langton, interview with the authors, June 1998.
18. 'They're Playing My Theme' in *Radio Times* 7–13 October 1995, p. 10.
19. Carl Davis, interview with the authors, June 1998.
20. A certain Christel von Lassberg drowned herself near Goethe's house with an obligatory volume of the novel in her pocket.
21. See Steven Marcus: 'Language into Structure: "Pickwick Papers" Revisited', in *Daedalus*, number 101, 1972.
22. A term to characterise results of behaviour, like the Fat Boy's, from eating and sleeping too much.
23. David Nokes: 'It Isn't in the Book', *Times Literary Supplement* 26 April 1996.
24. Kate Lock: 'Its Austenmania', *Radio Times*, 13 July 1996.
25. See Robin Nelson: *TV Drama in Transition: Forms, Values and Cultural Change*, Manchester: Manchester University Press 1997, p. 125.
26. Jon E. Lewis and Penny Stempel: *The Ultimate TV Guide*, Orion 1999, p. 80.
27. By Fay Weldon, it starred Elizabeth Garvie and David Rintoul, was produced by Jonathan Powell and directed by Cyril Coke.
28. Even to the extent of including a controversial seduction scene.
29. *Emma* was a United Film and Television production, for Meridian Broadcasting, in association with Chestermead Ltd. and A&E Network, New York.

30. Information provided by Ros Borland, Commercial Manager, BBC Drama, Amanda Knott, Deputy Commercial Manager, BBC Drama and Martin Rakusen, Commercial Executive, BBC Rights Agency, in interviews with the authors, May 1998.
31. Associated Book Clubs marketed Emma Tennant's work as: 'The adventures of Jane Austen's favourite heroine continue in this superb sequel from the author of *Pemberley.*'
32. 'Making the Right Moves: Stylish Emma Bed Linen' in Bournemouth *Evening Echo* 16 October 1996.
33. Desmond Christy: 'Jane's Fighting Clips' in *Guardian* 23 November 1994; See Allison Pearson: 'Pride and Prejudice Down the Ages', *Observer* 12 October 1995; Lucy Ellman: 'I Can No Longer Contain Myself', *New Statesman Society* 20 October 1995; Fay Weldon: 'Star of Stage and Screen' *Guardian* 12 April 1995; Andrew Culf: 'TV and Film Vie Genteelly for Jane Austen Blockbuster', *Guardian* 13 October 1995; Catherine Bennett: 'Hype and Heritage' *Guardian* 22 October 1995; Keith Thomas: 'Retrochic' *London Review of Books* 20 April 1995; Andrew Culf: 'Pride Wins Over Prejudice' *Guardian* 13 March 1996; Dan Glaister: 'Film Locations Make Most of Period Charm', *Guardian* 21 May 1996 and Maev Kennedy: 'Darcy's Pride Fuels Record' in *History Tours* 6.

6 The *'Pride and Prejudice* Effect'

1. David Nokes: 'It Isn't In the Book', *Times Literary Supplement* 26 April 1996.
2. Quoted in Kate Lock: 'Battle of the Bodices' in *Radio Times*, 1 September 1996.
3. Jonathan Swift: *Gulliver's Travels*, Part Two, Chapter Two.
4. Anthony Hayward: *The Making of Moll Flanders*, Boxtree 1996, p. 11.
5. Daniel Defoe: *Moll Flanders* 1721, J.M. Dent 1968, pp. 163–4.
6. Ibid., p. 19.
7. Andrew Davies, interview with the authors, May 1998.
8. Jon E. Lewis and Penny Stempel: *The Ultimate TV Guide*, Orion 1999, p. 234.
9. Andrew Davies, comment quoted in *Radio Times* 23 November 1996.
10. Ibid.
11. Ibid.
12. Andrew Davies, quoted in Sue Birtwistle and Susie Conklin: *The Making of Jane Austen's 'Emma'*, Penguin Books 1996, pp. 57–8.
13. Ibid.
14. Cf Ronald Hutton: *The Stations of the Sun*, Oxford, Oxford University Press 1997, p. 332.
15. Blurb on the cover of the proprietary video cassette.
16. This is not the place to dwell upon it, but it is nonetheless revealing that in showing respect for a Princess particularly associated with notions of a break with previous, stuffy, hidebound conventions, Michael Fish suddenly and uncharacteristically adopts the of garb of fogeyism.
17. Jonathan Miller: *Subsequent Performance* and cf Robert Giddings, Keith Selby and Chris Wensley: *Screening the Novel*, Macmillan 1992, pp. 16–20.
18. Quoted in *Radio Times* 16 November 1996.
19. Martin Rakusen, Commercial Executive, BBC Rights Agency interview with the authors, October 1998.

20. Anthony Trollope: *Autobiography* 1883.
21. New Year's Revolution in *Radio Times* 4 January 1997, p. 26.
22. Steven Waddington, quoted in Kate Lock: 'Ivan-Who?' in *Radio Times* 25 January 1997, p. 20.
23. John Brooke-Little: *Royal Ceremonies of State*, Hamlyn 1980, p. 58.
24. See Maggie Brown: 'False Steps' in *Media Guardian* 18 February 1997.
25. Martin Rakusen, Commercial Executive, BBC Rights Agency, interview with the authors, June 1998.
26. Ibid. *Rhodes*, which similarly had a very modest reception in the UK when first transmitted in the Autumn 1996, was subsequently shown all over the world and has earned £772 477.
27. Joseph Conrad: *Nostromo: A Tale of the Seaboard* (1904), Garden City: Doubleday, Page 1925, p. 77. Cf David Simpson: *Fetishism and Imagination: Dickens, Melville, Conrad*, Baltimore, Johns Hopkins University Press 1982, pp. 93–116.
28. Joseph Conrad: *Nostromo* 1904 Part 1, Chapter 6.
29. Joseph Conrad: *Nostromo* 1904 Part 3, Chapter 11.
30. Jonah Raskin: *The Mythology of Imperialism: Rudyard Kipling, Joseph Conrad, E.M. Forster, D.H. Lawrence and Joyce Cary*, New York, Dell 1971, p. 15. Cf Edward Said: *Culture and Imperialism*, Chatto and Windus 1993, pp. 159–60 and 197–200.
31. 'Are You Sure That's Wise?' in *The Box* April 1997.
32. Martin Rakusen, Commercial Executive, BBC Rights Agency, interview with the authors, June 1998.
33. ITV Midland Bank Drama Premieres publicity, 1997.
34. Ibid.
35. Ibid.
36. Ibid.

7 Boz Rides Again

1. Anthony Powell: *A Buyer's Market* 1952, Chapter 2.
2. Anthony Powell: *Temporary Kings* 1973, Chapter 1.
3. David Thomas: 'Times of Their Lives' in *Radio Times* 4 October 1997.
4. John Spurling: 'Dancing Partners' in the *Guardian* 8 October 1997.
5. Martin Seymour-Smith: *Who's Who in Twentieth Century Literature*, Weidenfeld and Nicolson 1976, p. 290.
6. Henry Fielding: *Tom Jones*, Book v, Chapter 7.
7. Cf Henry Fielding: Preface to *Joseph Andrews* 1742.
8. Henry Fielding: *Tom Jones*, Book ii, Chapter 1.
9. See Arthur Murphy: *An Essay on the Genius of Henry Fielding* 1762 and Hugh Blair: *Lectures on Rhetoric and Belles Lettres*, 1783, Volume 3.
10. Henry Fielding: *Tom Jones*, Book viii, Chapter 1.
11. Henry Fielding: *Tom Jones*, Book xv, Chapter 5.
12. Quoted in Alison Graham: 'The Day Rain Stopped Play' in *Radio Times* 15 November 1997.
13. It is an interesting coincidence that the Revd. Primrose is thrown into prison for debt.

14. There are distinct echoes in *Pickwick Papers*, chap. 51, when Pickwick sees the Dutch clock and the bird-cage on his arrival at the Fleet. It is Sam Weller who explains 'Veels within Veels, a prison in a prison' – an echo of *A Sentimental Journey*. It recalls the poignant episode when Yorick weeps to see the starling in the cage because it reminded him of the prisoner in the Bastille.

15. Jean Paul Richter (known as 'Jean Paul') 1763–1825, the chronicler of the quaint, cosy unchanging charm of harmless provincialism, a master of the wayward discursive and observant whimsicality, his works were very widely read in early nineteenth century and his influence endured (very strong in *The Old Curiosity Shop*) *Leben des vernuuegten Schulmeisterleins Wuz* (1793) and *Hesperus, oder 45 Hundesposttage, eine Biographie* (1795), (much imitated passages of landscape description, self consciously detailed and beautiful) and the unfinished *Flegeljahre* (1805), full of wit, irony and arabesques of humour.

16. Martin Rakusen, Commercial Executive, BBC Rights Agency, interview with the authors, June 1998.

17. See Sue Lonoff: 'Charles Dickens and Wilkie Collins' in *Nineteenth Century Fiction*, 35 (1980) and T.S. Eliot: 'Wilkie Collins and Dickens' in *Selected Essays* 1932.

18. Catherine Wearing, interview with the authors, April 1998.

19. Ibid.

20. G.K. Chesterton: Preface to *Our Mutual Friend*, Everyman's Library Edition 1906, reprinted in *Chesterton on Dickens*, edited by Michael Slater, Dent 1992, p. 209.

21. See F.B. Pinion, *A Hardy Companion: a Guide to the Works of Thomas Hardy and their Background*, Macmillan, London, 1968, pp. 46–7.

22. R.L. Purdy, *Thomas Hardy, A Bibliographical Study*, Oxford University Press, London, 1954, pp. 71–2.

23. By this time, Hardy knew the 'fearful price' he had to pay 'for the privilege of writing in the English language'. See, 'Candour in English Fiction', in Harold Orel, *Thomas Hardy's Personal Writings*, University of Kansas Press, 1966; Macmillan, 1967, London, pp. 150–1.

24. This was published in *The Fortnightly Review* in May 1891 as 'The Midnight Baptism: A Study in Christianity'.

25. Thomas Hardy, *Tess of the d'Urbervilles: A Pure Woman*, (1891), Macmillan, London, 1974, p. 150. Subsequent references are to this edition, and will be given in the text wherever possible.

26. Meridian 1998: dramatisation in two parts of 90-minutes each. Tess (Justine Waddell), Alec (Jason Flemyng), Angel (Oliver Milburn), Narrator (Gerald James), director of photography: Richard Greatrex, film editor: Peter Davies, composer: Alan Lisk, script executive: Gwenda Bagshaw, adapted by: Ted Whitehead, producer: Sarah Wilson, director: Ian Sharp.

27. The cast included: Paloma Baeza (Bathsheba Everdene), Nathaniel Parker (Gabriel Oak), Natasha Little (Fanny Robin), Jonathan Firth (Sergeant Troy) and Nigel Terry (Mr Boldwood).

28. Quoted in Jane Rackham: 'Far From the Modern Crowd' in *Radio Times* 4 July 1998.

29. Ibid.

30. See F.B. Pinion, *A Hardy Companion: A Guide to the Works of Thomas Hardy and their Background*, Macmillan, London, 1968, p. 28.
31. See Keith Selby, 'Hardy, History and Hokum', in *The Classic Novel: From Page to Screen*, (eds Robert Giddings and Erica Sheen), Manchester University Press, Manchester, 1999.
32. *Radio Times*, 23 October 1998.
33. Andrew Davies, interview with the authors, August 1998.
34. Ibid.
35. *Saturday Review*, BBC Radio Four 7 November 1998.
36. Martin Rakusen, Commercial Executive, BBC Rights Agency, interview with the authors, May 1999.
37. Ibid.
38. See John Sutherland: *Is Heathcliff a Murderer?: Puzzles in 19th Century Fiction*, Oxford, Oxford University Press 1996, pp. 66–72.
39. Charlotte Brontë, letter to W.S. Williams, 28 October 1847.
40. John Forster, review of *Vanity Fair* in *The Examiner*, July 1848.
41. Thackeray: *Vanity Fair* Chapter 53.
42. Ibid., Chapter 54.
43. See Andy Beckett: 'Blonde Ambition': 'They are feisty, female, moderately talented and very successful. And they all learned their trade at the Sylvia Young Theatre School' in the *Guardian* 19 May 1999.
44. Rupert Smith 'She's Sexy, Sexy, Scheming and Very, Very Sharp' *Radio Times* 31 October 1998, p. 25.
45. Andrew Davies, interview with the authors, August 1998.
46. Ibid.
47. *Radio Times* 10 April 1999.
48. Arthur Hugh Clough, letter 9 February 1849, Jane Welsh Carlyle letter 17 May 1849.
49. Alan Bleasdale, interview with the authors, May 1999.
50. David Lean's *Oliver Twist* 1948 was banned in USA because of objections raised by Alec Guinness's portrayal of Fagin. It was initially judged 'antisemitic' and was not granted a production seal of approval by the motion Picture Association of America until 21 February 1951 after British Lion Classics had made 'extensive cuts'. Robyn Karney (ed.): *Chronicle of the Cinema*, Dorling Kindersley 1995, p. 406.
51. *Oliver Twist*, Chapter 51 *'Affording an Explanation of More Mysteries Than One, and Comprehending a Proposal of Marriage with No Word of Settlement or Pin-Money'*.
52. Interview with Alan Bleasdale in United Productions WBGH Boston press publicity.
53. See Alan Bold and Robert Giddings: *Who was Really Who in Fiction*, Longman 1987 p. 116 and J.J. Tobias: *Prince of Fences: The Life and Crimes of Ikey Solomons* (Heinemann, 1974).
54. Interview with the authors, June 1999.
55. Ibid.
56. Ibid.
57. See Christopher Hibbert: *The Making of Charles Dickens* (Longman 1967), pp. 35ff.

8 The Albatross which was Really a Phoenix

1. See Fred Inglis: 'Brideshead Revisited revisited: Waugh to the knife' in Robert Giddings and Erica Sheen, editors: *From Page to Screen: Adaptations of the Classic Novel*, Manchester, Manchester University Press 1999, pp. 163–80.
2. Report on the publicity launch of Alan Bleasdale's dramatisation of *Oliver Twist*, 'ITV Puts Magic Back into Dickens with $5m Makeover for Fagin' in the *Guardian* 6 July 1999.
3. Some interesting answers are suggested in Lib Taylor: 'Inscription in *The Piano*' in Jonathan Bignell, editor: *Writing and Cinema*, Harlow, Essex, Addison Wesley Longman 1999 pp. 88–101. See also Stella Bruzzi: 'Tempestuous Petticoats: Costume and Desire in *The Piano*, in *Screen*, Vol. 36, number 3 Autumn 1995.
4. *The Piano*, by Kate Pullinger was published by Bloomsbury April 1994. See Kate Pullinger: 'How I Returned *The Piano*' in the *Guardian* 20 March 1994.
5. *Mutiny on the Bounty* 1932, *Men Against the Sea* 1934 and *Pitcairn's Island* 1934.
6. Susan King: 'Jane Eyre Follows Successful Path Blazed by *'Pride and Prejudice'*, in *Los Angeles Times* 17 October 1997.
7. 'Faces Behind the Figures' in *Forbes Magazine*, 25 March 1996, Vol. 157, issue 6, p. 112.
8. Paul Bauman: 'Flytes of Fancy' in *Commonweal*, 26 January 1996, Vol. 123, issue 2, p. 6.
9. Quoted in Bill Borrows:'Fat Profits', *The Guide, Guardian*, 29 August 1998, p. 12.
10. *BBC Annual Report and Accounts 1996–97*, p. 51.
11. 23 December 1996.
12. Kate Lock:'Battle of the Bodices' in *Radio Times* 1 November 1996.
13. 'Are You Sure That's Wise? Things We Wish They Really Hadn't Done', *The Box* April/May 1997.
14. F.R. Leavis's influential book on the English novel, *The Great Tradition*, published in 1948 and never out of print, lauded George Eliot, Henry James, Joseph Conrad, D.H. Lawrence at the expense of other novelists, including Dickens whom Leavis at that time regarded as merely as an entertainer. He revised and retracted these opinions in *Dickens the Novelist*, which he wrote jointly with, Queenie Leavis, in 1971.
15. The BBC will usually have a website for current major television drama productions and www.bbc.co.uk/Dickens is the Corporation's Dickens website.
16. Lisa Buckingham, 'Lights, Cameras and Bankroll' in *Guardian* 27 August 1994.
17. See Vanessa Thorpe: 'It's All Down to the Vision Thing: BBC at the Crossroads' in *The Observer* 23 May 1999.
18. The series was narrated by Dame Judy Dench, and ended Monday 23 December 1996.
19. *Victory at Sea*, made by NBC in 1952 in 26, 25-minute episodes. It narrated the role of naval warfare in the Second World War and made superb use of newsreel footage, with a popular music score by Richard Rogers.

20. *The Great War*, shown on BBC Television, in 26 episodes of 40-minutes each, was written by John Terraine and produced by Tony Essex. It was remarkable for its use of actuality material projected at the right speed and for excellent interview material.

21. A successor to *The Great War* made by the BBC, rather portentous in tone with dour commentary by Sir Michael Redgrave, again the series made very good use of actuality material.

22. Produced by Jeremy Isaacs for Thames Television in 26, 50-minute episodes, with commentary by Laurence Olivier.

23. *Alistair Cooke's America* was produced by Michael Gill for BBC Television in 13, 50-minute episodes. An internationally bestselling series, as was the book which went with the series, widely used in educational institutions, it has assumed the authenticity of orthodox history. See Robert Giddings: 'Paradigm Regain'd: Alistair Cooke, Disneyland and America' in Robert Lee, editor, *A Permanent Etcetera: Essays Presented to Eric Mottram*, Pluto Press 1992.

24. *The Ascent of Man*, BBC/Time-Life, written and presented by Jacob Bronowski, surveyed the various ideas which have guided or misguided humanity during past ages shown in 13, 50-minute episodes.

25. *Churchill's People*, BBC/MCA, based on Churchill's *History of the English Speaking People*, 26, 50-minute episodes of dramatised, romantic historical pageant.

26. *Civilisation*, BBC series of 13, 50-minute programmes, written and presented by art historian, Kenneth Clark, presenting the history of Western artistic endeavour.

27. *Seapower*, BBC 1981. Military history of naval warfare, shown in seven 30-minute episodes just before the Falklands war, presented by Lord Hill-Norton, Admiral of the Fleet.

28. *Ireland: A Television History* (1981), made the BBC and RTE and shown in 13, 50-minute episodes. Written and presented by Robert Kee, produced by Jeremy Isaacs.

29. *The Troubles* (1981), made by Thames Television in four 50-minute episodes, written by Taylor Downing and narrated by Rosalie Crutchley.

30. Richard Dimbleby: *Broadcaster by his Colleagues*, BBC 1966, pp. 75–6.

31. Quoted in Jonathan Dimbleby: *Richard Dimbleby*, Hodder and Stoughton 1975, p. 232

32. *All Our Working Lives*, a BBC oral history of industrial life, changing technology and changing times in the twentieth century, produced by Angela Holdsworth. Eleven 50-minute episodes, with enchanting musical score by Carl Davies presented history from the point of view of ordinary people and was quietly convincing, deeply moving and memorable. A gem of a series, of a kind easily overlooked.

33. *All Our Yesterdays*. This was a documentary series made by Granada Television, which was transmitted in weekly 20-minute episodes from 1960 until 1973, made up of newsreel film introduced by Brian Inglis.

34. See Tina Ogle: 'Sisters Who Did it for Themselves' in *Radio Times* 19 June 1999.

35. See Geoffrey Reeves: '*Tumbledown* (Charles Wood) and *The Falklands Play* (Ian Curteis): The Falklands Faction' in George Brandt, editor: *British*

Television Drama in the 1980s, Cambridge, Cambridge University Press 1993, pp. 141–61.

36. *A Horseman Riding* by BBC (1978) dramatized by Alexander Baron; *To Serve Them All My Days* (1980) and *Diana* (1983) both dramatized by Andrew Davies for the BBC.

37. *Poldark* (BBC, 1977–79).

Select Bibliography

BBC Annual Reports, Accounts and Handbooks

Bennett, Tony, Susan Boyd-Bowman, Colin Mercer and Janet Woollacott (eds), *Popular Television and Film: A Reader*, BFI and Open University, 1986

Black, Peter, *The Biggest Aspidistra in the World*, BBC Publications, 1972

Bloom, Clive (ed.), *Literature and Culture in Modern Britain*, Volume 1, Longman, 1992

Brandt, George, *British Television Drama*, Cambridge, Cambridge University Press, 1981

Brandt, George (ed.), *British Television Drama in the Nineteen-Eighties*, Cambridge, Cambridge University Press, 1993

Bridson, D., *Prospero and Ariel*, Gollancz, 1972

Briggs, Asa, *The Birth of Broadcasting: the History of Broadcasting in the United Kingdom*, Vols 1–5, Oxford, Oxford University Press, 1961–1978

Briggs, Asa, *The Golden Age of Wireless, the History of Broadcasting in the United Kingdom*, Vol. 2, Oxford, Oxford University Press, 1965

Briggs, S., *Those Radio Times*, Weidenfeld & Nicolson, 1981

Cockburn, Claud, *The Devil's Decade*, Sidgwick and Jackson, 1973

Coulton, B., *Louis MaNiece in the BBC*, Faber and Faber, 1980

Day, Gary (ed.), *Literature and Culture in Modern Britain*, Longman, 1997

Drakakis, J. (ed.), *British Radio Drama*, Cambridge, Cambridge University Press, 1981

Felton, Felix, *The Radio Play: Its Technique and Possibilities*, Sylvan Press, 1949

Fleming, Tom (ed.), *Voices Out of the Air: The Royal Christmas Broadcasts 1932–1981*, Heinemann, 1981

Gascoigne, Bamber, *The Making of 'The Jewel in the Crown'*, Granada, 1983

Giddings, Robert, Keith Selby and Chris Websley, *Screening the Novel: the Theory and Practice of Literary Dramatisation*, Macmillan, 1990

Gielgud, Val, *British Radio Drama 1922–1956*, Harrap, 1956

Halliwell, Leslie and Philip Purser, *Halliwell's Television Companion*, Grafton Books, 1987

Harboard, Jane and Jeff Wright, *Forty Years of British Television*, Boxtree, 1992

Harboard, Jane and Jeff Wright, *Forty Years of British Television*, Boxtree, 2nd edn, 1995

Hickman, Tom, *What Did You Do In the War, Auntie?* BBC Publications, 1995

IBA Television and Radio: Yearbooks of Independent Broadcasting

Leapman, Michael, *The Last Days of the Beeb*, Allen & Unwin, 1986

Lewis, Jon E. and Penny Stempel, *The Ultimate TV Guide*, Orion, 1999

McIntyre, Ian, *The Expense of Glory: the Life of John Reith*, Harper Collins, 1993

Mowat, C.L., *Britain Between the Wars 1918–1940*, Methuen, 1968

Nelson, Robin, *TV Drama in Transition*, Macmillan, 1997

O'Connor, Alan (ed.), *Raymond Williams on Television: Selected Writings*, Routledge, 1989

Reith, John, *Into the Wind*, Hodder and Stoughton, 1949

Rodger, Ian, *Radio Drama*, Macmillan 1982

Scannell, Paddy and David Cardiff, *A Social History of Broadcasting*, Vol. 1, 1922–1939, Blackwell, 1991

Self, David, *Television Drama, An Introduction*, Macmillan, 1984

Sieveking, Lance, *The Stuff of Radio*, Cassell, 1934

Snagge, John and Michael Barsley, *Those Vintage Years of Radio*, Pitman, 1972

Vahimagi, Tise (ed.), *An Illustrated Guide to British Television*, Oxford University Press, 1994

Vahimagi, Tise (ed.), *An Illustrated Guide to British Television*, 2nd edn, Oxford University Press, 1996

Index